Contents

How and Why Children Hate

Companion volume:

How and Why Children Fail
Edited by Ved Varma
ISBN 1 85302 108 3
ISBN 1 85302 186 5 pb

of related interest

Grief in Children
A Handbook for Adults
Atle Dyregrov
ISBN 1 85302 113 X

Six Theories of Child Development
Revised Formulations and Current Issues
Edited by Ross Vasta
ISBN 1 85302 137 7

Group Work with Children and Adolescents
Edited by Kedar Nath Dwivedi
ISBN 1 85032 157 1

Play Therapy with Abused Children
Ann Cattanach
ISBN 1 85302 120 2
ISBN 1 85302 193 8 pb

How and Why Children Hate

Edited by Ved Varma

Foreword by Martin Herbert

Jessica Kingsley Publishers
London and Philadelphia

First published in the United Kingdom in 1993 by
Jessica Kingsley Publishers Ltd
116 Pentonville Road
London N1 9JB

Copyright © 1993 the contributors and the publisher
Foreword copyright © 1993 Martin Herbert

British Library Cataloguing in Publication Data
How and Why Children Hate: Study of
Conscious and Unconscious Sources
I. Varma, Ved P.
155.4

ISBN 1-85302-116-4
ISBN 1-85302-185-7 pb

Printed and Bound in Great Britain by
Biddles Ltd, Guildford and King's Lynn

Foreword

On any night of the week the television viewer can be guaranteed many vivid, visual reminders of the hatred that fuels 'man's inhumanity to man'. Be it on the news, in a film or documentary, the images of violence, sadism and abuse – the outward and visible signs of hostility, prejudice and rejection come flickering from the TV screens in countless homes. Where does this denial of our common humanity, this gross insensitivity to individual suffering and sensibility have its source, its beginnings? The origins must be powerful as hatred is universal and so pervasive. It manifests itself in child abuse, in class and racial prejudice, in the cruelties of war and religious intolerance. The roots of hatred, sad to say, can often be traced to infancy and childhood. It seems a sacrilege to suggest that the children we love, the children who can be so loving, should have in them the seeds of the indifference, cruelty and violence which are the accompaniments of hatred. I have always found it difficult when looking at a baby – so pure, vulnerable and innocent – to imagine that life and biology have the potentiality to transform this infant into an active participant a future equivalent of today's ethnic cleansing or yesterday's Holocaust.

And yet hatred underlies much of the wanton cruelty, violence and vandalism which seems to be on the increase among children. Bullying, sibling abuse and parent abuse are of increasing concern to professionals. It is critical for society to understand (if it is to mitigate) the psychological and social processes that give rise to such hatred, and the distinguished writers (from several disciplines) who contribute to this book *How and Why Children Hate*, edited by Dr. Ved Varma, make a valuable contribution to this understanding. Their journey of inquiry into the reasons why children hate takes them into the intra-psychic world (e.g. the unconscious) of childhood and the external worlds of influence on their thinking and feeling – the family, parent, the cultural ethos of class and racial prejudice, religion, even nursery rhymes. This is a worthy project indeed; its insights into the human conditions of love and its relative, hate, will be of value to a wide audience.

Dr Martin Herbert

This book is dedicated by the editor, with affection and esteem, to Derek Ganley, Renate Hiller-Grodszinsky and Desmond Davies.

Introduction

As Robin Higgins says elsewhere in this book, 'hate is a complex affect or sentiment involving sadism, rage, anger and envy'. It is therefore very disturbing and destructive. Yet we all hate from time to time. Mrs Barbara Dockar-Drysdale writes (Personal Communication) that Dr D. W. Winnicott says hate is present in normal development; it therefore has a very important part to play in the development of the individual and an inability to hate could be as serious as inability to love. These matters are not sufficiently discussed and the editor feels, thinks and finds that there is too much hatred in the world. And children probably hate more than adults. Paradoxically, children are also more amenable to improvement and treatment.

Hence this book. It discusses how to recognise and handle hatred in a practical, purposeful way. The contributors include three child psychiatrists, five psychologists, two psychotherapists, one sociologist and an education-alist. They are all recognised and experienced experts in their fields. It is therefore an invaluable book for students and practioners in these fields.

Ved Varma
London

Further Reading

Klein, M. (1957) *Envy and Gratitude*. London: Tavistock Publications.
Varma, V. (1992) (ed.) *The Secret Life of Vulnerable Children*. London: Routledge.

Other books edited by Ved P. Varma

Stresses in Children (1973) London: University of London Press.

Advances in Educational Psychology Vol. 1 (1973) (co-editor Professor W.D. Wall) London: University of London Press.

Psychotherapy Today (1974) London: Constable.

Advances in Educational Psychology Vol. 2 (1974) (co-editor Mia Kellmer Pringle) London: Hodder and Stoughton.

Piaget, Psychology and Education (1976) (co-editor Professor Phillip Williams) London: Hodder and Stoughton.

Anxiety in Children (1984) London: Croom Helm/Methuen.

Advances in Teacher Education (1989) (co-editor Professor V. Alan McClelland) London: Routledge.

The Management of Children with Emotional and Behavioural Difficulties (1990) London: Routledge.

Special Education: Past, Present and Future (1990) (co-editor Peter Evans) Lewes: Falmer Press.

The Secret Life of Vulnerable Children (1991) London Routledge.

Truants form Life: Theory and Therapy (1991) London: David Fulton.

Prospects for People with Learning Difficulties (1991) (co-editor Professor Stanley Segal) London: David Fulton.

Vulnerability and Resilience in Human Development (1992) (co-editor Professor Barbara Tizard) London: Jessica Kingsley.

Coping with Unhappy Children (1993) London: Cassell.

Management of Behaviour in Schools (1993) Harlow: Longman.

CHAPTER 1

Hate in Nursery Rhymes
Captive Audience; Essential Message

Robin Higgins

'What?' cried Job in the middle of his trials. 'What? Shall we receive good at the hand of God and shall we not receive evil?' As evil is the shadow of good, chaos the shadow of order, hate is the shadow of love. From our earliest days, we cannot escape the presence of hate. We have to come to terms with it and know it inside and out. Nursery rhymes are one means which assist us to do so.

A note about hate

Hate is a complex affect or sentiment involving sadism, rage, anger and envy (Rycroft 1968, Berke 1985). It is aroused by the experience of frustration, and in its most stark and uncompromising guise by events which are felt to threaten life. Hate, because it arises at those times when life is felt to be threatened, is particularly active in states of vulnerability such as infancy, or for a mother immediately after giving birth when she finds herself landed with a dependent vulnerable creature whom she often both adores and fears.

Again hate, if sustained and unresolved, entails revenge. Unresolved hate, resentment and revenge can in themselves be life-threatening, so it is of particular importance that hate should find some permissible outlet if the natural childhood experience of tit for tat (Jung and Kerenyi 1963) is not to turn into the vicious crippling circle of resentment and revenge.

The period of special vulnerability, along with the time when the vicious spiral can still be averted, coincide with the period we are particularly concerned with in this chapter: the period of the nursing couple and their nursery rhymes.

Hate and the nursing couple

During and immediately after foetal life, the establishment of its own rhythms is of vital significance for the infant. So hate and its behavioural concomitant of rage may explode over (temporary) distortion of rhythms or over faulty rhythmic entrainment. Mother and infant rhythms may become jarringly out of joint. The infant's hate and rage is a direct attempt to restore the balance.

In this sense, hate is the complement of love a necessary opposite as distinct from indifference, which arises when the complementarity of hate and love has failed. In nursery rhyme lore, indifference goes under the guise of 'don't care' and (*pace* the Miller of Dee) is given short shrift:

> Don't care didn't care
> Don't care was wild
> Don't care stole plum and pear
> Like any beggar's child.

> Don't care was made to care
> Don't care was hung:
> Don't care was put in a pot
> And boiled till he was done.

Blake fully appreciated that, in the context of love, hate is an essential ingredient when he wrote:

> My friendship oft has made my heart to ake.
> Do be my Enemy for friendship's sake. (Blake 1978)

For any of us to enjoy a robust and reliable world of our own, we have to endure the repeated experience of hating the person we love and, out of these successive bouts of hate, resurrecting that person inside us in an increasingly complex, less black and white, pattern (May 1985).

For infant and mother, there are two sides to this resurrection: hate and its resolution for the infant; hate and its resolution for the mother.

The love of mother for infant and infant for mother tend to be taken for granted. Why would one go to all the trouble of having an infant if one promptly rejected it as soon as it was born? Why on the infant's part should one hate the owner of the breast (or the bottle) that feeds, the person on whom one is so totally dependent?

Neither of these questions, as it turns out, is as rhetorical as they might seem. The sad fact is that some parents do reject their own child, sometimes precisely because of the trouble its nine months' coming has caused them. Equally there are some infants who hate the breast or hand that feeds, sometimes precisely because of the highly dependent position that they find themselves in.

First, we consider the infant. When in the womb, and immediately after birth, we take the first steps in making some sense of our world, we have to transform chaotic, fragmented and unrelated impressions into images and experiences that are encompassable and that in the course of time we can recognise, remember, and share with others.

This transformation closely involves the person we have for nine months been part of. In these early months, as the small system attached to the greater, we have been constantly drawing our nourishment from her blood-stream and putting back into it waste-products for detoxification. We continue this two-way traffic in the same way after the umbilical cord is cut, though with psychic rather than somatic events. We hand the chaotic and unencompassable feelings with which we are saddled over to our mother and hope to receive them back from her in a modulated form that begins to have some coherence.

Hate forms an essential ingredient of these unencompassable feelings and, indeed, is one of the reasons for their being unencompassable. Instances abound of the murderous phantasies an infant may harbour towards its parents (see, for example, Klein 1988,1989).

So, the reasons why infants may hate their mothers are because the transformation of hate is an essential path of growing by encompassing the chaotic; because without hate there is no resilience; and because the only person usually available for the infant to hate is the long-suffering mother.

The reasons why mothers may hate their babies have been well rehearsed by Winnicott (1978): from the start, the infant is not her own; it endangers her body, interferes with her private life; it hurts her at times by, for example, biting and chewing on her nipples; it treats her like an unpaid skivvy, showing scant appreciation for anything she does for it; it is small and vulnerable and horribly dependent and if she fails it at the start, the pay back will last for ever. Perhaps the most unarguable reason of all is that the mother realises she's in a trap. For her infants to grow free of her, she has no option but to carry for a while the hatred they dump on her like their stools.

Clearly, then, in the nursing couple, the mother and baby, there is a lot of hate lurking around and a deep need for permissible outlets to modulate, transform, and express it.

How does the mother endure transform and hand back these feelings of hate and rage? The simple answer is in reverie; in tuning into her own and her infant's feelings and living with them, carrying them. A more detailed answer probes into the nature of reverie; its character of being there, a presence when the other feels most alone, a support without intruding. A more detailed answer also examines the different forms reverie may take; the dreaming container, enchantment. The particular form addressed in this chapter is the crooning of nursery rhymes.

The nursery rhyme and reverie

The nursery rhyme has come to be used down the centuries as one means containing the various emotions which occur between infant and parent, especially the mother. The central emotions for containment are love and its inverse: hate. Their mode of being articulated and contained lies both in the singing and the content of what is sung.

When mothers sing to their children, they hold and rock them as part of themselves. For a while, time and outside events become immaterial. Rhymes and rhythms take over like a mantra. These are moments of enchantment when each is absorbed into the other, united by the power of sound.

A key experience throughout our life, stemming from the first nine months of symbiotic existence, is that of being held. This experience, like any other, has an opposite. Here the opposite is not being held and not being held may mean being allowed to move independently, or being dropped (Higgins 1989).

The child's fear of being let down finds a counterpart in the adult's fear of being tied to the baby. Many young mothers feel quite overwhelmed by the degree to which the infant is dependent upon them. They sometimes experience a great urge to be rid of this beloved burden, an urge which often fills them with anxiety and guilt. They are by no means always relieved of this burden within and without by the many well-meant admonitions from relatives friends and experts.

The first point about dependency on the part of mother and infant, then, is the excitement and fear of being no longer held. Nursery rhymes voice the possibility quite openly:

> Rock-a-bye-baby on the tree top
> When the wind blows the cradle will rock.
> When the bough breaks the cradle will fall
> Down will come baby, cradle and all.

Appropriately, the words are sung to a variant of the rebel tune of Lillibulero. Or again:

> Catch him crow! Carry him kite!
> Take him away till the apples are ripe;
> When they are ripe and ready to fall,
> Here comes baby, apples and all.

Or again:

> Humpty Dumpty sat on a wall.
> Humpty Dumpty had a great fall.
> All the king's horses and all the king's men
> Couldn't put Humpty together again.

And here's a riposte for the child (again sung to a much closer version of Lillibulero):

> There was an old woman tossed up in blanket
> Seventeen times as high as the moon.
> Where she was going I couldn't but ask it,
> For in her hand she carried a broom.
> 'Old woman, old woman, old woman', quoth I;
> 'O whither, O whither, O whither so high?'
> 'To sweep the cob-webs from the sky,
> And I'll be with you by and by'.

Sometimes the adult's exasperation becomes more explicit. In the *Naughty Baby's Song*, peace is sought by intimidation, through threats of bogeymen of either English (Oliver Cromwell in the shape of Black Old Knoll) or, as here, European extraction:

Baby, baby, naughty baby,
Hush, you squalling thing, I say.
Peace this moment, peace, or maybe
Bonaparte will pass this way.

Baby, baby, he's a giant,
Tall and black as Rouen steeple,
And he breakfasts, dines, rely on't,
Every day on naughty people.

Baby, baby, if he hears you,
As he gallops past the house,
Limb from limb at once he'll tear you,
Just as pussy tears a mouse.

And he'll beat you, beat you, beat you,
And he'll beat you all to pap,
And he'll eat you, eat you, eat you,
Every morsel, snap, snap, snap.

Here another over-burdened and, in this instance, single parent coasts towards non-accidental injury:

There was an old woman who lived in a shoe.
She had so many children she didn't know what to do.
She gave them some broth without any bread
And whipped them all soundly and put them to bed.

Sometimes adult exasperation takes a more ambiguous, envious turn, harking back to memories of one's own idealised infancy when a smug and unassailable dependency was seemingly ours to be enjoyed:

What does the bee do?
Bring home honey.
And what does Father do?
Bring home money.
And what does Mother do?
Lay out the money.
And what does baby do?
Eat up the honey.

Blake was well aware of the ambiguities, not merely in love and hate but in the apparent innocence of dependence:

> O the cunning wiles that creep
> In thy little heart asleep.
> When thy little heart does wake,
> Then the dreadful lightnings break. (Blake 1948)

Or again:

> My mother groan'd, my father wept;
> Into the dangerous world I leapt,
> Helpless, naked, piping loud,
> Like a fiend hid in a cloud. (Blake 1948)

Some lullabies broach the breaking of dependence in an apparently gentle, repetitive fashion akin to the game of peep-bo that children often set up for the same purpose. Such lullabies may be full of cornucopial promises, intended to suggest the ever open arms, the ever available breast. Both the next two instances come from America:

> Hush you bye, don't you cry,
> Go to sleep, little darling.
> When you wake, you shall have cake
> And drive those six little horses...

And here a more extensive list of replacements is promised should the first gift turn out to be faulty:

> Hush little baby don't say a word
> Mama's going to buy you a mocking bird.
>
> If that mocking bird don't sing
> Mama's going to buy you a wedding ring.
>
> If that wedding ring turns brass
> Mama's going to buy you a looking glass.
>
> If that looking glass gets broke
> Mama's going to buy you a billy-goat...

And so on. The reiterated images of fragility and breakage are balanced by reiterated assurances of repair, the whole set of stanzaic conditionals being accompanied by a throbbing, dance-demanding pulse. In these reassurance lullabies, the overall aim is to establish a trust which breeds trust and which overcomes fear, anxiety and hate on both sides.

An alternative interpretation would see the reassurance as a mask for hate and the cornucopial promises as a form of bribe.

The lure of the wild

Besides the bald statement of being dropped, besides the intimidation of the bogeyman, besides the ambiguous envy of dependence or the equally ambiguous assurance of reparation, a further way in which hate is expressed in nursery rhymes may be seen in the theme of *The Flight from Home*.

In one sense, this theme is a sophisticated extension of the bough breaking under the rocking cradle. The purposeful escape involves conscious intention on both sides; hate prompts kicking and being kicked out:

> What makes you leave your house and land?
> What makes you leave your money O?
> What makes you leave your new-wedded lord,
> To go with the wraggle-taggle gypsies O?
>
> What care I for my house and land?
> What care I for my money O?
> What care I for my new-wedded lord?
> I'm off with the wraggle taggle gypsies O!

Or more simply:

> I won't be my father's Jack
> I won't be my mother's Jill,
> I'll be the fiddler's wife
> And have music when I will.
> T'other little tune, t'other little tune,
> Prithee love, play me t'other little tune.

So much for the child's leap to independence. What about the adult's? Sometimes the response is equally straightforward, as in the case of the king who:

> Had three sons of yore
> And kicked them through the door
> Because they wouldn't sing.

But on other occasions, in attempting to deal with their fears about the child's dependence and with the many bonds that they find the child stirs in them, adults may take special pains (and pleasure) in weaving stories to impress on the child the vulnerability which goes with this dependence:

> My dear, do you know
> How a long time ago,
> Two poor little children
> Whose names I don't know,
> Were stolen away
> On a fine summer's day,
> And left in a wood,
> As I've heard say...
>
> And when it was night
> So sad was their plight
> The sun it went down,

And the moon gave no light.
They sobbed and they sighed
And they bitterly cried,
And long before morning
They lay down and died...

The dangers of the passage through the wood are hammered home in stories like *Little Red Riding Hood,* or the *Erl King.* Here's Blake again:

'Father! father! where are you going?
O do not walk so fast.
Speak father, speak to your little boy,
Or else I shall be lost',

The night was dark, no father was there;
The child was wet with dew;
The mire was deep and the child did weep,
And away the vapour flew. (Blake 1948)

So, it is not uncommon for children to be given mixed messages about taking steps towards independence. On the one hand, get off my back and stand on your own bottom (as one mother was once heard instructing her child). On the other hand, the child is warned against trespassing outside the cosy domestic domain, predicted perils being used to consolidate the imposition of parental choice:

My mother said I never should
Play with the gypsies in the wood:
If I did, she would say
Naughty little girl to disobey.

Your hair shan't curl and your shoes shan't shine,
You gypsy girl, you shan't be mine.
And my father said that if I did
He'd rap my head with the teapot-lid.

The lure of the wild inside the home

The spirit of hate, rebellion and independence, then, may prompt children to escape from home and a parent to kick them out or give them mixed messages about the dangers of leaving. But there are several routes along which the ambiguous feelings of hate and rebellion pull them back into the home.

One particular route, emphasised by Melanie Klein, is the hate which is stirred up by a sense of exclusion from the so-called primal scene; that painful experience where children encounter the parents making love, and no longer know where and to whom they belong.

Goosey, goosey gander,
Whither shall I wander?
Upstairs and downstairs
And in my lady's chamber.
There I met an old man
Who would not say his prayers.
I took him by the left leg
And threw him down the stairs.

The sense of exclusion not only arises between child and adult but between male and female as partners, and more generally. The hate engendered by the primal scene is a potent source of sexual rivalry and sexual battles. In several nursery rhymes, the focus on gender distinctions prepares for the rivalry, complacency and disdain in nursery warfare and beyond:

What are little boys made of?
Frogs and snails
And puppy dogs' tails
That's what little boys are made of.

What are little girls made of?
Sugar and spice
And all that's nice
That's what little girls are made of.

What are young men made of?
Sighs and leers
And crocodile tears
That's what our young men are made of.

What are young women made of?
Ribbons and laces
And sweet pretty faces
That's what our young women are made of.

Not surprisingly in such ambiguous preparations, the elderly are the last who can expect to be spared:

What are old women made of?
Bushes and thorns
And old cow's horns
That's what old women are made of.

Which prompts an Andy Capp, Alf Garnett type of riposte:

Who are you? A dirty old man.
I've always been so since I began.
Mother and Father were dirty before me
Hot or cold water has never come o'er me.

Peering into the future hazards of the marriage mart, the unromantic ethos of nursery rhymes includes the complaint of the woman who idolizes and is then let down by her man:

> There was a lady loved a swine
> Honey quoth she
> Piggy-hog wilt thou be mine?
> Hoogh, said he.
>
> I'll build for thee a silver sty
> Honey, quoth she
> And in it thou shalt lie
> Hoogh said he.
>
> Pinned with a silver pin
> Honey quoth she
> That thou may go out and in
> Hoogh, said he.

(One is reminded of Robert Graves' question: 'Why have such scores of lovely gifted girls married impossible men?' (Graves 1974).)

The same realistic, if sardonic, ethos paints a different marital state, this time the hen-pecked man speaking through the mouth of the woman:

> I had a little husband,
> No bigger than my thumb;
> I put him in a pint-pot
> And there I bade him drum.
> I bought a little horse,
> That galloped up and down;
> I bridled him, and saddled him
> And sent him out of town.
> I gave him some garters
> To garter up his hose,
> And a little silk handkerchief
> To wipe his pretty nose.

In his collection of nursery songs in 1849, Halliwell includes the ballad of Lord Randal who returns to die in his mother's arms after being poisoned by his treacherous sweet-heart (Halliwell 1970). Before he dies, his mother dots the i's and crosses the t's on how he proposes to dispose of his worldly goods. This particular aspect of the sexual battle, which involves the jealousy of two generations (lover and mother), crops up in many different versions, whether 'my boy' is Randal, Billy, Tammy, King Henry, my dear son, or my bonnie wee croodin' doo.

Hate in loss and disaster

Another type of exclusion (and the hate which goes with it) arises from a general and not specifically sexual sense of deprivation and loss. Nursery rhymes could be said to prepare children for some of the shocks they may at any time have to face, either inevitably like illness and death or unpredictably like being caught in a sinking ship (Yule 1991) or having one parent murder the other (Black and Kaplan 1988). Cock Robin is a nursery rhyme figure who endures deprivation and death: on one occasion when the north wind is blowing and he has to hide his head under his wing to keep himself warm, and on another when he's killed and is mourned by all the birds of the air who fall a-sighing and a-sobbing on receiving the news.

Once again, in nursery rhymes, the children are reminded of their vulnerability to loss:

> When I was a little boy I lived by myself,
> And all the bread and cheese I got I laid upon a shelf;
> The rats and the mice they made such a strife
> I had to go to London town to buy me a wife.
> The streets were so broad and the lanes were so narrow
> I was forced to bring my wife home in a wheelbarrow.
> The wheelbarrow broke and my wife had a fall,
> Farewell wheelbarrow, little wife and all.

Loss may take less extreme forms, as with the Three Little Kittens who lost and then found their mittens and so were able to enjoy their pie (withheld by their mother until the mittens were found). It may also carry heavier symbolic overtones which may refer to loss of identity, as in the case of the Old Woman who fell asleep on the king's highway, had her petticoats snipped up to the knee by the Pedlar, and then, when apparently unrecognised by her own dog, suffered serious doubts as whether she be herself or someone else. A somewhat similar situation occurs in the riddle of

> Little Nancy Etticoat
> With a white petticoat
> And a red nose;
> She has no feet or hands
> The longer she stands
> The shorter she grows. (Answer: a lighted candle.)

Or the overtones may hark back to gender differences and castration, as in the case of the Three Blind Mice, who in addition to their sight lost their tails to the knife of the farmer's wife, or Little Bo-Peep whose sheep went tail-less when she fell fast asleep on duty, and who in her efforts to amend her delinquency didn't rest but

> Went over hill and dale-o
> And did what she could

As a shepherdess should
To tack to each sheep its tail-o!

Loss is often contingent on a disaster:

Ladybird ladybird
Fly away home.
Your house is on fire
And your children all gone:
All except one
And that's little Ann
And she's crept under
The frying pan.

In these circumstances, the hate in loss is apt to be transmuted into black humour:

There was a man, he went mad.
He jumped into a paper bag;
The paper bag was too narrow,
He jumped into a wheelbarrow;
The wheelbarrow took on fire,
He jumped into a cow byre;
The cow byre was too nasty,
He jumped into an apple pasty;
The apple pasty was too sweet,
He jumped into Chester-Le-Street;
Chester-Le-Street was full of stones,
He fell down and broke his bones.

Similar sequences of tragic farce may be found in *The Little Disaster* (Crane 1974), *The Blue-tail Fly* (a lengthy version of *Jack Sprat*) (Halliwell 1970) and *The Ploughboy Song*, starting 'My daddy is dead but I can't tell you how' and listing the series of foolish decisions subsequently made by the surviving son. Black humour sometimes combines with ghoulism, spookies, and sadistic jokes:

Fee Fie Foh Fum
I smell the blood of an English (or Christian) man.
Be he alive or be he dead
I'll grind his bones to make my bread.

Such jokes may include amusement at a phobic object, as in *Little Miss Muffet* and the spider, or observations on ruthless nature as in *The Fox Went Out*, *The Frog and the Crow*, or Mrs Bond's preparations of Dilly ducks for her customers' dinners.

At other times, sadism reaps its own reward. When, in the story of Jack and Jill, the latter came in and did grin

> To see Jack's paper plaster;
> Her mother whipt her across her knee
> For laughing at Jack's disaster.

And, in another instance, the price of sadism is ostracism.

> Tom tied a kettle to the tail of a cat
> Jill put a stone in the blind man's hat,
> Bob threw his grandmother down the stairs;
> And they all grew up ugly and nobody cares.

Later stages of expressing hate through nursery rhymes

As they grow older, children can still find in nursery rhymes means for expressing some of the frustration and hate which they experience in trying to sort out the world. Many of the verses have *non sequiturs* and tangle-talk that humorously reflect these painful confusions of learning.

> Spring is sprung
> De grass is riz.
> I wonder where dem birdies iz?

> De little birds is on de wing.
> Ain't dat absurd?
> De little wing is on de bird.

> A man in the wilderness asked of me
> How many strawberries grow in the sea?
> I answered him as I thought good
> As many red herrings as grow in the wood.

> If all the world was paper,
> And all the seas were ink,
> And all the trees were bread and cheese
> What would we have for drink?

> If all the world were sand-O
> Oh then what should we lack-O
> If, as they say, there were no clay,
> How should we take tobacco?

In verses such as these, the child can laugh at some of the frustrations of being confused. There's the same sense of making up one's own language, a bridge back to babbling, or to those moments when we half persuaded ourselves that a scribble was the equivalent of adult writing.

Eventually children turn their hate on the nursery rhymes themselves. They kill them off in parody, puncturing adult attitudes they find excessively pious or authoritarian. The White Paternoster

> Matthew Mark Luke and John
> Bless the bed that I lie on.
> Four corners to my bed,
> Four angels round my head;
> One to watch and one to pray
> And one to bear my soul away

becomes

> Matthew Mark Luke and John,
> Went to bed with their trousers on.
> Mark cried out in the middle of the night
> Oh, my trousers are too tight! (Opie and Opie 1967)

As the Opies point out, this parodying of nursery rhymes implies some dismantling of the loving, secure atmosphere in which they were originally learnt. The parodying forms part of an inevitable attack on the parental system which the child has to outgrow (Opie and Opie 1967) but the parodying may also pick up some of the original hate which is embedded in the song and which was around at the time of listening to it, when the child was a captive audience. These elements of hate, absorbed at the time in a state of pre-verbal awareness, are repressed and then some seven years later may be re-found, re-played and developed. Their expression may well aid and be aided by the rough and tumble of the play-ground.

In escaping from one tradition (the loving acceptance of the nursery rhyme), children plunge headlong into another (the parody of the rhyme). The different socio-psychological sets going with each tradition represent different points on the spiral of human development. Perhaps the essential feature of these different sets is that through them children take back into themselves the hate they handed over for a while to the other on whom they were dependent.

The final kill?

In the past, a clearly marked cycle existed for the transmission of nursery rhymes from one generation to the next. This cycle of transmission entailed a gap of anything between twenty and seventy years, the gap being the period which elapsed between the time the rhyme was heard in childhood and the time it was relayed to subsequent generations (Opie and Opie 1967).

More recently, at any rate in Western Europe and American families, this cycle has been disrupted as a result of the many social changes affecting family life.

Who sings nursery rhymes today? Working mothers and nurturant fathers? Third Age grandparents? Au pairs and baby-sitters? Is the singing of nursery rhymes a dying occupation, replaced by radio, TV, and videos? Are nursery rhymes going the way of folk-song and in danger of becoming fossilised, collections for museums of infantilia?

If they exist, how do today's singers approach the naked hate which is apparent in many nursery rhymes and which as we've seen can act as the catalyst for growth? Is there a tendency to bowdlerise the rhymes under the impression that the child should be spared the stark experience of hate whilst being exposed to the steady stream of filtered violence on the TV screen?

If the singers and songs no longer exist, what permissible outlets for hate have replaced them? And what are the consequences of this change for individuals and society?

References

Berke J. (1985) Envy loveth not. *British Journal of Psychotherapy 1,* 171–86.

Black D. and Kaplan T. (1988) Father kills mother. *British Journal of Psychiatry 153,* 624–30.

Blake W. (1948) *Poetry and Prose of William Blake.* Edited by Geoffrey Keynes. London: Nonesuch.

Graves R. (1974) *Poems selected by himself.* London: Penguin.

Halliwell J.O. (1970) *Popular Rhymes and Nursery Tales of England.* (First published in 1849). London: Bodley Head.

Higgins R.N.T. (1989) *How to Get in Touch with Childhood.* Chapter on Multiple Adolescences. Unpublished manuscript.

Jung C.G. and Kerenyi C. (1963) *Essays on a Science of Mythology.* New York and Evanston: Harper Torchbook.

Klein M. (1988) *Envy and Gratitude.* London: Virago.

Klein M. (1989) *The Psycho-analysis of Children.* London: Virago.

May R. (1985) Internalisation in narcissism: the problem of disillusionment. *British Journal of Psychotherapy 1,* 187–96.

Opie I. and Opie P. (1967) *The Lore and Language of Schoolchildren.* Oxford: Oxford University Press.

Rycroft C.F. (1968) *A Critical Dictionary of Psychoanalysis.* London: Nelson.

Winnicott D.W. (1978) *Through Pediatrics to Psycho-analysis.* Paper on Hate in the Countertransference. London: Hogarth.

Yule W. (1991) Children in shipping disasters. *Journal of Royal Society of Medicine 84,* 12–15.

Readers can refresh their memories of the rhymes used by referring to various sources, including:

Crane W. (1974) *The Baby's Bouquet.* (First published in 1877). London: Pan Books.

Lomax, A. (ed.) (1964) *The Penguin Book of American Folk-Songs.* London and Baltimore: Penguin Books.

Opie I. and Opie P. (1985) *The Oxford Dictionary of Nursery Rhymes.* Oxford: Oxford University Press.

Poston, E. (1971) *The Baby's Song Book.* London: Bodley Head.

CHAPTER 2

Unconscious Communication of Hatred Between Parents and Children

Francis M. J. Dale

For most of us, the notion that children, let alone small babies, are capable of such a strong emotion as hate is a shocking, even unacceptable thought. It is, I would suggest, only a little more acceptable that parents can hate their children. However, if we care to look for it, the evidence that hate can and does exist between parents and children is not difficult to find.

Although baby battering is not a new phenomenon, it is rightly causing much concern amongst child care professionals, social workers, doctors, the police and the public in general. In addition, there would seem to be a steady increase in the reporting of cases of emotional, physical and sexual abuse.

Because parents exert such a powerful and dominant influence over their children, it is easier to notice and to accept that what should be a loving and benign relationship can sometimes be perverse, sadistic and cruel. It is precisely because of this imbalance of power that, when children hate, it is often less obvious and harder to detect.

Hatred in babies

Before we can understand *how a baby can hate and why*, we will need to develop some insight into the unconscious components of its relationship to the object of its desires – the mother. However, the object of the baby's desires can only be known in relation to the cognitive and perceptual development of the infant. A new born baby, for example, does not have the same experience of its mother at birth as it will have after six weeks – when its eyes can focus – or at twelve months when it can take the enormously significant step of beginning to communicate about its thoughts and feelings with words. The baby at twelve months *would not recognize* the picture it had of its mother in the first days and weeks after birth.

Initially, it will only know about a kaleidoscope of *sensations*: warmth, touch, smell, the rhythmic sound of the mother's voice, harsh or soft light. Some of these sensations will tend to please or comfort the baby and these will be responded to and actively sought after. Gradually, from being discrete experiences, perhaps even fragmentary and unconnected, *patterns of sensation* will emerge and coalesce to form *an expectation in the baby for certain types of experience*. The most important of these expectations will centre around the 'feeding experience'.

Thus, the first and by far the most important 'object' of the baby's desires will be the experience of the *mother as breast*. All the infant knows of its mother at this early stage is the sensation of the erect nipple/mount contact – the flowing, filling warmth of milk leading to fullness and satiation. Somewhere, too, there will be the reassuring sound of the mother's voice.

Therefore the first object, the first relationship, is not to the whole mother but to a part of her, an aspect of her. In other words, it is to the breast. For the infant, the mother *is* the breast.

Not only is the mother the breast, but the very survival of the baby depends on its establishing a satisfactory and dependable relationship to it early on. Before bottles and baby milk became a substitute for the breast, if the breast failed the baby, then it died.

It is not the actual breast which is important so much as what it brings the baby into contact with and represents. For example, bottle fed babies still have most of the experiences and sensations associated with the breast: the nipple in the mouth, the warmth and smell of the mother's body, close eye and skin contact, the feeling of being held and contained and the sound of the mother's voice.

It stands to reason, therefore, that any disruption to this vital bond between the baby and the breast is experienced as potentially catastrophic. The most common disruption occurs when the baby needs the breast (here, not just the breast as a physical object but all the things it stands for in the baby's fantasy) and finds that it is not there. The expectation of the breast will lead the baby to search for it. If this fails then it will cry in an increasingly distressed way until eventually it will begin to scream and to show the most intense kind of distress with its whole body.

By this stage most babies are also exhibiting signs of anger, if not rage. If the mother reappears now, the baby may reject her, even 'attack' her, and she may need to spend some considerable time in trying to make contact again and to reassure the baby.

Here, the baby clearly has a dilemma. The 'going away mother' has become the 'bad' or hated mother. But she is also the 'good' mother who loves, comforts and understands the baby. It is just not possible for a baby or small child to reconcile loving and hating the same person; the very person on whom it depends for its survival.

It solves this dilemma by keeping the two opposite and incompatible sets of feelings for the mother separate. If you like, it 'gets rid of' the bad mother whom it hates in order to protect its relationship with the good mother from being threatened or even destroyed by its hateful impulses. Of course, an infant cannot in reality destroy its mother with angry or hateful feelings, but because its capacity to discriminate between fantasy and reality is so limited (and will be for many years) the thought, *in fantasy*, is equated with the deed.

Unconscious mechanisms of defence

The question we now need to address is how the infant or small child gets rid of, avoids, or disposes of the bad mother or bad part of her (e.g. the breast) so as to preserve and keep safe its experience of her as a good object or person. Before answering this question, however, we need to understand that the good and bad aspects of the mother are not initially experienced as being separate from the baby; the baby's experience of the mother is not differentiated from its experience of itself. Infant and mother have a merged identity. As a consequence of this, the baby's hatred of the bad mother/breast is also experienced as hatred of *those parts of itself* which are identified with her.

Thus the baby needs to protect not only the good aspect of mother from attack, but also its subjective experience that it contains *within itself*, elements of the bad mother. The baby achieves this by 'splitting'. This is an unconscious process whereby thoughts or feelings which are unacceptable to the 'core' sense of self (the central ego), or which are incompatible with the good mother, are split away and expelled. The mechanism by which they are expelled is called projection and although sometimes affects, thoughts or experiences can be evacuated into an inanimate object, they are mostly projected into a person or a 'part' person (i.e., the breast).

The person, or part person, in psychoanalytic terms called the 'part object', is usually the frustrating or 'bad' mother. Thus what is split off from the subjective experience of the baby is both the connection between the bad and good mother (i.e. as both belonging to the same person) and ownership of those parts/aspects of the self which are identified with the bad mother. Of course, the baby does not *actually* get rid of the 'bad' mother; but in the baby's phantasy life, where external reality and internal experience are not properly differentiated, the baby *experiences* its wishes – including the wish to 'do away with' the bad mother – as fact.

The sequence of events probably develops in the following way. The mother/breast frustrates the baby. Unless good or reparative experiences intercede, frustration turns to anger and then to hate. This hate, or the part of the self which feels hatred, is then expelled or projected out of the self and into some object/person which can receive or contain it.

However, although in the short term splitting and projection serve to rid the baby of its bad experiences and to protect its relation with the good mother, this primitive form of defence creates problems in its own right. First, in getting rid of unwanted parts of the self, the baby is depleting itself. It's a bit like jettisoning the cargo of a ship in order to keep it afloat, when without the cargo the ship is worthless. Second, in phantasy, the attacks on the bad object/mother threaten to turn it/her into a terrifying figure – very much like the giants, monsters and witches of children's dreams and fairy stories – who, the child fears, wants to retaliate and punish the child. Thus the baby gets rid of an internal bad figure whose 'badness' persecutes it from within, only to set up an external figure who threatens it from the outside.

'Normal hate'

You may think I have painted a picture in which the child is assailed from all sides by monstrous figures full of vindictiveness and hate from which there is no escape. However, the bad mother and the good mother, although split and kept separate from each other in the child's phantasy in reality, originate and coexist in the same person – the mother (or part person – the breast). Because of the original splitting of the object into good and bad parts, the mother who comes to comfort the child is now perceived *only* as the good mother. The baby can then offset the experience of the bad mother by internalising or reintrojecting (i.e. taking back inside) good experiences and good mothering which lessens its persecutory fear and its need to keep projecting out and 'losing' parts of the self which are felt to be bad.

In order to see how these processes operate in babies, we will need to look at the baby's changing relationship to its mother as development and maturation proceed.

It was Sigmund Freud who introduced the general public to the notion that the emotional and mental life of the infant was moulded and expressed according to the developmental stage it had reached. He outlined three stages: oral, anal and genital. He demonstrated, both from the direct observation of infants and from retrospective material from adult patients, that these developmental stages had a *psychological* as well as a physiological significance for the way the infant understood and related to both its internal and external world.

Hate in the oral stage

In the oral stage, not only is the baby's physiological need for food met through the mouth and breast but, as outlined above, also its emotional and psychological needs. The baby 'fastens on to the world', and holds itself together, with its mouth. Babies who are denied access to the breast respond in much the same way that you or I might do if someone choked off our supply of air. They show every sign of a desperate struggle for survival. Fortunately, from a purely physical point of view, babies can survive without food for longer than they can without air. But from a psychological point of view, the loss of the breast is an equivalent experience. The baby is in a struggle for survival.

In the normal run of things the baby finds the breast again. A sense of wholeness, connectedness and relief push away the memory of the absent breast and the panic which ensued. However, it is inevitable that there will be times when the baby will be frustrated and it will show its anger in the best way it knows how – with its mouth. Screaming, refusing food (or sicking it up) and later, biting, are all oral ways of showing anger.

Hate in the anal stage

Although orality never loses its importance, with increasing cognitive and physiological maturation the anal region begins to assume primacy. The unconscious significance of faeces for the child are twofold. Firstly, they represent the first 'gift' that the infant can offer the parent(s). Although you or I might not be exactly enamoured with being presented with faeces as a sign of affection, they are the first concrete acknowledgement of the love the child has for its parents. Faeces are the end product of the food which the mother or father gives the child and proof of the integration and creative capacity of its insides.

Conversely, faecal products can also represent badness, anger, anxiety and 'falling-apartness'. Children become sensitized at a very early age to the fact that the whole arena of when, where and how they 'do their business' has important consequences in gaining parental approval and acceptance, or disapproval and rejection. 'Poos' are something parents just cannot ignore. This fact gives the child power. Poos can be given or withheld. They can be good or they can be bad. They can be safe or they can be dangerous. They can be an offering, or they can be a weapon.

A child who is angry with its parent therefore has a very powerful way of showing it at its disposal. Passive anger can be seen with children who withhold their faeces. This could be seen as withholding their love, or fear of the badness and 'mess' which is felt to be contained in their 'bottom' or insides.

A more active expression of 'anal hate' is defecating where and when one isn't supposed to; for example, into a clean nappy or into one's pants. Here the child is literally as well as metaphorically putting their shit into their parents. There are some expressions used in adult speech which, although crude, perhaps pithily express unconscious knowledge of the anality in people's aggressiveness: for example, the expressions, 'Don't shit on me' or calling someone an 'arsehole' or 'little shit'.

Hate in the genital stage

With the introduction of the genital phase, we enter what Freud believed was the crucial battleground in which children and parents attempted to resolve their contradictory feelings of love and hate for each other. He named it the Oedipus Conflict after the Greek tragedy by Sophocles in which Oedipus kills his father and marries his mother.

Briefly, Freud outlined the child's dilemma in the following way. Initially, the infant behaves as if there were only two people in the world – itself and mother. Then along comes father and he clearly has claims on mother too. Not only that, but he clearly shares a kind of intimacy – which the child can sense even if not understand – from which it is excluded. The dyadic or two person relationship has expanded to include the father and become a triangular relationship.

Conflict was there before but it was nothing compared to the conflict which now ensues. Ignoring unconscious guilt, in one sense it would be easy if neither the child nor the mother felt any affection for the father. But the child who hates the father for encroaching into its monopoly of mother also loves and values the father. The dilemma is resolved (only ever partially) in a variety of ways.

For the boy, it is primarily by identification with the father. In some ways the father is a more powerful, exciting and intriguing figure than the mother. The exclusive relationship with the mother can be to some extent compensated for by developing a similarly exclusive relationship with the father. After all, son and father are *the same*. They both have a willy and one day the boy will be big and powerful like his dad. The son can identify with the father in ways in which he can't with his mother. In addition, in *unconscious* identification with the father, the son can have the same intimacy with his mother that his father does. He too can become her 'husband', her protector, her 'little man'.

For the girl, the situation is different. She can identify with her mother. She is the same sex. In one sense, like with the male child, she 'loses' mother in having to share her with daddy. In another sense, she keeps mummy by identifying with her and becoming her in a way that is not possible in the boy's case. In identification with the mother, the girl both keeps her but also replaces her. As with the boy's desire to get rid of the father, this creates unconscious guilt, for the girl also needs and loves her mother.

With both sexes, the identification with the parent of the opposite sex – in the boy's case to *possess* the mother, in the girl's to *identify with her* – are the source of much anxiety. This is because in both cases the identification has the unconscious significance of having replaced, for the boy, the father in mother's affections, and for the girl, the mother in father's affections.

With such powerful and contradictory forces operating within the child in relation to its parents, one can see why defences are primarily aimed at keeping hateful thoughts and impulses unconscious.

Clinical example 1: The paper witch

I would now like to give an example of how the process of splitting and denial operated as a defence against the hated or bad mother in a little boy who came from a very loving and stable background. He was nearly six years old when his mother had to go into hospital for an internal operation. Both parents prepared him carefully for the admission, explaining what was going to happen, how long his mother would be in hospital and when he could visit, as well as arranging for his grandmother to come and help look after him.

During the evening of the day before his mother was to be admitted to hospital, this boy woke up screaming. As he was being comforted by his father, the boy told him that he had been having a nightmare in which he had been fighting with a paper witch. At the point at which he began to feel he was losing the battle he woke up terrified.

It is the context in which this little boy and this dream that makes it interesting and gives it significance. Earlier that same evening, he had been making paper cut-outs with his mother. Also, he had resisted being taken in to see his mother after the nightmare. We can now piece together the unconscious symbolism behind the nightmare. The boy's mother was going to have something cut out of her. The mother he loved (the good mother) was going to be both absent and 'cut up'. The absent or 'going away mother' was thus turned into a bad mother.

Making the paper cut-outs was experienced at an unconscious level as cutting up or attacking the 'bad going away mother'. This anxiety could be managed while he was awake and clearly in relation to his good mother, but not when he was asleep and his conscious capacity to keep the 'bad' and 'good' aspects of his mother separate failed.

The significance of his failure to keep the 'bad' and 'good' aspects of his mother apart was, first, that the bad mother – the witch – became a persecuting and attacking figure threatening to overwhelm and destroy his good mother, and second, that she would punish him for his unconscious attacks on her as the 'bad going away mother'.

The point I am making here is that this is the situation with respect to 'normal hate' – when it is a transitory situation, or where it is only an aspect of the mother which is hated or attacked. The little boy in question never became aware of what was a passing hate for his mother who was, from his point of view, abandoning him. they both survived the hate because the fundamental relationship between them was, and remained, one of love and acceptance. If you like, the good mother was far more powerful and well established than the bad mother.

Clinical example 2: 'Ghostbusters'

This second example of 'normal hate' relates to a case in which a boy of six was referred to a Child Guidance Clinic because of nightmares. He would regularly wake up in great distress and his parents had difficulty in pacifying him. Significantly, he was completely unable to recall any detail from his nightmares. He did remember, though, that they had started shortly after he had seen a video of one of the 'Ghostbusters' films. Fortunately, I had seen the film and could see that there was a clear link between the main theme of the film and a traumatic and life threatening event from this boy's infancy.

In the film, an agent of the Devil steals a new born baby from its mother and places it on a dias or altar where it is to be possessed by the Devil so that he can manifest in human form. The mother meanwhile is desperately trying to force a way into the building where her baby is imprisoned.

. In reality, when this boy was born, he was found to have a congenital abnormality of the oesophagus whereby it terminated in his throat rather than connecting to his stomach. In order to save his life he had to be operated on immediately but, in the process, was separated from his mother. Through gross mismanagement, she was prevented from seeing her son for the next three days.

The parallels are obvious. The boy was 'stolen' from his mother. He was placed on a 'dais or altar' (the operating table) where he was to be 'sacrificed' to the 'Devil' (i.e., operated on by the surgeon). His mother was prevented from 'rescuing' her baby by the doctors who stopped her from having access to him.

It isn't hard to imagine that a new born baby would probably experience such traumatic surgery as a murderous attack and the mother who 'allowed' it as a figure of hate. It doesn't matter that in reality the surgical intervention saved its life, or that the mother was distraught at being prevented from being with her baby. The reality, from the baby's point of view, is what will affect its experience and its perception of events.

In the case of this boy, although later events helped to repair the emotional damage, a residue of unresolved anger and anxiety remained which hadn't been dealt with. The understanding he gained concerning his infantile trauma, and being able to hear how distressing it had been for his mother, helped him to get in touch with a great deal of repressed anger towards his mother which he had never been able to openly express before.

For both of them, this paved the way towards a more open and expressive relationship where anger was no longer seen as so destructive and annihilating. He could now 'hate', be angry with the mother who allowed this to happen to him, because the mother *who didn't abandon him* showed him that she could tolerate his anger.

But what of relationships where this is not the case? Where perhaps the mother hates the child, either in fantasy or in reality?

Pathological hate

Hate is pathological when it is the main component, either conscious or unconscious, in one's relationship with oneself (i.e. with respect to internalised object relationships) or with other people and when it isn't culturally approved. Hate *is* actually approved and seen as 'normal' in certain situations, for example in times of war. In these situations, the individual or group remains 'healthy' and normal by being able to project its hate or rejected qualities into the hated object – the enemy. This kind of hate always has to be strongly defended against and severe unconscious prohibitions are set up to prevent knowledge of it from becoming conscious. Unless there is a complete breakdown of the defences erected against the hateful impulses

– as in some forms of psychosis – the feelings of hate remain hidden, disguised or projected elsewhere.

Some defences against hate

Splitting and projection

This is a very primitive form of defence and one which was perhaps most clearly defined by Melanie Klein, a psychoanalyst who worked primarily with children. Freud believed that the ego arose from the need to cope with unconscious processes which sought to express themselves without regard to external reality (what he termed primary process). With an immature ego, not yet sufficiently differentiated from these powerful and chaotic unconscious impulses, these were defended against through the mechanism of splitting. Whenever unacceptable thoughts or impulses threatened the ego-self they would be split off *with the part of the self which had been contaminated by them*. In this way the integrity of the remaining part of the ego-self would be preserved. It would also of course be depleted. Continued splitting can result in the complete fragmentation of the self.

Clinical example 3

A thirteen-year-old boy was referred to me suffering from hallucinations, bizarre thought processes and paranoid delusions. He believed that other children in his school hated him and wanted to kill him, and he would become terrified and quite hysterical if anyone came near him. As I worked with him, I came to understand the unconscious meaning of his delusions of persecution. My patient was in a merged or symbiotic union with his mother. That is, in his imagination, he felt to all intents and purposes, that he and his mother were 'inside' each other and had no separate identities. He had never been out of the house by himself in thirteen years. Consciously he idealised his mother – couldn't live without her; 'If she died, then I would die'. However, unconsciously, he hated her and wanted to kill her.

This thought was so unacceptable to his conscious ego-self that it had to be split-off and projected into other children so that they had the murderous impulses and not him. Having disowned these impulses, he now experienced them as originating in these other children and being directed at him. His murderous impulses were now 'trying to murder him'. In one sense, of course, this is a perfect defence. From being the murderer, he is now the victim. The direction of the murderous impulses has been reversed, so how can he be blamed? On the other hand, having lost touch with his hate, it cannot now be resolved.

Repression

Once an ego-self has become more or less permanently established, as an alternative to splitting, unacceptable thoughts or impulses can be repressed; that is, actively denied access to consciousness. Here, instead of being projected outwardly they are, as it were, 'pushed into the basement and shut away'. Everyone uses repression to some extent but the greater the emotional charge of that which is being repressed – for example, hate – the greater must be the amount of energy at the service of repression. Repression uses energy and it also requires 'psychic space' into which repressed impulses can be shut away.

Hate which is repressed doesn't go away. It gets put into storage. Therefore continued repression of hateful impulses can lead to a situation where one's insides are experienced to be full of badness and where the reservoir of energy available for normal, healthy functioning and creativity is depleted. Repression, as a defence against hate, works well as long as there is 'enough space in the basement'. Once it is filled, however, there is a very real risk of it spilling over.

Clinical example 4

Mrs James was a professional woman in her mid forties who came into therapy because of severe depression. She recounted a childhood that could have come straight from a Dickens novel. The family had lived in absolute poverty and squalor. The father was an alcoholic who physically and verbally abused his wife, and of whom his children lived in terror. My client had no difficulty in getting in touch with her hatred and contempt for her father. Her mother however, could do no wrong. She idolised her, almost to the point of veneration.

There were some indications, though, that hinted at another story. For example, when she first began in therapy she said to me, 'Whatever you do, you must never criticise my mother'. Naturally, this raised the question as to why she needed to make such a point of stressing this. If she was so sure in her opinion regarding her mother's virtues, why did she need to be so defensive about any criticism of her?

It gradually became clear that Mrs James's unconscious attitude towards her mother was one of hate. She despised her mother for staying with her father, for her passivity and acceptance of such a dreadful life, for her failure to protect her children, and for her emotional coldness. Mrs James could never remember ever being held by her mother or spoken to tenderly.

When she finally became consciously aware of how much she hated her mother, the shock of the realisation almost drove her to suicide. This was due, in part, to the fact that she had set her mother up inside herself as an idealised person who gave some meaning and purpose to her life. It was hard for her to see that, as an abused and emotionally deprived child, she had *created the mother she needed.* This idealised mother never existed in reality. However, without the fantasy of the good mother, she felt empty inside and that life wasn't worth living.

This brings us to the question of how – and whether – unconscious hate can be acknowledged in a constructive way without the need to employ the kinds of defences which deny and distort the reality of the way we relate to ourselves and others.

Reaching love through hate

In an interesting article entitled 'Hate in the Counter-transference', the psychoanalyst and paediatrician D.W. Winnicott addresses the issue of how psychotherapists need to be able to deal with the hate which exists in themselves before they can deal with the hate which they will encounter in their patients: '...the patient can only appreciate in the analyst what he himself (i.e., the analyst) is capable of feeling' and, 'Above all he must not deny hate that really exists in himself' (Winnicott 1976).

This asks a great deal of the psychotherapist, just as it does of the mother (or father) when they come across hatred in their child. With deeply disturbed children or patients, it seems as thought they can only reach love through hate. They don't want to hate or be hated, but as Winnicott suggests, they need to have the experience of their hate being received, of it being tolerated, of it being survived; and of themselves surviving the hatred they find in their parents (or therapist): '...the analyst's hate is actually sought by the patient and what is then needed is hate that is objective. If the patient seeks objective or justified hate he must be able to reach it, else he cannot feel he can reach objective love' (Winnicott 1976).

Parents who hate their children

I have outlined above some of the underlying dynamics when children hate their parents and some of the defences they employ in keeping the hate unconscious. But what of the situation when it is the parent who hates the child?

In my experience, parental hate falls into two categories. In the first, and most common, the parent's hate for the child comes about in response to the projection into the parent of feelings of intense rage, despair or persecution which they child's immature ego cannot cope with.

This will occur most frequently with respect to very small children and babies, or older children with a low threshold for frustration and poor ego strength. Most parents do not act upon this hate because they come to recognise that it comes from the child and doesn't really 'belong' to them. This is frequently the state of affairs when parents feel like strangling or hitting a screaming child. Here, the parent is experiencing within him or herself the frustrated rage and hate which their child is experiencing but can't manage.

With some parents and children, however, the situation is reversed – it is the parents who project their infantile feelings into their children. What they cannot tolerate is what their children represent regarding *their own* infantile relationship with their parents.

Clinical example 5

Mr 'Antonucci' was a very hard-working father of four and a self-made businessman. He originally asked for help in coping with his son Marco who exhibited obsessional symptoms, paranoid delusions and suicidal behaviour. In the course of a family meeting, Mr Antonucci described a recent event in which he had become so angry with Marco that he had packed his bags ready to leave home. He had taken Marco to the dentist only to find that when they were called in to the surgery Marco had vanished. Mr Antonucci described how humiliated he had felt and how he could have 'murdered Marco'. I suggested to Mr Antonucci that for him to leave home just because his son was frightened of the dentist seemed to be an overreaction and wondered if this didn't point to it having some hidden significance for him. In a flood of emotion, Mr Antonucci suddenly recollected a similar situation with respect to his mother when he was the same age as Marco. She had taken *him* to the dentist and he had been terrified. When he had wanted to run away, she lost her temper and slapped him about the face and head.

On the surface it would appear that Mr Antonucci's anger and frustration were directed towards his sone because he had embarrassed and humiliated him. But the unconscious component related to the fact that this incident so closely mirrored a similar event in his childhood in which he had been humiliated by his mother. The hatred he had felt for his mother had been successfully repressed until the incident with his son – which so closely mirrored the earlier event – threatened to 'undo the repression'.

The anger he felt towards his son had two elements to it. On the one hand, he was angry because his son's behaviour threatened to reveal his unconscious hate of his mother, and on the other because, as a parent, in losing his temper with his son he was in identification with the 'bad mother'. He was doing to his son what his mother had done to him.

Clinical example 6

This second example should clarify this process further. A young mother managed to get her young son admitted to hospital because he was so hyperactive she could not manage him. She more or less implied that if the hospital couldn't 'cure' him then she would have to have him put into care. When we discovered that she had been given up by her mother when she was the same age as her little boy, it became clear that, unconsciously, she was rejecting not her little boy but the possibility of being reminded by him of all her unresolved feelings at being abandoned by her mother.

> Many such parents, when confronted by these 'replica situations' which mirror their own infantile experience, come to relate to their children as a kind of persecuting presence from the past and are driven into identifying both with their children and the abusing parents at the same time. In identifying with the demands or distress of their 'real' children, they are once again threatened with coming face to face with still unresolved issues from the 'child inside them'; whilst in identifying with their parents, they feel as adults, unjustly accused and blamed by their children's behaviour. (Dale 1990)

The effect of this kind of unconscious hate is an important factor in understanding the very high incidence of abused children coming from families where one or other of the parents has themselves been abused. Again, it has to be understood in terms of an unconscious defence whereby unacceptable experiences are split off and projected into someone else.

In the case of a parent who was abused as a child it often happens in the following way. The experience of being abused, because it is so damaging and unacceptable, cannot be properly acknowledged or though about and hence remains as an unresolved emotional trauma *inside the child* – inside the parent. When a child of the abused parent comes close enough to mirroring the situation in which the parent was abused (it might have reached the same age at which the parent was abused) there is an unconscious tendency to recreate the abuse in one's own child. In this way, the pain of the original abuse gets projected out of oneself but only to perpetuate the cycle of abuse in one's own children.

I must repeat, this is not a conscious process. Very few parents *consciously* put their children into abusing situations. I well remember the acute distress of a mother who, because she had been abused, was very careful not to allow her daughter to get into any situation where she might be at risk of abuse. However, the one neighbour she thought she could trust turned out to be an abuser.

Conclusion

In this chapter, I have tried to show how the communication of unconscious hatred between parents and children needs to be understood from various perspectives and why defences are necessary in order to keep this hatred unconscious. I have also attempted to demonstrate the importance of being able to understand the psychodynamic processes which evoke hate and which can be used to lessen its destructive consequences.

References

Balint, M. (1979). *The Basic Fault*. London and New York: Tavistock Publications.

Dale, F.M.J. (1990) Chap. 6. The psychoanalytic psychotherapy of children with emotional and behavioural difficulties. In Varma, V.P. (ed.), *The Management of Children With Emotional and Behavioural Difficulties*. London:Routledge.

Fairbairn, W.R.D. (1978). *Psychoanalytic Studies of the Personality*. London: Routledge and Kegan Paul.

Guntrip. H. (1982). *Personality and Human Interaction*. London: The Hogarth Press.

Guntrip. H. (1980). *Schizoid Phenomena Object-Relations and the Self*. London: The Hogarth Press.

Klein, M. *et al*. (1952). *Developments in Psychoanalysis*. London: The Hogarth Press.

Milner, M. (1977). *On Not Being Able to Paint*. London: Heineman.

Milner, M. (1969). *The Hands of the Living God*. London: The Hogarth Press and The Institute of Psycho-Analysis.

Stafford-Clark, D. (1967) *What Freud Really Said*. Pelican.

Spillius, E.B. (1988). *Melanie Klein Today* (Vol. 1). London and New York: Routledge.

Symington, N. (1986). *The Analytic Experience*. London: Free Association Books.

Winnicott, D.W. (1968). *The Child, The Family and the Outside World*. London: Pelican.

Winnicott, D.W. (1980). *Playing and Reality*. London: Penguin.

Winnicott, D.W. (1987). *Home is Where We Start From*. London: Penguin.

Winnicott, D.W. (1976). *The Maturational Process and the Facilitating Environment*. London: The Hogarth Press.

Wolheim, R. (1974). *Freud*. London: Fontana/Collins.

CHAPTER 3

The Family Scapegoat
An Origin for Hating

Christopher Dare

This chapter is concerned with children who are treated as though they are
irretrievably bad and blamed for all the tension and strife in the family.
Children in such a position often show difficult or disturbed behaviour which
may become extreme. They are especially prone to become full of rage and
hatred. They are frequently referred to a child or adolescent psychiatry team.
The parents believe that the child is psychiatrically ill but they often show
an uncertainty as to whether that might mean the child is mad or brain
damaged. Sometimes a child in such a position seems improbably free from
disturbance to the child mental health professionals. More often they have
behavioural difficulties, troublesome or annoying in themselves but seeming
to evoke from the family a level of criticizing concern far in excess of that
warranted by the behaviour. Characteristically, the parents attribute ill will
to such children and declare that they have been difficult to understand,
unresponsive to discipline, defiant and ungrateful since they were very little
or even since birth. The psychiatrist may be able to appreciate the family's
difficulties if the child is indeed overactive, out of control, quite unresponsive
and out of touch with reality. In the cases being described here, however, the
psychiatrist is put in a dilemma: the children so ill-described by their families
look miserable, may be pathetically trying to please and to the observer's eye
no worse than other children in the family. Indeed, sometimes the child so
complained of is notably the best behaved of the children.

The picture can best be portrayed with a specific example. A family of
young school children were being interviewed by a psychiatrist. The parents
complained that their oldest son (an eleven-year-old) was always on the go,
restless, constantly noisy, destructive, unsocial and unrepentant for his
wrong acts. The parents reiterated that they were sure that he was a
hyperactive child. Peter, this child, sat motionless throughout the interview,
whilst his eight-year-old sister and five-year-old brother played rowdily,
happily, blithely uninterested in the discussion. The psychiatrist, after half
an hour, commented that he had not seen Peter move and asked what the
mother and father made of that.

'Ah!' said the mother, perhaps quite triumphantly, 'You may not have seen him move but I can tell you that his *mind* is overactive!'

'Oh!' said the psychiatrist.

Later, when the psychiatrist said that he was at a disadvantage in understanding the problem because Peter had been so still and well behaved in the session, the father said:

'We knew that he would be like that. No one ever believes us. He's trying to show us up!'

'How difficult for you all', the psychiatrist cautiously replied.

The scapegoat

There is, in every-day life, a notion of a *scapegoat*, a person who can be 'picked upon' and made to take the blame for a misfortune or tragedy. The word has been taken into social and group psychology but is rarely given any precision. Psychoanalytic writers pointed to the quite exact meaning of *scapegoat*, in its biblical origins, as a sacrifice. In Leviticus it is described as a yearly event in which a goat is forced to leave the herd and the tribe to wander in the desert, taking the sins of the tribe away from themselves. The goat was, in effect, symbolically laden with the ills of the tribe, driven from the tribe to fend for itself or die within the desert; thus the tribe was freed from its ills. Many social circumstances – fear and denigration of strangers and foreigners, for example – display a parallel process very clearly. The social process seems to rely upon a psychological mechanism observed when someone sets about freeing themselves from bad or unwanted attributes by ascribing them to others:

It's not me being bad tempered this morning, it's you! Miserable lot!

This psychological process corresponds closely to the psychoanalytic idea of projection.

In the early days of family systems therapy, the patient was commonly thought of as a sort of family scapegoat. For example, Ackerman (1974) discusses scapegoating as a *family role*. He sees the family as *doing* it to the child:

Since people make one another sick... Clinically we observe troubled families in which the child is scapegoated and made vulnerable for a breakdown. (p.49)

Ackerman repeatedly likens scapegoating to prejudice and conceives of it as an attack by one person on another. He understood scapegoating within the family as being capable of being redirected to an outsider. This is very important. The psychiatrist seeing Peter felt a great sympathy for the little boy. He seemed so miserable, isolated and his parents were quite unable to see him as doing anything right. However, the psychiatrist knew that it was a total waste of time trying to evoke sympathy for Peter within the family. If they felt so strongly that it was necessary to protest about their oldest son to a psychiatrist, going through all the paraphernalia of GP's letter, waiting list and so on, then they could not possibly yield to the psychiatrist's viewpoint easily. They knew their son so much better. The psychiatrist, sympathetic to Peter would, they rightly might guess, be unsympathetic to them. His sorrow for Peter would arouse hostile anger in them.

The idea that the person whom the family considers to be the problem, the patient, is always a scapegoat has unfortunate consequences. The notion carries with it a sense of blaming the family, as though they were making their child into a patient. The idea of the patient always being a scapegoat denies the reality of children sometimes having difficulties to which the family are responding. Families, if they become aware of the professionals seeing them as the cause of their child's problems, consider can quite rightly consider themselves to be misunderstood. They can see themselves as being scapegoated!

This overuse of the term *scapegoating* seems to have led to its disuse. The subject became one of the casualties of the association between family therapy and the anti-psychiatry movement (Cooper 1967). This is unfortunate and, from time to time, it is resurrected because of the need to describe very real clinical situation, such as, when a family present a much blamed child such as Peter. This can produce children who hate.

Epstein and Bishop (1981) define scapegoating as a:

> maladaptive and unique function... a functional process which involves a family member's becoming an active recipient of negative affect and/or negatively perceived attributes on a continuing basis. The scape-goating process serves the special purpose of providing a displacement mechanism, i.e. a means of avoiding conflict in other threatening areas. The scapegoat is active in drawing attention onto him/herself and is not simply a passive victim of other family members. (p.460)

This is a rather simplified description but it does emphasise that scapegoating arises as the result of an interaction between an individual family member and the family as a whole, expressing certain problems through their relationship with the individual.

Some of the characteristics which indicate that a child is a scapegoat have already been mentioned; these and others are summarised in Table 3.1.

Features of scapegoating in childhood

1. An emphasis has already been put on the extent to which the family's complaints are in excess of that which seems warranted by the scape-goat's actual behaviour. Making this judgement is never easy. As a rule it is best, in any therapeutic relationship, to proceed as though what

Table 3.1: Clinical characteristics of scapegoating

1. The family complaints are in excess of the child's behaviour
2. Present complaints date since birth
3. Said to be like Jekyll and Hyde
4. Good behaviour is said by the parents to be there only to deceive
5. Other people do not know what the child is really like
6. If treatment is successful another child becomes the problem
7. Siblings join in the complaints against the scapegoat
8. There are no extenuating circumstances
9. The patient is on the edge of the family
10. If a parent has left the family the scapegoat is said to be like the absent parent

people say is the truth, to their knowledge. It is unwise to disbelieve the complaints of the parents. An outsider will never know the whole of what goes on in a family. It is also the fact that children can be deceitful and, in any case, can be angels in one setting and devils in another. However, a child is probably being scapegoated when it is subject to an unmitigated tirade; when the complaints are non-stop and when the details that are told me do not seem to tally with the emotional reaction produced. The absence of any excuse or sympathy for any aspect of their life situation also characterises a scapegoated child.

2. Not only may the complaints made about a child be different from the actual behaviour: the parents may say that the child has been noticed to be difficult, oppositional and misbehaved since birth. Peter's mother said that she had 'sensed' the evil in him as soon as she saw him, after a prolonged and frightening birth. She immediately recognized him as being a strong character.

Now, it is certainly true that babies can have strong and distinct characters. Some are born with or acquire a high level of irritability from adverse experience; for example, some forms of brain injury during or shortly after birth. It is also true that a mother, worried about the responsibility of her first baby, can feel discouraged and thwarted by the infant who does not respond to her care, not seeming contented and peaceful. It is quite natural to see the baby as willful and oppositional when tired and harassed, but to hold a long term view that the child is contrary and disparaging is to endow the baby with adult qualities, quite inappropriately. This endowment seems rather to come from outside the child; from the mother, the father or perhaps the grandparents. Such a babe is *destined* to become a scapegoat if the adult attitudes continue unchanged.

3. Alongside of the grievances that the parents hold against their child is a strong sense of bewilderment. This is often compounded by the transformations from time to time, by moodiness or bad temper, that seem meaningless. Such features may not be unusual. The process of scapegoating is to be suspected when the variability is adduced as further evidence of the child's wickedness and untrustworthiness. This may openly be referred to as being like a 'Jekyll and Hyde'.

4. In a non-scapegoated child, the Jekyll and Hyde state could be viewed sympathetically, being seen as bewildering and uncomfortable for the child also. In a scapegoating family, the incomprehensibility of the variations in the child's mood or behaviour is seen as part and parcel of the *deceitfulness*. These accusations are so often used to discredit the good qualities of the child – their success at school, their kindness to friends or their stoicism. It can be extremely difficult for the child mental health worker to tolerate such accusations. This is especially so because it is easy to understand; children who are repeatedly told that they are untrustworthy, wicked, deceitful and incomprehensible soon become bad-tempered, lacking in confidence and feeling hopeless about themselves. It is no wonder that good qualities come to be in short supply.

5. Parents who scapegoat maintain their belief in their children's universal badness by implying the misplacement of any positive value that is identified by others: outsiders are unaware of the reality of the children, which is only truly known by the parents themselves. This applies, especially, to any outsider who shows the slightest sympathy or exoneration of the child. Most workers in the child mental health team have a strong tendency to empathise with the plight of children in difficulties and they above all arouse the mistrust of the parents who take such a negative view of their child.

6. As will be described later, children who are determinedly scapegoated are extremely difficult to help. The experienced therapist will know that there is a painful consequence of apparently successful treatment of the first child to be scapegoated: often, and soon, the family return with equally intransigent denunciation of another child. Now the first child presented is often portrayed as a model of goodness and reason. This is especially the case if the first child has been seen in effective individual therapy, learning to manage itself in such a way as to avoid the parent's trend to see it as so hopelessly bad. Such a child feels less hated, and acts less hatefully. Whole family treatment can, occasionally, help the family change so that no scapegoat is needed. Such contrasting circumstances are suggestive of a dominantly family process whereby a the problems complained of in the scapegoat are a result of a *family* need, not of an established process in an individual. The scapegoat's hatefulness follows from its frustration and anger at being seen as bad. When another child is proposed as the problem when a

former child improves, the complaints are reproduced with a depress-
ing exactness. Furthermore, the parents show no realisation that they
are using just the same words and phrases to depict the new problem.
If the therapist suggests that at one time they had said that the now
complained-about child was pleasurable, good tempered and well behaved, the parents will be scandalised, saying that the child had always
been impossibly bad.

7. The process whereby one child can be freed of blame and another be
set up as the family problem is probably well known to all the family
members. To avoid themselves becoming the scapegoat all family
members tend to join in the family attitudes to the chosen child. This
is especially so for anyone who sees themselves as particularly vulnerable, for example the same sex sibling or a companion step- or half-sib-
ling. It is another of the painful processes for the outside observer; it
seems such a betrayal and abandonment for the scapegoated child by
those who know only too well what it is like.

8. The complaints of a scapegoating family against the chosen sacrifice do
not derive from chance ill will and malice, although it sometimes
seems so. The family have a strong need to have a sacrifice so that a
danger to the family as a whole is seemingly avoided. The commonest
danger seems to be the fear that the marriage will break up in mutual
parental denunciation but there may be other dangers. One common
theme is a belief that the chosen scapegoat represents someone in the
history of the family who is, in reality or in mythology, destructive.
The absence of any extenuating explanation or exoneration of the
scapegoat is an important element in avoiding contamination by the
evil of the danger to the family. Hatred is mobilised under the extreme
fear of a catastrophe. Unfortunately, in a tragic sense, scapegoating
'works': the family does feel free of the danger whilst the scapegoat is
unremittingly identified as the problem. The therapist who offers reason or mitigation of the child's hatefulness is feared as someone wishing for the destruction of the marriage or the family. Extenuation
would break down the strength of the protection offered by the piling
of all evil on to the scapegoat.

9. The original biblical scene entailed evicting the sacrificial animal from
the tribe. The scapegoated child is always threatened with eviction and
it sometimes happens that the family finds a way to get rid of the
child. Some boarding schools are used in this way if the family has the
resources or can persuade someone else to pay. Local authority reception into care sometimes occurs as a result of the scapegoated child
acting in a flagrantly hateful way. Sometimes a local authority social
services department will be horrified at the level of pain and rejection
that the child receives and it will see it as constituting emotional abuse
requiring reception into care. Regularly, of course, physical abuse is,
perpetrated against the child by a parent or parents; this leads to re-

moval of the child. Surprisingly, perhaps, eviction is unusual. Usually the scapegoated child lives miserably on the edge of the family.

It is also true to say that the child *chosen* as the scapegoat has been, for other reasons, on the periphery of the family. The clinical impression is that step-children, adopted children and foster children are all more vulnerable to being scapegoated, if the family has the need. Likewise, a child handicapped by physical or learning disability can become pushed to the edge of the family and so liable to scapegoating, but only in those families that can use such a mechanism and have a need for it. Sometimes the vulnerable child has a psychiatric disorder – an adolescent with a schizophrenic disorder, for example. Odd, incomprehensible, difficult and annoying behaviour can lead to a child being partially rejected, coming to exist on the edge of the family and then for reasons outside of themselves subject to scapegoating. Paradoxically, an ill or handicapped child may become the central figure of the family. The need for special care and help can understandably lead a family to concentrate most of their resources onto one such child. The feeling of being such a focus is not always experienced as benign or helpful. To be at the centre of the family can detract from the child feeling a real member of the family. Such a child may behave in an angry and apparently ungrateful manner, leading in turn to the sort of rejection and anger that makes the child feel is unfair. If, for other reasons, the family is a scapegoating one, a process of further attacking and denigrating the disturbed child can lead to a self perpetuating cycle. The fact that the child has been the focus of such care makes it even less likely that actual rejection will occur. The family become fixed in the most cruel cycle of mutual hatred and hurtfulness. This vicious circle produces some of the most difficult, hating and disturbed children ever seen by a child psychiatric team.

10. So far, there has been some discussion both as to why scapegoating oc-
    curs and why a particular child is the subject and becomes full of re-
    sentful hate in the process. A special case occurs when a parent has a
    reservoir of resentment and hate against an absent partner. Most com-
    monly the absent partner is a deserting male and the co-habitation or
    marriage breaks up in betrayal, hurt, rage and fierce misery. This proc-
    ess is commonly associated with the deserted partner falling out of
    love into a blind hate. The deserting man is seen as having been totally
    bad: the breakup of the marriage as entirely his fault. The deserted
    partner, whether male or female, denies any responsibility for the part-
    nership failure. Some of this is based on truth, some on a process of
    projecting all the bad feeling and problems of the relationship onto the
    other person. Clearly this is akin to, if not the same as, scapegoating. A
    child in the family, especially one that resembles the departed partner,
    is critically vulnerable to scapegoating. Of course the children of the
    marriage may not wholeheartedly agree with the way the partners at-

tribute blame for the failure of the relationship. Even if a child or children accept that the partner is blameworthy they may not stop loving and needing their deserting parent. The continuing loyalty of the child for the absent father may be enhanced if he or she was a favourite of the missing parent. The remaining parent may see the child as resembling the now hated betrayer in looks and/or personality. The scene is set for the child to become a scapegoat. The potential is realised if, on beginning a new partnership, the fresh-made couple run into difficulties. Foremost will be the woman's fear that her new partner will turn out like the former one. The new partner will fear that he will suffer the same fate as his predecessor. To heap all potential blame onto the children is especially possible because the child or children most identified with or fond of the absent parent may well resent the new partner; they may suspect and mistrust him. This may grow to an incipient hatred, the flames being fanned if the child becomes identified as the cause of any of the troubles of readjustment to the new family organisation.

Expressed emotion and the measurement of blame

So far the descriptions in this chapter have been clinical, from the experience of seeing many families. However, as a result of a formal research study it has recently become possible to imagine a measurement of some aspects of scapegoating in families. Leff and Vaughn (1985) have described a method of measuring the communication of certain feelings in families. They interviewed the relatives of adult psychiatric patients, tape recording the conversations and making scientifically accurate measures of criticism, warmth and hostility. They also estimated the emotional involvement of the relative in the patient and judged the amount of positive comments made to the patient. We have shown that this measure can be derived from family interviews (Szmukler et al. 1987).

Table 3.2 shows the results of a study of a group of eight families, each containing an adolescent patient considered by the criteria outlined in this chapter to be scapegoats. Tables 3.3 and 3.4 give the comparable scores in a group of anorexic and bulimic patients. What is obvious is how much criticism and hostility are communicated to this group of scapegoated children. Likewise, of course, the children receive very little warmth from their parents. This scientific measurement supports the clinical judgement. It also shows that a patient, even one with the obnoxious symptoms of bulimia, does not necessarily excite high levels of criticism and hostility. It suggests that there is something special going on in scapegoating families; something more than the presence of a child or adolescent with psychiatric symptoms. Another quality of the families emerges from inspection of the measures of the expression of emotion: the parents show no more warmth for each other, on average, than do the parents of eating disorder patients.

Table 3.2: Expressed emotion in families containing a scapegoated adolescent (The mean scores of a sample of 8 families)

	CC	H	EOI	W	+
Father to child	8.2	1.6	1.1	0.1	0
Mother to child	11.8	2.2	2.3	0.8	1.0
Father to mother	0.3	0	0	0.6	0
Mother to father	0.3	0	0	0.6	0

CC = critical comments; H = hostility; EOI = emotional overinvolvement; W = warmth; + = positive remarks

This table shows, in bold type, high levels of criticism and hostility from both father and mother to the scapegoat child. It also shows very low levels of criticism between father and mother. The column marked EOI shows that there is a level of involvement of mother to the child which is higher than that of the anorexic or bulimic patients in Tables 3.3 and 3.4.

Table 3.3: Expressed emotion in families containing a anorexic adolescent (The mean scores of a sample of 30 families)

	CC	H	EOI	W	+
Father to child	1.6	0	0.6	1.9	0.4
Mother to child	2.2	0.2	1.0	2.4	0.6
Father to mother	0.9	0	0	0.7	0.1
Mother to father	1.6	0.2	0.1	1.2	0

CC = critical comments; H = hostility; EOI = emotional overinvolvement; W = warmth; + = positive remarks

This table shows low levels of criticism and minimal hostility as occurring within anorexic families. There is a low level of emotional over-involvement but higher levels of warmth than in families with a scapegoated child.

Table 3.4: Expressed emotion in families containing a bulimic adolescent (The mean scores of a sample of 6 families)

	CC	H	EOI	W	+
Father to child	4.3	.3	2.7	2.7	1.0
Mother to child	2.6	0	1.4	2.6	1.0
Father to mother	1.2	0	0	.6	0
Mother to father	3.6	.6	.6	.8	.6

CC = critical comments; H = hostility; EOI = emotional overinvolvement; W = warmth; + = positive remarks

This table shows higher levels of criticism from father to child than in anorexic families, but not nearly as high as in scapegoating families. There are possibly higher levels of criticism between parents, especially the mother to the father. Emotional over-involvement also seem to be significantly warmer to their child in comparison to the mothers of bulimic patients.

Scapegoating parents do show a very low level of criticism for each other, in comparison with the parents of eating disorder patients. This might be a clue as to the presence of a mechanism – a technique of blaming a child in order to avoid blaming each other.

The successful treatment of a scapegoat

Mr and Mrs M married in their late twenties. He is a youth group leader working in a suburban project for disturbed and delinquent youths, for whom he has created a strict but often successful regime. There is a glitter of violence and anger in his eyes that controls unruly boys but which troubles some of the mental health workers that have met him. He is a tall and athletic man; indeed, his prowess as a footballer still earns him respect from his clients. He was born to a family that was struck by a pair of premature and tragic deaths. When Mr M was a toddler, his paternal uncle was killed in action in Malaysia. His father died when he was ten years old. His brother committed suicide at the age of nineteen, whilst 'on the run' when he had inadvertently and foolishly become entangled in a marijuana smuggling operation. He seemed to have felt himself to have been responsible for his own upbringing after his mother's death.

Mr M was apprenticed as a panel beater but on qualification he immediately became a worker in a street project for young people at risk on the streets of Soho (this was two years after his brother had died). Subsequently he trained as a psychiatric nurse and learned something of how his wish that he could have saved his brother had influenced his chosen career.

Mrs M was thought by herself and her husband to come from a much more stable, less tragic but rather cold and distant family. She was the only child of her parents. They had been washed up rather than having actively and wilfully settled on the South Coast, having come to Britain from India in 1948. Both her grandfathers had been in the middle ranks of the Indian Civil Service. Mrs M still had a trace of the laconic trailing speech of that caste. Her own mother had felt herself to be considered unimportant in comparison with her older brother and this was thought by Mr and Mrs M to account for her decidedly critical attitude to men in general and towards her son-in-law in particular. When Mrs M's own children were little, she realised that she was extremely unsure of herself as a mother. Later she came to tell of her parents having left her to look after herself much of the time. She began to realise, with some bitterness, that they had had a tradition of servants and nannies looking after children, not the actual parents. She felt that she had in fact been neglected. This served as a source of considerable covert anger, especially against figures in authority.

Mrs M had taken a degree in English Literature at the university in her home town and had eventually 'drifted' into teaching English as a foreign language to students from abroad.

As a couple, Mr and Mrs M had had a rather close relationship. They both, it seems, felt themselves to be set apart from other people. They clung to each other rather like strangers in a strange world. Early in their marriage they came to avoid rows at all costs, they said, because they both though that bad temper was simply unnecessary. From the beginning, they had an earnest commitment to the task of parenting and found their first child, Tony, to be a considerable worry. For all his life they had been aghast at the intensity of his capacity both to oppose them and to be unhappy. Mr M's profession was accepted by both parents to give him an expertise in children and families. From time to time Mrs M allowed herself a quiet satisfaction that her husband was so confounded and infuriated by Tony.

Harry's birth, three years after Tony's, was beset by obstetric complications and his early months were a time of anxiety to his mother and father but, to their surprise, he was a compliant, sweet tempered and independent person from his first year of life.

When Tony was five years old the family sought help on account of his naughtiness and unhappiness. They had recently converted within their original Church of England religion to a rather evangelistic movement. This brought them great happiness and support and they both commented, unprompted, that the church gave them a better experience of a loving family than they had had before in their lives. Seeking help for Tony was precipitated by someone in the church telling them that she could not see how *they* could have such a naughty child as their oldest son. When they saw the psychiatrist, he affronted them by his relaxed acceptance of what they thought was Tony's cheekiness. They were even more put off when the social worker seeing the parents, whilst the psychiatrist 'played' with Tony, implied that they were too strict and had too high expectations of good behaviour.

The psychiatrist offered to see Tony a few times, suggesting that they should have regular talks with the social worker. They refused. They continued to believe that Tony was in need of more discipline. They also took him to a spiritual healer, and later said that it was because they thought that Tony had a deep spiritual defect. To their annoyance the spiritual healer seemed not to think that there was much wrong with the little boy, and offered to pray that they might be more tranquil about their son.

The family returned to another child mental health team when Tony was ten years old. They said that in the previous visit they had expected that the psychiatrist would tell them that Tony was psychiatrically ill, would have taken into hospital for tests and would have given him medicine to make his brain work more slowly. Instead, they said, the psychiatrist had told them that Tony was normal and he had asked a social worker to see them, to teach them to treat him softly. They had tried that but it had made Tony even worse. Now he was quarrelsome and naughty in the family, rude and abusive to his mother and lacked concentration at schoolwork. At school he was said to be the 'victim of his own reputation'. If there were problems in class he was sure to be in the middle of them and assumed to be their source. It was the school problems that had determined his referral because they were apprehensive about his capacity to make the transfer to secondary school at the age of eleven.

At the first interview the parents were seen to be a serious, harassed looking couple. Mr M had a sternness which fitted with his description as to how he conducted himself in his job whilst Mrs M was a dour shy woman. Tony was a sad, persecuted, clumsy and rather plump pre-adolescent. Harry was attractive, blue eyed and blond. He was somewhat nervous, largely silent, declining to talk with the therapist, mostly grinning charmingly and looking anxiously to mother to speak for him.

In the first session of therapy, the facts of the parents' worries about Tony emerged. The parents were pessimistic about their relationship with Tony and they were mostly negative about him. There were high levels of criticism and disapproval of Tony. He seemed to be scapegoated.

After a while, the therapist began to concentrate on Tony's feeling that he was, all the time, being 'got at'. The therapist thought that it would be unwise to focus upon the parents' unremitting antagonism to their son. Tony, in turn, made little attempt to deny the parent's specific accusations against him, although he tried always to lighten the intensity of their general criticisms. He did this not in an argumentative or assertive way but in a gloomy, dogged hopeless manner. He seemed to know that there would be no changes in attitudes towards him but that he had to try to get some mitigation, if only to avoid the worst consequences. In trying to express this state of mind and to speak for Tony's fatalism, the therapist said to Tony, 'It's as though you feel that you are cursed'.

Tony agreed, and the therapist began to ask whether or no there had been any good fairies at Tony's christening or whether it had been only bad witches. Tony was, initially, astonished at the phrasing of the question and began to brush it aside, but then he took it to heart and said that there were probably none.

The therapist began an exploration of the balance of good and bad fairies at the christenings of the other family members. Mother had had a few loving or even helpful fairies, and Harry had been attended by mostly good fairies. In this discussion the father revealed, to the therapist's relief, that he saw himself as largely cursed. He went over the deaths in his family history (which had been unmentioned in the first treatment). In the course of unraveling the dreadful series of tragic deaths, Tony eventually said:

> It's the men that are cursed. Dad and I, we have all bad fairies at our christenings.

The therapist was attempting to help the family invent a myth to sustain the treatment, avoiding confrontation with their view as to Tony's nature. He offered a 'therapeutic myth' to the family as a method whereby the dilemmas of the family, expressed as a need to have a scapegoat, are organised into a metaphorical tale. A myth 'frames' the family reality, as Minuchin and

Fishman (1981) have expressed. It can be seen as a part of a family's way of understanding themselves or, as with Tony's family, it can be given an explicit form by the therapist. This understanding gives family members (or individuals) a hold on what the therapy is about that can sustain them through an uncomfortable time, giving up the need to have someone to hate.

Tony was able to hold on to the idea of men being cursed, so that at the beginning of the new phase of treatment he did not see the therapist who was, for the time being protecting the parents, as simply getting at him. It was also a way of understanding Tony (and his father) that Harry could appreciate; he had already begun to disparage his brother and, to a lesser extent, his father. This attitude came directly from Mrs M's own mother; it is an early stage of a sibling joining in with the family to scapegoat his brother, fending off the same fate for himself. The male therapist could also easily have been made to feel discredited by the little boy and made into a scapegoat himself.

The therapist had suggested that the family lived by a myth that men were bound to have had only bad fairies at their christening. Tony, as scapegoat, became the embodiment of the masculine badness, thereby protecting Mr M and Harry from this fate. Although this invention had helped the family enter therapy and had engaged the interest of the two children, it was no sort of cure.

The family rather soon developed a pattern of coming once every three or four weeks for sessions that had a rather consistent pattern. They would enter with some subdued barracking from a sheepish and yet defiant Tony. Mr M would try hard not to complain about his son, wishing rather to report on an observation of his own whereby he had identified some defect or lapse in himself and had allowed Tony to get away with a piece of dominating, obnoxious behaviour, provoking a sequence of Mr M trying to reason with his son but finding himself in an escalating confrontation. The end point would be that Tony felt bullied and attacked by his father, and Mr M indeed felt a potentially violent bully, unable to control his elder son's misbehaviour that could so easily dominate the house. Mr M struggled to describe these scenes in a way that would reflect at least as much discredit upon himself as upon his son. He would invite his wife to join in, in like vein. She, however, did not see that her behaviour could be compared to her son. She was reluctant to contradict her husband openly but often had a look of troubled defiance, often glancing at the therapist as if she hoped that he would take a more sensible line and see that the simple truth was that Tony was seriously ill behaved. It was as though she was more confident of herself in seeing Tony as the problem.

The children had a pattern to accompany their parents' fixed sequence. Harry came into the room next to his mother, often clinging to her and often whispering some aside to her, looking at the therapist. When the therapist asked him to make his contributions to the whole room, Harry would either ask his mother to speak for him or would say that it was something that he only wanted to talk of to his mother. Mrs M learned not to speak for Harry and over the months became irritated with his repeatedly doing the same thing, but Harry did not stop doing it for many months. When he did say aloud what he had been whispering, it would come out that he was describing something that Tony had done at which he expected his mother to become annoyed. When later in treatment he found that he could not interrupt he would flop over his mother's lap, claiming he needed to sleep, but doing so in such a way that he was totally distancing himself from the procedure of the session.

Tony looked glum and sullen whilst his parents described his episodes of misbehaviour, scowling, hiding his head by pulling his anorak up over his eyes and muttering occasionally audible disclaimers of having ever done anything of which his parents spoke. Soon, Harry would 'wake' and watch Tony, subtly egging him on to more noisy and noticeable distracting behaviour. Nods, gestures, threats and mouthing would be exchanged between the boys.

Not surprisingly, Tony would eventually be turned upon by his parents and told to quieten down and not to upset his brother. It took some hours of observation (that is, two months of therapy) before the therapist was able to see that Harry was quite clearly as provocative as his brother, (in this particular setting the therapist was sorely missing one-way screen or video recording to help him disentangle what was going on in this family), but what Harry did was either so low in amplitude that it was hardly visible to the adults or it had a quality of innocence that was equally protective.

The therapist made two types of intervention, which both had to be repeated in different ways and on many occasion. One was to get the parents to treat the exchanges between the boys as unnecessary interruption that had to be ignored. Over some weeks the parents implemented this strategy. Not surprisingly the boys increased the noisiness of their interactions to the point of viciously kicking and pinching each other. Here too it was striking that Harry's spitefulness seemed equal to but invisible in comparison to Tony's. This was subject to the therapist's second type of intervention, which was simply to point out how Harry had a style of doing things that were in the main similar to Tony's activities but which were somehow much less defiant and overt in their delivery and therefore had none of the obnoxious quality.

Mr M took a lead in accepting what the therapist said and tried to give his wife the benefit of the insight, in such a way as to fuel her sense of frustration and skepticism. Harry was absolutely scandalised that anyone could doubt his innocence, but here again his protest seemed real innocence whilst Tony's very similar indignation seemed hopeless.

Neither the direct instruction nor the verbal information about the therapist's perception of the children being more similar than the overt picture, had immediate effects. However, over the weeks and months, these two interventions, and a number that were less often repeated, were associated with a change in both the family relationships and the degree to which Tony got into trouble. He began to do well at his new school and had longer periods without his parents feeling themselves driven to despair.

Of course, at the end of treatment, the family still had concerns about the present and fears for the future. The therapist would not have been surprised to hear from them again, when Tony was a teenager. Alternatively, they might have come complaining about Harry. However, this did not happen.

Acknowledgements

The measures of Expressed Emotion reported in this chapter were undertaken by Danie Le Grange and Mathew Hodes to whom the author owes thanks. He also acknowledges the generous support of the Medical Research Council.

References

Ackerman, N.W. (1974) Prejudice and scapegoating in the family. In Zuk, G.H. and Boszormenyi-Nagy, I. (eds.) *Family and Disturbed Families*, p.48–57. Pal Alto: Science and Behavior Books.

Cooper, D. (1967) *Psychiatry and Anti-psychiatry*, London: Tavistock.

Epstein, N.B., Bishop, D. (1981) Problem-centered systems therapy of the family. In Gurman, A.S. and Kniskern, D.P. (eds.) *Handbook of Family Therapy*, chapter 12, p.444–482. New York: Brunner/Mazel.

Leff, J.P. and Vaughn, C. (1985) *Expressed Emotion in Families*. New York: Guilford.

Minuchin, S. and Fishman, H.C. (1981) *Family Therapy Techniques*. Cambridge, Massachusetts: Harvard University Press.

Szmukler, G., Berkowitz, R., Eisler I., Leff, J. and Dare, C. (1987) A comparative study of parental 'Expressed Emotion', in individual and family settings. *British Journal of Psychiatry*. 151: 174–8.

CHAPTER 4

Child Abuse and Hatred

Kedar Nath Dwivedi

An eleven-year-old boy was referred to our clinic by the Department of Social Services. He was the eldest of five children, all of whom had different fathers. He came across as a very bright, perceptive and alert child, and appeared caring and protective towards his younger siblings. As he had been found attempting to sexually assault another child the social services department and the police had become involved. Through our clinic the family received regular family therapy sessions and the boy also attended weekly group therapy sessions. Over a long period of treatment he began to comprehend and overcome the damaging influences of his past experiences and their effect on his current problematic behaviours.

His habit of fire-setting was the most dangerous one. It turned out that he would deliberately set fire especially to tyres or heaps of tyres (for example, tyre mountains or rubbish tips) which belonged to a particular company – the company for which his sexually abusive father had worked. This was the way he tried to express the mountain of his hatred towards the father's abusive acts. Hobson (1989) has compiled some very moving accounts provided by the victims of abuse. For example:

> My father was a large man who was physically very powerful. When he hit me I was flung the length of the room. He was a respected man, a manager who owned his business. My mother was a quiet, cold woman who worked part time because she wanted to, not because she had to. When I was small she undressed me and locked me in the coal bunker. When she took me out she told me off for being dirty and put me in a red hot bath of water... I was seven when my father first raped me. I was nine when he had anal intercourse with me. His visits to my room were part of my life. At 14 I had a miscarriage. After that I tried to commit suicide several times. I was put in a psychiatric hospital for several months when I was 17. When I left home at 18 my brothers and sisters turned against me. I was the one who was in the wrong. I was the guilty party and nothing I said or did made them change their minds because they did not want to lose their security and their parents. I lost everything. It was though everyone in my life had suddenly died. (An account given by a 19-year-old shop manageress, p.98)

I used to stay awake at night looking at the lamp post and the stars and the moon. I could not hear him enter my room. I felt cold as my blankets were removed. He did not say anything to me. I *hated* him. I felt useless. I felt he owned me. I felt guilty as I tried not to feel pleasure, but the more I tried to hold my feelings the greater the pleasure. I thought I heard him laugh. (An account given by an 18-year-old male nurse, p.95)

Elliot (1986) wrote about an eleven-year-old girl who reported that she was made pregnant by her father and made to have an abortion. As she did not want to become pregnant again she took a cork from a wine bottle, smeared it with butter and inserted it to prevent herself getting pregnant again. But this did not prevent her father abusing her and the cork got pushed further into her body. When she tried to get it out with the help of a coat hanger, she got hurt and started to bleed. The father then made her have oral sex. Even her younger sister was made to sit and watch this. Her mother knew what was going on but only called her names.

I was asked to see a fifteen-year-old girl who had been taken into care and was living in a children's home. She referred to her parents as 'that man' and 'that lady' and was full of intense hatred for them. She described them as 'evil' and 'monsters' and did not want even to see them. The intensity of her feelings were magnified by the mechanism of narcissistic disorder (see later) instituted so early in her life. This led to such a blind hatred and an addiction to hatred so intense that it became too difficult to work with.

The extent of the problem

In western culture, ill treatment of children was not really recognised as a social problem in the past. It is only recently that this has come to be regarded as child abuse and a problem. Violence to children was justified for centuries on educational, remedial and religious grounds. Instances of barbarous treatment of children from medieval times abound, including infanticide, mutilation, flogging, starvation and exploitation (Mause 1976). There was a deeply entrenched notion of parents having the full right to treat or punish their children as they saw fit, because the children were the property of their parents.

The idea that childhood is separate from adulthood emerged as late as the 17th century. Babies, if they survived babyhood, became little adults, except a few favoured ones. In Britain, therefore, even as recently as a century ago, the abuse of children by parents was considered to be culturally acceptable and the belief in parental right existed until the end of the last century. In 1880 Lord Shaftesbury did recognise the enormity and indisputability of this evil, but the state was still reluctant to intervene in family affairs: 'so private, internal and domestic a character, to be beyond the reach of legislation' (Shaftesbury, quoted in Pinchbeck and Hewitt 1973). Instead, he tried to improve the conditions for children at work. In fact, some 67 years after the introduction of legislation to protect animals, the first Charter for children appeared in 1889 (Meadow 1989). Thus, only by the end of the 19th century did the state take powers to intervene to protect children with the Prevention of Cruelty to and Protection of Children Act in 1889.

Child abuse is generally regarded as a western phenomenon, although some degree of parental violence to children is universal. The term 'Battered Baby Syndrome' was coined by Kempe (Kempe *et al.* 1962) to draw attention to the size and seriousness of this problem. In April 1976, The Royal College of Psychiatrists was asked to submit evidence to the Parliamentary Select Committee considering this problem. This evidence (Scott 1977) emphasised that there is not one but a whole range of syndromes with many types of parents, children, causes and treatments.

According to the NSPCC, the reporting of figures of parental violence to children in Britain grew steadily in the late 1970s and early 1980s. In 1983 in England and Wales, 7038 children were reported physically abused. One child a week was found to be dying. Due to this, child abuse became the fourth most common cause of infant death. Similarly, in the United States of America, the number of reported cases increased dramatically from 60,000 in 1968 to 1 million in 1978. In New York City alone, nearly 150 children die due to child abuse each year. The number of child abuse cases is estimated at between 15,000 and 18,000 per year in Germany and nearly 50,000 per year in France, where there are nearly 500 deaths per year (Hobson 1989). The reporting of cases has been significantly influenced by public awareness; for example, the setting up of a hotline in 1971 in the state of Florida increased the number of reported cases from 17 in 1970 to 19,120 in 1971.

There is now an increased public awareness along with professional recognition of the problems and society's unwillingness to tolerate such behaviours. For more than a decade corporal punishment in general has been significantly less acceptable. In spite of this, it seems that nearly 90% of parents smack their children and nearly 600 children die due to child abuse in the UK every year (Frude 1990).

It was estimated that between 1 April 1989 and 31 March 1990 numbers on registers increased by about 7%. The estimated number of children on the register as a rate per thousand children under the age of eighteen has risen from 3.8 at 31 March 1989 to 4.0 at 31 March 1990. In that period there has also been a reduction of population aged under eighteen. Younger children are more likely to be on the register than older children. In 1990 the highest rates were found in the age groups 1–4 years (5.7 per thousand), 5–9 years (4.7 per thousand) and under one year (4.2 per thousand). The representation on the registers then decreased with age. The estimates also indicate that there were more girls (4.3 per thousand) than boys (3.8 per thousand) on the registers (Department of Health 1991).

A child is considered to be abused if he or she is treated by an adult in a way that is unacceptable in a given culture at a given time; child rearing practices do vary between countries and cultures and between different sub-cultures and different times in the same country.

Physical abuse or non accidental injuries include soft tissue injuries to the skin, eyes, ears, internal organs, ligaments and bones and also burns and scalds. Such injuries are mostly violent episodic and may be repetitive. Sometimes there is a history of long term deliberate injury, including suffocation and poisoning. *Neglect* includes the failure to provide the physical circumstances, food, care and love that are essential for a child's normal growth and development and neglecting to protect from any kind of danger. *Emotional abuse* includes mental cruelty, scapegoating, excessive criticism, hostility and rejection. Scapegoating and related issues are discussed at length elsewhere in this volume. *Sexual abuse* includes the involvement of children by older persons in the following types of sexual activities: exposure (for example, during sexual acts, pornography and exhibitionism), touching of sexual parts (for example, child or adult genitalia and post-pubertal female breasts), sexual intercourse (oral, anal or vaginal; acute assault and chronic involvement) and other sexual acts (for example, ejaculation of semen onto the child's body, sado-masochistic acts) (Royal College of Psychiatrists 1988).

Each local government and health authority in England and Wales has a Child Protection Register (previously known as At Risk Register). All children living in the area who are found to be abused or at risk of abuse are placed on this Register. Many of these Registers are managed by the National Society for Prevention of Cruelty to Children (NSPCC) and their combined data forms a Research Register to estimate the national picture.

At 31 March 1990, 43,900 children were estimated to be on Child Protection Registers in England; a rate of 4.0 children per 1,000 population aged under eighteen years. Of these children, 25% were in the care of local authorities, a further 8% on supervision orders and 1% under place of safety orders. The reasons for their registration were as follows: 42% grave concern, 26% percent physical abuse including combination categories (23% physical abuse alone), 16% sexual abuse including combination categories (14% under sexual abuse alone), 16% neglect including combination categories (13% neglect alone), 5% emotional abuse (Department of Health 1991).

Nearly 4% of children up to the age of twelve years are brought to the notice of professional agencies such as Social Services Department of NSPCC because of suspected abuse. Each year, at least one child in a thousand under the age of four suffers severe physical abuse such as brain haemorrhage, bone fractures, mutilation and severe internal injuries. A minimum mortality rate is 1 in 10,000 children and many cases are unde-tected; thus nearly four children die each week as a result of abuse or neglect. The notification of suspicion of child abuse has increased nearly 20 times in the last 10 years. Although some of the reports are proven to be unfounded, the number of proven cases is four or five times that of a decade ago. Until a few years ago there was widespread reluctance to accept the fact that children were also being sexually abused. In Britain, reported cases have risen steeply in the last few years from a handful in the late 1970s to 7119 new cases registered in 1987. The sharpest rise came in 1986 with a 127% increase.

Child sexual abuse appeared as an epidemic of the 1980s. NSPCC statistics represent cases of sufficient severity, although they may not be proven. Accordingly, the rate of sexual abuse incidents in 1986 was 0.57 (in contrast to 0.27 in 1985) per 1000 children under the age of 17 years. Eighty per cent of the sexually abused children were girls and 18% were less than five years old. The mean age was 10 years 2 months. The estimated number of new cases in a year in England and Wales was 6333 in 0–16-year-old children (Creighton 1987).

Markowe (1988) provides a very good methodological critique of the UK data on child sexual abuse and concludes that the information that is available is open to criticism because it is invalid and is not representative of the general population. This makes estimating a figure for the national prevalence of child sexual abuse an unsatisfactory exercise. As is apparent from several studies, much of the child sexual abuse never reaches the attention of professionals. The abuse is not disclosed to anyone at all, so officially collected statistics will always underestimate the extent of the problem: an iceberg phenomenon.

A MORI interview survey (Baker and Duncan 1985) of a nationally representative sample of all adults aged 15 years and above in Great Britain revealed that 10% of subjects reported having been sexually abused before the age of 16 years (12% of females and 8% of males). The risk was not associated with any specific social class category. The younger respondents reported significantly more abuse than older respondents. Twenty three per cent were repeatedly abused by the same person and 14% were subject to multiple abuse by a number of people. Fifty one per cent of the experiences reported as abusive involved no physical contact but 44% did, although without sexual intercourse. Five per cent reported full sexual intercourse. Forty nine per cent of abusers were known to the victims and 14% of all the reported sexual abuse took place within the family.

A general practice survey of female patients aged 20–39 years revealed a 42% positive history of childhood sexual abuse (Nash and West 1985). Similarly, a survey of female students revealed a 54% positive history of childhood sexual abuse (Nash and West 1985). The BBC Childwatch viewers were also invited to complete a questionnaire and 90% of those who replied had a positive history of childhood abuse (BBC 1986).

The reason for the problem

It has been very difficult to comprehend fully why some people abuse children. Most behaviours are products of a convergence of both outer and inner forces. The interactions between such forces can be extremely complex and at various levels. One of the frameworks that can be used to make sense of such a complexity is the General Systems Theory. This theory originated in the field of cybernetics (von Bertalanffy 1968). As the models of natural sciences in the 19th century were rather naive, mechanistic, reductionistic and 'either/or' models, Ludwig von Bertalanffy proposed an alternative model in 1945 which unified the natural and social sciences in a single theoretical framework. The Society for the Advancement of General Systems theory was established in 1954.

A *system* is composed of component parts and their interactions. As nothing exists in isolation but rather in a hierarchy of systems, the systems are therefore made up of subsystems and are themselves parts of supra systems. Every subsystem, system and supra system has boundaries with characteristic permeability for communication and feedback between different parts. All events, therefore, are better understood in terms of circular rather than linear causality.

One can thus conceive of inner intrapsychic processes influencing individuals who are also influenced by outer systemic forces such as family, school and work systems, which in turn are influenced by the larger supra systems creating a socio-cultural and politico-economical context for organisational (for example, family) functions. Social circumstances such as unemployment, poverty, single parenthood, social isolation, poor accommodation, ill health and unwanted number of pregnancies and children are bound to produce frustrations which may cause even the most normal of parents to lash out. Poverty can change attitudes, personalities and behaviour; thus economic hardship can also lead to considerable emotional deprivation.

Current theories about child abuse emphasise the influences of social processes such as the stresses of modern life, the use of physical punishment to elicit obedience and the nature of family organisation which hastened to isolate parents with their heavy child care burdens (Gil 1973). It is also clear that cultural forces can modify the propensity of large numbers of adults to be sexually interested in children. There is a tendency in the capitalistic society to sexualise children in the media and elsewhere (Vermeulen 1981). It is possible that such media portrayals and the culture they represent may stimulate adult sexual interest in children. Child pornography also stimulates sexual interest in children (Baker 1978). Exposure to pornography involving children creates new converts; it elicits sexual arousal in people who would not otherwise have become aroused. Themes of sexual activity amongst adults may also be mixed with themes of sex with children, and masturbation with this kind of material can induce arousal, attraction and addiction for children in such consumers. Thus sexual abuse needs to be seen within a social and cultural framework. There also appears to be a degree of moral confusion about sex. The current sexual revolution has pushed towards 'all is permitted'.

Brandt and Tisza (1977) proposed a concept of 'sexual misuse' including all sexual stimulation inappropriate for the child's age, level of psychosexual development and role in the family. Such an experience interferes with or has the potential for interfering with a child's health and development. Bolton *et al.* (1989) provide a model of abuse of sexuality describing a continuum of environments that range from the promotion of normalised sexual development to those which eliminate the possibility of normal development and mention the following points on that continuum: predominantly nurturing environment; evasive environment (evading answering questions); environmental vacuum (no exposure to any sexual information); permissive environment (very open and honest approach); negative environment (punished for exploring); seductive environment (exposure and suggestive teasing); and overtly sexual environment. In western capitalistic culture power can be equated with economic control; it can also influence the gender role and power differences. The tyranny of a father's use of economic sanctions and personal force can easily lead to mother's powerlessness and dependency and therefore to her inability to protect her children. Her feelings of powerlessness, frustration and anger towards her husband may transfer into violence and exploitation towards her children who may be the only ones over whom she still has any power.

The anthropologist Edmund Leach (1968), in his 1967 Reith Lecture, shocked his audience by referring to the family as 'an emotional gas chamber' (quoted by Marinker 1976, p.119).

> Today the domestic household is isolated. The family looks inward upon itself, there is an intensification of emotional stress between husband and wife, and parents and children. The strain is greater than most of us can bear. Far from being the basis of the good society, the family with its narrow privacy and tawdry secrets is the source of all our discontents.

In an extended family set up in a different cultural context, for example in an Asian family, the intricate protective relationships between several family members tend to augment the protection against abuse. On the other hand, the nature of western family organisation is such that there is a constant negotiation for power distribution and therefore perpetual proneness to conflict. Sex and violence within the family can therefore be used as weapons to control each other's behaviour, express strong feeling and resolve such conflicts. Child abuse can therefore be a symptom of a dysfunctional family system. It may also be an attempt at defending against threatened disintegration of the family system – a kind of homeostatic function.

Child abuse is a manifestation of the disintegration of generational boundaries. Abusive parents are described as adults who are rather immature and cannot empathise with their children. They may also have very unrealistic expectations about their children's abilities. The child may be treated as if he or she were a parent figure. Thus, the child may be expected to satisfy the needs of the parents for love and nurturance of which they were deprived in their own childhood. Such an unconscious role reversal is bound to lead to frustration and aggression because a child is bound to fail in this enormous task *and the parents would perceive this as a wilful rejection*. Thus the child's lack of mastery of a skill is misperceived as wilful hostility, requiring punishment.

Physical abuse

As regards physical abuse of children, Frude (1990) found very little by way of sex difference either in victims or in perpetrators. However, the victims are usually young (the majority younger than five years) and the parents are also young with poverty, low employment status, low educational level, poor living conditions, single parenthood, marital instability, social isolation, drug and alcohol abuse. Younger children are physically more vulnerable than older children. Babies and young children can cry a lot, can be very demanding and can arouse high anxiety in parents. They are also very difficult to control by threatening, begging, cajoling or reasoning. Similarly, young parents may be immature and resentful of costs and may have unwanted pregnancies, accommodation and finance difficulties and poor confidence in dealing with the baby.

Abusive incidents are more likely to occur in the context of customary high aggression, unresolved disciplinary problems and poor parent–child relationships. Parents tend to lack warmth and empathy; they tend to judge children's behaviours as bad and feel aversive towards many of these behaviours. These children may have developmental difficulties and may also be aggressive and non-compliant; thus a vicious cycle is set up as children become more attention seeking, immune to negative sanctions, resistant to positive goading and difficult to manage. As abusive parents lack disciplining skills, they tend to attend to bad behaviours and unwittingly reinforce them. They also tend to ignore good behaviours, which can therefore become extinguished. The style of these parents' normal punishment is rather harsh and they tend to flare up rather easily. As anger also accumulates, the child's single act may lead to explosive outbursts (Steele and Pollock 1968). The sequence of events leading to abuse usually begins with a behaviour of the child, such as refusing to eat, wetting, stealing, lying, aggressiveness, etc. which the parent finds aversive and interprets as wilful hostility, for example, 'He is crying deliberately to get at me'; 'He looks at me as if to say just try and feed me' (Brandon 1976); 'When he cried all the time it meant he didn't love me, so I hit him' (Steele and Pollock 1968).

Welldon (1991) describes the concept of a perverse motherhood with an urge to be in complete control of and to merge with the other; to desire and intend to engulf the other person; to dehumanise, intrude into and invade the other. Such a perverse behaviour is brought about by poor individuation and emotional instability and is precipitated by lack of support and a feeling of powerlessness. Thus, the only power available to her is through her exclusive emotional and physical authority over her baby.

According to Browne (1989), the situational stressors in relation to family violence are made up of the following four components:

1. Relations between parents and grandparents; inter marriage; marital disputes; step-parent/cohabitee or separated/single parent.

2. Relations to children, such as spacing between births, size of family, parental attachment to child, and parental expectation of child.

3. Structual stress – poor housing, unemployment, social isolation, threats to parental authority, values, and self esteem.

4. Stress generated by the child (or other dependant) – for example, an unwanted dependant; one who is incontinent, difficult to discipline, often ill, physically deformed, or retarded; one who is temperamental, is frequently emotional, or very demanding.

These situational stressors are mediated by the family relationship and are 'buffered' if the relationships are secure. If such a buffering is not available because the family relationships are rather insecure and anxious, then 'episodic overload' (for example, child misbehaving, having an argument etc.) can easily lead to physical or emotional lashing out. This, in turn, will further damage the overall family relationships, thus escalating the vicious cycle resulting in constant stress, repeated assaults and very fragile relationships. Browne (1989) concludes that, since all stressors and background factors are mediated through the interpersonal relationships within the family, it is these relationships that should therefore be the focus of work on prevention, treatment and management of family violence.

The early writings on abuse attempted to attribute such behaviours to some form of mental illness. Similarly, the victims were often described as mentally incompetent (Meiselman 1978). These attempts have not been convincing and though a small minority of abusers may be clinically mentally ill the current consensus is that most physical abusers do not exhibit any psychotic or other features of any major mental illness (Finkelhor 1979; Russell 1984). Instead, they may have various psychological inadequacies which limit their parenting abilities. Such inadequacies may be in the form of lack of social skills, social competence, confidence, self esteem, impulse control, maturity, frustration tolerance and autonomy. These inadequacies can often be traced to abuse and/or neglect in their own childhoods, leading to a cycle of abuse.

Sexual abuse

Child sexual abuse is also a manifestation of the disintegration of generational boundaries, where a child is placed in a parental role which includes the sexual role of a spouse. Such a situation is more likely to happen when one of the parents is pushed out of the parent subsystem and a child is pulled in to fill the vacated position (Haugaard 1988). One of these patterns has been described as a 'pathological exaggeration of generally accepted patri-archal norms' (Herman 1981) where the father is in clear command of the home and is very dominant and abusive, while the mother has an emotional or physical illness and is very withdrawn and submissive. The mirror image of this is the situation where mother is described as dominant, angry and hostile and father as passive, dependent and treated more like a child than a parent (Greene 1977).

Alexander and Lupfer (1987) conducted a survey of 586 female under-graduate students. The students who had experienced incestuous sexual abuse rated their family structure as having greater power differences in their male/female relationships within the family. Thus management, treatment and prevention of family violence can only be achieved through these relationships.

Herman and Hirschman (1981) compared 40 women who had incestu-ous relationships with their fathers during childhood with 20 women whose fathers had been seductive but not overtly incestuous. More of the women who had experienced overt incest reported that their fathers had been violent and their mothers had been chronicly ill, disabled or battered. Untreated depression, alcoholism, psychosis or repeated involuntary child bearing were most commonly cited as causes of impaired maternal functioning.

The families with the problem of child sexual abuse may have very rigid family roles. Sometimes the mother may be rather permissive and may in a passive aggressive way encourage the role reversal between herself and her daughter and unconsciously offer the daughter as a buffer to the father. Mothers are also often the victims of sexual abuse in their childhood. Mother can induce the daughter into a maternal role through material indulgence and nurturing, coupled with expectations that the daughter will assume exceptional responsibility. This role reversal sets the daughter up as a replica of the maternal grandmother with whom the mother can then act out her displaced hostility by directing it towards the daughter (Kaufman et al. 1954).

Gelinas (1983) describes in detail one of the patterns involved in the development of incestuous relationships. Accordingly, there are many fami-lies in which a child may function as a parent. Such a child, usually a girl, may end up doing most of the cooking, cleaning, laundry and also looking after of children and even the adults. This process is called 'parentification' (Gelinas 1983). When she grows up she is usually drawn to men for whom care taking is very important. These may be men who in their childhood were emotionally deprived due to their mother's depression, other illnesses or death. Such men are insecure, dependent, emotionally immature and nar-cissistic. They may even be involved in petty crimes. Thus a complementary relationship between a caring woman and a dependent man can become very strong until the arrival of a child. The mother who has already been a surrogate mother to her siblings, to her parents and to her husband may now feel depleted and exhausted. She becomes concerned and preoccupied with the emotional needs of her child and, instead of caring for her husband, tries to lean on him; he feels abandoned, having to compete with his child. Therefore he escalates his demands for attention and affection, thus perpetuating the vicious cycle.

As more children arrive on the scene the dynamic becomes desperate and, if there is an older child, usually a female, available to share some of the mothering responsibilities, mother feels able to give up some of her caring duties. The child slowly assumes various responsibilities out of her loyalty to her mother. As the father is neither confident nor resourceful enough to form outside relationships and his relationship with his wife is already dried up, he starts to slide into an inappropriate relationship with his already parentified daughter.

Thus the outer systemic forces can converge with the inner sub-systemic or intrapsychic processes to produce behaviours as final common pathways. This is equally applicable to both constructive and destructive behaviours.

Hence individual deviances and intrapsychic factors are also important in sexual abuse. It is suggested that many perpetrators of incestuous child sexual abuse have a primary sexual arousal pattern to children, even though they may also have sexual relations with adults. A study into the predictors of re-offence among child molesters found that sexual deviance was the only significant predictor of recidivism. The measure of deviant sexual arousal was based on laboratory measures of sexual preferences using penile plethysmography (Barbaree and Marshall 1988). Thus, incestuous perpetrators may be more like other child molesters except for their choice of victims (Lanyon 1986).

Fathers may also present their sexual behaviours towards the child as a vehicle for affection, attention and power in an otherwise emotionally impoverished atmosphere. There may be different intrapsychic pressures acting upon abusive fathers, for example, a history of emotional deprivation, identification with the perpetrators, victimisation, arrested development, trauma, lack of social skills, marital problems, intense need to relate to a child at an emotional level, paedophilic dependence upon children for sexual arousal with masturbatory conditioning and fantasies, disinhibition due to drug, alcohol or stress or due to rationalisation or commercial gains such as pornographic trades Maisch (1972) found a heterogenous profile of offenders. They rarely suffer from any recognisable mental illness (Lukianowicz 1972) but alcoholism has been recognised as a problem common to many incestuous fathers (Virkkunen 1974). Alcohol may not create sexual feelings towards a child but can serve to reduce internal inhibitions about the act.

In some people with certain personality disorders, there is a possibility of certain feelings such as dread of adult sexuality, self-doubt, depression and intense tension to be displaced in the sexual act. Through this act the childhood experiences may be relived in an attempt to resolve them largely through the facility of dominating others – a domination that was unavailable in their family of origin (Bell and Hale 1971). Severity of the personality disturbances may be directly related to the number of offences the person commits (McCreary 1975).

With regard to sexual traits, opinions have been rather contradictory. Some men are found to be undersexed, others oversexed. Some experts think that these men are unconscious homosexuals, others think that they are uninhibited heterosexuals (Nelson 1982). Howells (1981) found dominance and submission as characteristics which paedophiles both admire and feel to be important characteristics in people.

Paedophiles tend to be obsessive collectors of child pornography. Some perpetrators have been known to hold records of a thousand or more children who have been victims of their paedophiliac careers. Child pornography has now grown to the extent that it is one of the largest international rackets and is used as a tool to introduce children to sexual abuse (Tate 1990). Child pornography records the actual abuse of children in magazines, videos and films and can range from explicit nude photographs to oral, anal and genital sex. Children may be shown bound, tortured and mutilated. It is believed that even children's murders have been filmed and sexual abuse of their bodies after death has continued.

Hard core child pornography became widely available from 1969 to 1979 when Denmark legalised its production and other nations were lax in pursuing the existing laws. Over the last ten years the controls on commercial production and distribution have been tightened but there has been a rise in home made child pornography with the general availability of video cameras.

Boys are not immune to sexual abuse and assault (Vandir Mey 1988). Many are raped by people they know and trust; for example, father figures, teachers, youth leaders, priests, stepfathers, and also by casual acquaintances. Assault by strangers and gangs is also common and many lives have been shattered by these experiences. In the family dynamics of western culture, there is always a struggle for power and the problem of power imbalance. Male sexual abuse has therefore been hypothesised as a form of scapegoating in which men use other men to establish their power and masculinity where they have been deprived of conventional means to such power (i.e. through women).

Whether or not true paedophilia occurs in females is not immediately clear. It may be disguised as caring. Groth and Birnbaum (1978) point out that nearly three quarters of male paedophiliacs choose female victims while one quarter choose male victims. Bolton et al. (1989) describe three categories of female offenders against male children:

1. *Exploration/exploitation*. Usually young offenders (16 or above) for example babysitters, anxious, socially unskilled.

2. *Personality disorders/severe abuse history*. Usually adults or adolescents with poor adjustment, aggressive, self-destructive, depressed etc. They

usually abuse female children but may also abuse male children as well.

3. *Developmentally arrested or regressed*, maybe single or married or divorced but not self sufficient, and are usually isolated with a history of sexual abuse; fixated, regressed paedophiles, self initiated love affairs, victims.

Boys constitute between 12 and 33% of sexually abused children who are reported. Of these, 6 to 50% are abused by parents or step parents. Different categories of families have been described, for example

1. *Homosexual families.* For example, a latent homosexual who punishes his son for the son's acting out behaviour.

2. *Promiscuous families*, with a chaotic lifestyle where several children of both sexes may be sexually abused.

3. *Physically abusive families*, where sexual abuse becomes an extension of physical abuse or physical abuse facilitates sexual abuse.

4. *Families with a history of alcohol or drug abuse.*

Less protectiveness may be extended towards potential sexual victimisation of male children as people may be more concerned about female victims than male victims. Males are socialised to be strong and to take care of themselves, therefore male victims may be more reluctant to report their own victimisation because they may have more to lose in reporting (Finkelhor 1986). It violates the male ethics of self reliance and raises the stigma of homosexuality. This is why both professionals and parents may sometimes ignore the warning signs of victimisation when they are present. More parents prepare female children than male children for this danger. In a study by Lands (1956), 44.1% of female but only 26.8% of male victims' parents had prepared them against sexual assaults. Male victims also have more difficulty seeking out help and protection (Brandt and Tisza 1977). In recent years the number of male children being reported as victims of sexual abuse has risen. A 1985 study of the prevalence of child sexual abuse in Great Britain found that 8% of the males surveyed had been sexual abuse victims (Baker 1985).

Juvenile offenders

Sexual abuse is not only committed by adults but also by children and adolescents (Ryan 1986). Margolin and Craft (1990) found that adolescent non-parental care givers (for example, baby sitters) in comparison to older care giver cohorts were observed to commit substantially more sexual abuse and the nature of sexual abuse they committed was more likely to involve intercourse and physical assault. The literature on physical and sexual violence has long noted the over-representation of perpetrators who are between fifteen and twenty-four years of age (Amir 1971, Dube and Herbert 1988, Eisenhower 1969, Katz and Mazur 1979, Russell 1986). Crime statistics indicate that as many as 30% rapes and 56% percent of child molestations are committed by sexual perpetrators under the age of eighteen (Fehrenbach *et al.* 1986). Most of these adolescents are diagnosed as suffering from conduct disorder (Kavoussi *et al.* 1988). Young offenders are usually not offered treatment and may be ignored or their offence may be passed off as experimentation, adolescent adjustment reaction, sex play or normal adolescent aggressiveness. If there is no intervention or treatment, such a behaviour may persist and escalate into adulthood offending (Johnson 1988).

A study conducted on 47 boys (4–13 years old) who molested children younger than themselves and took part in a treatment programme specially designed for child perpetrators in Los Angeles found that coercion was used in all cases. Of these boys, 49% had been sexually abused and 19% had been physically abused, and their perpetrators had already been well known to them. There was a history of sexual and physical abuse and also of substance abuse in the families of the majority of these children (Johnson 1988).

SIBLING OFFENDERS

With the increasing number of blended families, step siblings of different ages and foster children and the absence of a biological bond, sibling sex contact takes a new meaning (Kempe and Kempe 1984). Fifteen percent of females and 10% of males in Finkelhor's college student sample were able to verify sibling sexual abuse (Finkelhor 1980). This may be an expression and demonstration of resentment, anger, aggression or hatred towards the sibling. Outside forces such as parental neglect may also intensify sibling rivalries. Poor caring may lead to an inability to control aggressive impulses and younger siblings may be considered as intruders.

FEMALE PERPETRATORS

As it is hard to believe that women can also commit such acts, the incidence of sexual abuse by women on male and female children has been underestimated (Banning 1989). Finkelhor and Russell (1984), analysing the results of the American Human Association study, reported the incidence of female perpetrators in 13% of girl victims and 24% of boy victims and also reported studies based on self reports of the general population of adults recalling their childhood experiences indicating that about 20% of male and 5% of female child victims were abused by women.

The women perpetrators have not been studied properly and are therefore poorly understood. However, there is a strong history of sexual victimisation in childhood (McCarthy 1986). Though the vast majority of female victims do not become sexual offenders, those that develop severe pathology become victims, such as prostitutes or marry child molesters or wife abusers. It seems that boys identify with the aggressor and become offenders and girls remain victims, possibly identifying with their mothers. The consequences of serious child sex abuse, therefore, can be devastating, although different for men and women. Hawton and Roberts (1981) concluded from a survey that attempted suicide is very common in parents who abuse their children.

The effects of abuse

The experience of abuse for a child can be very confusing and traumatic. Even in professionals, the story of child sexual abuse evokes dreadful, uncomfortable feelings and can lead to denial, revulsion or, at times, uneasy fascination. According to Finkelhor (1979) some 63% of sexually victimised children never told their experience to anyone.

A common method of inducing victims to participate in the abuse is the exercise of adult authority and the use of threats or physical force. There may be some aggression along with exhibitionism, fondling and kissing to start with, which may progress to oral sex and anal or vaginal intercourse. 'Then there was the pain of breaking and entering when the senses are torn apart. The act of rape on an eight-year-old body is a matter of "the needle giving because the camel can't". The child gives because the mind of the violator cannot' (Maya Angelou's *Autobiography* 1971, quoted in Brownmiller 1975, p.174). The abuse usually happens in the victim's own home, adding to their sense of disorientation and threat, so they have no safe space even at home (Burgess and Holstrom 1975). Times when father and daughter may normally express affection, playing together, and love may become imbued with the traumatic memories of sexual abuse.

It arouses a feeling of total revulsion, total fear and confusion as the body betrays its owner by its sexual desire. 'He sucked my breasts and I felt wildly excited and terribly angry. He entered me with his fingers and *a surge of hate combined with desire* rose' (Brady 1980, p.55). It may lead to a feeling of being poisoned by the semen, the feeling that the activity is wrong and shameful. It may be accompanied by physical violence, threats of violence, emotional abuse, petty humiliations and insults. It may induce a feeling of paralysis, preventing the victim from speaking or moving. there may also be an element of bribery and seduction. It may be associated with constant dread that it would happen again, or a sense of guilt. 'I had let it go on for so many years without telling someone. I was afraid that people would think it was my fault' (Butler 1978, p.30). As the victim moves into adolescence, the abuser may also become possessive and jealous. Some children wish to protect their powerless mothers from knowledge, feeling sorry for the mother. There may also be a sense of hostile betrayal, bitterness and lack of warmth.

> Although victims as young as four months old have been identified, incest is usually initiated when the victim is between four and 12 years old, with particularly high risk at four and nine. It is easy to gain the compliance of a young child by misrepresenting sex as affection or training by threats and bribes and by exploiting the child's loyalty and need for affection, desire to please and specially, trust of the parent.

Most children are not even aware of what the activity is that is being demanded and only gradually realise by the age of 10 or 11 that things are not what they should be. (Gelinas 1983, p.313–314)

At the age of four and five anal intercourse is often physically less difficult than vaginal and may be more frequent than previously suspected. The abuse is usually terminated by the victim around the age of 14 or 15, often by disclosure, threats to disclose or repetitive running away. (Gelinas 1983)

Jehu (1989a) reported the experiences of a series of 51 previously sexually abused women. The reactions of the victims when they were being abused were predominantly negative. More than two thirds of them reported each of the reactions of guilt, fear, helplessness, compliance, anger, avoidance, denial and dissociation. The abuse was kept secret for some period of time by 96% of victims, usually because of fear or disbelief, pain or anger. Eventually, 52% disclosed their abuse before they reached seventeen. Reactions of others to this revelation were overwhelmingly negative towards the victims. Only rarely was blame attached to the offender or accepted by the confidante. Some children do find the courage to tell someone who may be able to believe and facilitate further disclosure and initiate protective action; however, many children, because of various fears, try to keep this a secret. The professionals, relatives or friends may become suspicious through a variety of symptoms (listed below) suggestive of abuse.

1. *Genital and anal*: genital and anal bruising; scratching; tears; vaginal or anal bleeding; torn, stained or bloody underclothing; presence of sexually transmitted or venereal infections (including genital warts); pregnancy; various objects in orifices; genital itching; soreness; discharge; abnormally stretched orifices (especially anus); unusual odour around the genital area.

2. *General*: bruising and injury from coercion or undue force; difficulty walking or sitting; pain in passing urine; recurrent cystitis; emotional and behavioural consequences; flashbacks; sleeplessness; nightmares; memory impairment; guilt; depression; irritability; anxiety; hyper-alertness; morbid fears; phobic avoidance of men; frozen watchfulness; helplessness; loss of self-esteem; social isolation; regression (bed wetting, clinging, excessive separation anxiety); over eating or anorexia; disobedience; lack of concentration; psychosomatic responses (headache, abdominal pain, fake epileptic fits); excessive washing; antisocial behaviour; running away; substance abuse; psychotic breakdown; auditory hallucination; self mutilation and other suicidal behaviour; school refusal or educational problems or avoidance of P.E. or school medicals.

3. *Sexual behaviours*: precocious knowledge; disinhibited sexual behaviour; age-inappropriate sex play with peers; sexually provocative to adults or

peers; sexualised detail to artwork; sexual innuendo in written work; promiscuity and prostitution; sexual molestation as aggressor; identity confusion.

The effects of physical abuse

Kempe *et al.'s* study (1962) estimated 11% death and 28% permanent injury due to physical abuse, although subsequent follow up studies have quoted low death rates (Lynch 1978). But the problem of re-abuse, permanent physical damage and lifelong scarring, deformity or neurological abnormality remain. Martin *et al.* (1974) found that 53% of physically abused children had some neurological abnormality and one third of these had severe handicaps, particularly victims of recurrent severe shaking, including permanent visual impairment. There can also be a problem of growth failure and intellectual retardation, including developmental speech delay. In addition, physical abuse can lead to a number of personality and behaviour problems. Victims may find it difficult to relax and enjoy life. They may suffer from poor self esteem and from behaviours which make parents, teachers and peers reject them, and from social isolation. They are easily labelled as hostile and carry a high risk for both fostering and adoption breakdowns, making them feel not wanted by anyone.

The effects of sexual abuse

It is not the sexual activity *per se* that is so damaging, but the abusive context in which such an activity takes place. Well over half of all children have childhood sexual experiences with other children (Finkelhor 1979) but not all these become damaged or abusers. Leitenberg *et al.* (1989), in a study of current sexual behaviour and sexual adjustments in a sample of 433 college students in New England, concluded that a simple occurrence or non-occurrence of sexual activity among children during their developmental periods had little impact, either positive or negative, on later sexual adjustment during adulthood.

The abusive experiences, on the other hand, arouse strong feelings and can lead to fixation, repeated appearance in fantasy and, therefore, damage and perversion. Depending on the circumstances, the abusive experiences can arouse any of a variety of feelings. For example, the feelings of fear, insecurity, guilt, shame and embarrassment are often very common. There is usually a fear of the abuser and of what might happen. Guilt may also arise due to the fact that the activity might have been pleasurable, or due to the consequences of disclosures. There may also be feelings of self blame, self doubt, confusion about what has happened and why it is wrong, and even uncertainty about how to feel. There may arise a fear of internal damage, of AIDS, of becoming a homosexual. There is a feeling of having been betrayed both by abusers and carers. There may also be acute anxiety and feelings of being dirty, spoiled, disgraced, disgusted, angry, hostile, violent and full of hatred.

These overwhelming feelings can easily interfere with one's functioning and interpersonal relationships, and lead to a great deal of distress and psychiatric disturbance. At least the following areas need attention (Vargo *et al.* 1988) in offering help to such victims:

1. Damaged goods syndrome, i.e. the feeling of having been physically damaged, stigmatised and condemned.
2. Fear of reprisal, as the phrases like 'I will kill you if you ever tell' reverberate in the victim's mind.
3. Lack of appropriate social skills.
4. Loss of self mastery and control.
5. Intense anger which may be directed at the perpetrator, other family members for not having protected and the agencies for being too impersonal or invasive. The anger may also arise due to social rejection or lack of control. This anger may be turned inwards into depression.

Sexual assault out of the home is often totally unexpected and usually involves the use of threats or force. The child's feelings are greatly influenced by the feelings of the parents. In fact, parental response may be more extreme than that of the child. The intensity of parental alarm and the attempts to get the situation fixed and put it behind can be destructive. Because of their feelings of disbelief, embarrassment, grief, guilt, anger and fear, there may be an intense urge to 'get' the perpetrator. Stable families work through such events, but in the chaotic family this parental over-reaction may destroy the child's hope of putting the event in his or her past (Goodwin 1982). Adams-Tucker (1982), in a study of 28 sexually abused children ($2\frac{1}{2}$-to $15\frac{1}{2}$-year-olds), arranged their chief complaints of psychiatric disturbance in the following six clusters in decreasing order of severity. More than half of these children were admitted to psychiatric in-patient units because of their severe or extremely pathological behaviours.

1. Self destructive, suicidal, withdrawn, hallucinating.
2. Aggression, sex related complaints, running away.
3. Problems concerning school and oppositional difficulties with parents, siblings or peers.
4. Anxiety.
5. Psychosomatic complaints.
6. Sleep related complaints.

The long term consequences of sexual abuse include sexual, emotional and behavioral problems. Sexual problems include: sexual experimentation; homosexuality; sexual dysfunction; sexual stigmatisation; compulsive participation or avoidance of sexual activity; confusion over sexual and non sexual behaviour; compulsive masturbation; precocious sexual behaviour;

association of sexuality with aggression; adolescent pregnancy; seductive behaviour; prostitution; problems in marital sexuality; sexually transmitted diseases. Emotional problems include hopelessness; anxiety; personality and character disorder; guilt and shame; depression; poor self image; emotional instability; inhibition and fear of tenderness; anger towards and distrust of parents; feelings of betrayal; distrust of males; loneliness; hostility; poor sense of identity. Behavioral problems include runaway behaviour; poor social skills and unsatisfying social relationships; self destructiveness; suicide; delinquency; impulsiveness; alcohol and drug abuse; hyperactivity; compulsivity; fantasy and withdrawal; continued victimisation; perpetration of abuse as a parent.

Jehu (1989a and b) reported the findings of a series of 51 previously sexually abused women who entered therapy in a clinic at the University of Manitoba. Ninety four percent were found to be sexually dysfunctional. These sexual dysfunctions, according to Jehu, were due to mood disturbances, interpersonal problems and sexual stress that were associated with the earlier traumatic experiences of sexual abuse and its surrounding circumstances. Ninety two percent reported low self esteem, 88% reported feelings of guilt, 70% depressive episodes.

Many of these women also had interpersonal problems. The problems of interpersonal adjustment arise due to stigma, withdrawal from social contact and behaviour seeking rejection, for example physical or verbal aggression to create a barrier which leads to isolation or not getting married. Victims may marry a partner who exploits, dominates or physically abuses them, evoking anger, hostility and resentment, which is likely to disrupt the sexual response and satisfaction. Such domination by the partner may result in a power struggle in the relationship and the victim may not respond sexually because this would represent submission to her partner. Only 24 women were living as married but all of these were experiencing discord in their relationships. Ninety one per cent were oppressed by the partner, 33% physically abused by him, 68% feared men and 90% felt that no man could be trusted (Jehu 1989b).

Fear and anxiety reduce sexual functioning and satisfaction. Abuse can also lead to fear of intimacy. There may be a conscious or unconscious desire not to let anyone get close enough to hurt them again (Vargo *et al.* 1988).

Affection and sex may be split off from each other; therefore, there may be a craving for affection without sex. The more intimate the relationship the greater the likelihood of its re-capitulating the earlier traumatic experience with the offender who was emotionally close. Sexual activity can also become very stressful because of its associations with the history of abuse and, with various aspects of sexual anatomy, responses, activities, thoughts, fantasies and images. For example, the emotional response to the offender's penis could become generalised to include disgust at one's own clitoris, pubic hair, one's partner's penis, and even his nose (Jehu 1989b).

Jehu (1989b) has also listed the following common stress reactions.

1. *Emotional*: anxiety; fear; panic; feeling trapped; helplessness; vulnerability; disgust; revulsion; guilt; shame; anger; resentment.

2. *Cognitive*: re-experiencing traumatic events through intrusive thoughts; ruminations; obsessions; flashbacks; images; dreams; nightmares; dissociative reactions such as amnesia, de-personalisation, de-realisation and multiple personality disorder.

3. *Physiological*: muscle tension; sweating; rapid breathing; palpitation; dizziness; fainting; nausea; retching; vomiting; disturbances of eating, sleep, sex and excretion.

4. *Behavioral*: avoidance of stress situations and aggressive acts. Incest victims appear to be well represented among female psychiatric patients (Gelinas 1983).

Anger and hatred

Often sexually abused children have had no safe place to express their anger. Even parents and other caring adults may also discourage direct expression of anger from a child. Abused children often repress their anger and have few, if any, means of expressing appropriately. For many victims the only way they imagine they can get over the feelings is to seek revenge on the attacker. Many commit horrendous crimes against others and get involved in things like assault on a grand scale. Others may turn to prostitution in an effort to make punters pay for what has hitherto been taken from them.

> The anger is like a burning desire in my cheeks and the rage I feel inside grips me like a vice. I want to kill him for what he did to me. (Grove and Panzer 1989, p.160)

> When I am angry I don't know, it is all bottled up inside me. And I really stew and I am miserable for days and I tear myself apart and make myself sick and miserable. (Grove and Panzer 1989, p.249)

Providing a safe environment where the child is allowed and encouraged to express his feelings is an important step in eventually teaching abused children to manage their angry feelings in constructive ways. It is important to note that the expression of feelings is only one step in this process and not the major goal of therapy. Children should be helped to appreciate the fact that their angry feelings are a normal outcome of the abuse; that they are not bad because they are angry; that it is OK to be mad at somebody who hurts; that to be angry does not mean they have to hurt someone to feel better. They should also be helped to learn to recognise when they are getting 'mad' (for example tension, stomach upsets, confusion) and to learn constructive ways of venting anger (for example symbolic confrontation with abuser; producing stories, poems, pictures; helping other children to learn to protect themselves).

Group therapy is one of the most essential components of treatment of victims of abuse. There is often an intense degree of acting out in such groups, because the painful feelings associated with abuse are often dissociated and therefore need to be acted out. The group therapists learn of these affective experiences of abuse through the process of projective identification, i.e. by experiencing the feelings that are dumped into them (Dwivedi *et al.* 1992, Ogden 1979).

Some children who experience the extreme suffering of pain, torment and terror are able to keep some of these feelings alive even as they grow up. They are able to remember what it felt like when they were little, how afraid they were when their parents exploded, how they cried when they were taken away from their parents. Keeping in touch with these feelings helps to keep in touch with the injured child within and to prevent the blind repetition of that morbid past. This may help to protect one's child, with a feeling of 'I would not let my child go through what I went through myself as a child' (Fraiberg *et al.* 1980).

In many children the feelings of hurt, anxiety, shame and worthlessness are so overwhelming that these are pushed out of consciousness and are repressed. As they grow up they may still remember the incidents – childhood beatings, desertion, tyranny and rejection – in chilling detail, but the original feelings may undergo complete or partial repression. This repression leads to an unconscious alliance and identification with the fearsome figures. Such a pathological identification with the dangerous assaultative enemies of the ego is the phenomenon of *identification with the aggressor*. Thus, as a little child one may become so frightened that, in order to make oneself less scared, one may start talking and sounding like the one who is actually frightening.

Sexual abuse includes a history of being seen and treated as 'part objects', of seduction and emotional deprivation, of being prevented from individuating from parental figures and of being prematurely sexualised. This leads to a kind of perversion because compulsive activities take over the freedom in obtaining gratification. Perverse men and women may use their genitals to express their hatred towards symbolic sources of humiliation. Women may also use it against their own bodies or the objects of their own creation (for example a baby), motivated by a deep need for revenge (Welldon 1988, 1991).

Child abuse, narcissism and hatred

In narcissistic disorder there is an element of the grandiose as a defence against damaged self concept. This is achieved by stripping off and external-ising all bad traits. The person develops 'blind hatred' towards many others who are assigned subhuman status. Such a person does not recognise that others also have a right to exist or that these others have ever been good or kind to that person. There is a destructive readiness to injure others on the grounds that they are 'monsters' who have no right to survive (Horowitz

1989). Horowitz *et al.* (1984) proposed a 'three party person role relationship model', comprising a hero, a monster and a critic. Viewing others as monsters is a dissociative defence, in which the human qualities of a person are forgotten. There is also an illusion that the critic is totally admiring the hero, while totally loathing the monster. There is no guilt, fear or shame over hostility in this state and anger is an enjoyable energy. Through externalisation of all bad traits and idealisation of the hero, the self can attach and have an idealising transference. The self is elevated over the 'monster' who is bad, and so can safely feel contempt as well as disgust and rage towards these traits. Guilt, shame or fear of retaliation may come later with these traits and transition to some other state. Thus, at times, anger may be confusingly compounded with shame and anxiety (Kohut 1972). Another form is that of chronic embitterment or addiction to hatred. Childhood abuse is an important cause of the rising tide of Narcissistic Disorder and hatred and the The Narcissistic Disorder and important factor in the epidemic of child abuse.

Acknowledgement

I am most grateful to Lesley Curtress for her repeated and painstaking word processing of the manuscript, and to Phil Sullivan, Roger Gordon, Alec Clarke and Jess Gordon for their valuable suggestions.

References

Adams-Tucker, C. (1982). Proximate effects of sexual abuse in childhood: a report on 28 children. *American Journal of Psychiatry 139* (10): 1252–1256.

Alexander, P.C. and Lupfer, S.L. (1987) Family characteristics and longterm consequences associated with sexual abuse. *Archives of Sexual Behaviour,* 16, 235–245.

Amir, M. (1971). *Patterns of foreseeable rape.* Chicago: University of Chicago Press.

BBC (1986). Childwatch – overview of results from 2,530 self completion questionnaires. BBC broadcasting research (unpublished – quoted in Markowe 1988).

Baker, A.W. and Duncan, S.P. (1985). Child sexual abuse: a study of prevalence in Great Britain. *Child Abuse and Neglect, 9*: 457–467.

Baker, C.D. (1978). Preying on playgrounds: the sexploitation of children in pornography and prostitution. *Pepperdine Law Review, 5*: 816.

Banning, A. (1989). Mother–son incest: confronting a prejudice. *Child Abuse and Neglect 13*: 563–570.

Barbaree, H.E. and Marshall, W.L. (1988). Deviant sexual arousal, offence history, and demographic variables as predictors of re-offence among child molesters. *Behavioral Sciences and the Law, 6* (2): 267–280.

Bell, A.P. and Hale, C.S. (1971). *The personality of a child molester: an analysis of dreams.* Chicago: Aldine and Atherton.

Bolton, F.G., Morris, L.A. and MacEachron, A.E. (1989). *Males at Risk*. London: Sage.

Brady, K. (1980). *Father's Day*. New York: Dell.

Brandon, S. (1976). Physical violence in the family: an overview, in Borland, M. (ed.) *Violence in the Family*. Manchester: Manchester University Press.

Brandt, R.S.T. and Tisza, V.B. (1977). The sexually misused child. *American Journal of Orthopsychiatry*. 47: 80–89.

Browne, K. (1989). The naturalistic context of family violence and child abuse. In Archer, J. and Browne, K. (eds.) *Human Aggression: naturalistic approaches*. London: Routledge.

Brownmiller, S. (1975). *Against our Will: Men, Women and Rape*. New York: Simon and Schuster.

Burgess, A.W. and Holstrom, L.L. (1975). Sexual trauma of children and adolescents: pressure, sex, and secrecy. *Nurs. Clin. North Amer. 10* (3): 551–563.

Butler, S. (1978). *Conspiracy of Silence*. San Francisco: New Glide.

Creighton, S.J. (1987). *Child abuse in 1986: initial findings from the NSPCC's register research* (Research briefing no 8). London: NSPCC.

Department of Health (1991). Children and young persons on Child Protection Registers. Year ending 31 March 1990. Provisional feedback. Personal Social Services. Local Authority statistics. London: Department of Health.

Dube, R. and Herbert, M. (1988). Sexual Abuse by children under 12 years of age: a review of 511 cases. *Child Abuse and Neglect, 12*: 321–330.

Dwivedi, K.N., Brayne, E. and Lovett, S. (1992) Groupwork with sexually abused adolescent girls. *Group Analysis*, 25 (4), 477–489.

Eisenhower, M.S. (1969). *To establish justice to insure domestic tranquillity*. Final report of the National Commission on causes and prevention of violence. Washington D.C.: U.S. Government Printing Office.

Elliot, M. (1986) For Pity's sake help. *Community Care* (14 August) p.19.

Fehrenbach, P.A., Smith, W., Monastersky, C. and Beisher, R.W. (1986). Adolescent sex offenders: offender and offence characteristics. *American Journal of Orthopsychiatry 56*: 225–233.

Finkelhor, D. (1979). *Sexually Abused Children*. New York: Free Press.

Finkelhor, D. (1980). Sex among siblings: a survey of prevalence, variety and effects. *Archives of Sexual Behaviour, 9*: 171–194.

Finkelhor, D. (1986). Designing new studies. In Finkelhor, D. (ed.) *A Sourcebook on Child Sexual Abuse*. Beverley Hills, L.A.: Sage. pp199–223.

Finkelhor, D. and Russell, D. (1984). Women as perpetrators. In Finkelhor, D. (ed.) *Child Sexual Abuse: New Theory and Research*, 171–185. New York: The Free Press.

Fraiberg, S., Adelson, E. and Shapiro, V. (1980) Ghosts in the nursery: A psycho-analytic approach to the problems of impairment infant–mother relationship.

In S. Fraiberg (ed.) *Clinical Studies in Infant Mental Health: The First Year of Life.* London: Tavistock.

Frude, N.J. (1990). *Family Problems: A Psychological Analysis.* Chichester: John Wiley and Sons.

Gelinas, D.J. (1983). The persisting negative effects of incest. *Psychiatry 16.* (Nov) 312–332.

Gil, D. (1974). *Violence Against Children.* Cambridge, Mass: Harvard.

Goodwin, J. (1982). *Sexual Abuse: Incest Victims and their Families.* Boston, Mass: John Wright PSG.

Greene, N.B. (1977) A view of family pathology involving child molest – from a juvenile probation perspective. *Juvenile Justice,* 13, 29–34.

Groth, N. and Birnbaum, J. (1978). Adult sexual orientation and the attraction to underage persons. *Archives of Sexual Behaviour, 7*: 175–181.

Grove, D.J. and Panzer B.I. (1989). *Resolving Traumatic Memories: Metaphors and Symbols in Psychotherapy.* New York: Irvington.

Haugaard, J.J. (1988) The use of theories about the etiology of incest as guidelines for legal and therapeutic interventions. *Behavioural Sciences and the Law,* 6(2), 221–238.

Herman, J.L. (1981) *Father–Daughter Incest.* Cambrige, Mass: Harvard University Press.

Herman, J. and Hirschman, L. (1981) Families at risk for father–daughter incest. *American Journal of Psychiatry,* 138(7), 967–970.

Hawton, K. and Roberts, J.C. (1981). The association between child abuse and attempted suicide. *British Journal of Social Work, 11*: 4, 415–420.

Hobson, S. (1989). Battered and abused children in Great Britain, in Moorhead, C. (ed.) *Betrayal: child exploitation in today's world.* London: Barrie and Jenkins. pp92–113.

Horowitz, M.J. (1989). Clinical Phenomenology of narcissistic pathology. *Psychiatric Clinics of North America, 12* (3): 531–539.

Horowitz, M.J., Marmar, C., Krupnick, J. *et al* (1984). *Personality Styles and Brief Psychotherapy.* New York: Basic Books.

Howells, K. (1981). Adult sexual interest in children: considerations relevant to theories of etiology. In Cook, M. and Howells, K. (eds.) *Adult Sexual Interest in Children.* New York: Academic Press.

Jehu, D. (1989a). Mood disturbances among women clients sexually abused in childhood: prevalence, etiology, treatment. *Journal of Interpersonal Violence, 4* (2): 164–184.

Jehu, D. (1989b). Sexual dysfunctions among women clients who were sexually abused in childhood. *Behavioral Psychotherapy, 17*: 53–70.

Johnson, T.C. (1988). Child Perpetrators – children who molest other children: preliminary findings. *Child Abuse and Neglect, 12*: 219–229.

Katz, S. and Mazur, M. (1979). *Understanding the Rape Victim: A Synthesis of Research Findings*. New York: John Wiley.

Kaufman, I., Peck, A.L. and Taginri, C. (1954). The family constellation and overt incestuous relations between father and daughter. *American Journal of Orthopsychiatry, 24* (April): 266–277.

Kavoussi, R.J., Kaplan, M. and Becker, J.V. (1988). Psychiatric Diagnoses in Adolescent Sex Offenders. *Journal of American Academic Child Adolescent Psychiatry, 27* (2): 241–243.

Kempe, C.H., Silverman, F.M., Steele, B.F., Droegemueller, W.A., Silver, H.K. (1962). The battered child syndrome. *Journal of the American Medical Association, 181*, 17–24.

Kempe, R.S. and Kempe, C.H. (1984). *The Common Secret: sexual abuse of children and adolescents*. New York: Freeman.

Kohut, H. (1972). Thoughts on narcissism and narcissistic rage. *Psychoanalytic Study and Child, 27*: 360–400.

Lands, J. (1956). Experiences of 500 children with adult sexual deviants. *Psychiatric Quarterly Supplement, 30*: 91–109.

Lanyon, R.I. (1986). Theory and treatment in child molesters. *Journal of Consulting and Clinical Psychology, 54*, 176–182.

Leach, E. (1968). *A Runaway World: 1967 Reith Lectures*. BBC London. Oxford: Oxford University Press.

Leitenberg, H., Greenwald, E. and Tarran, M.J. (1989). The relation between sexual activity among children during pre-adolescence and/or early adolescence and sexual behaviour and sexual adjustment in young adulthood. *Archives of Sexual Behaviour, 18* (4): 299–313.

Lukianowicz, N. (1972). Incest. *British Journal of Psychiatry, 120*: 301–313.

Lynch, M.A. (1978). Annotation: the prognosis of child abuse. *Journal of Child Psychology and Psychiatry, 19*: 175–180.

Maisch, H. (1972). *Incest*. New York: Stein and Day.

Margolin, L. and Craft, J. (1990). Child abuse by adolescent care givers. *Child Abuse and Neglect 14*: 365–373.

Marinker, M. (1976) The Family in Medicine. *Proceedings of the Royal Society of Medicine*. 69, 115–124

Markowe, H.L.J. (1988). The frequency of child sexual abuse in the U.K. *Health Trends*, 20. 2–6.

Martin, H.P., Beezley, P., Conway, E.S. and Kempe, C.H. (1974). The development of abused children. *Advances in Paediatrics, 21*. Chicago Year Book. Medical Publishers, pp25–73.

Mause, L. De (Ed) (1976). *The History of Childhood*. New York: Souvenir.

McCarthy, L.M. (1986). Mother-child incest: characteristics of the offender. *Child Welfare*, LXV (5): 447–459.

McCreary, C.P. (1975). Personality differences among child molesters. *Journal of Personality Assessment, 39*: 591–593.

Meadow, R. (1989). ABC of child abuse: epidemiology. *British Medical Journal 298* (18th March): 727–730.

Meiselman, K.C. (1978) *Incest: A psychological study of causes and effects with treatment recommendations.* San Francisco: Jossey-Bass.

Nash, C.L. and West, D.J. (1985). Sexual molestation of young girls. In West, D.J. (Ed) *Sexual Victimisation.* Aldershot. Gower: pp.1–92.

Nelson, S. (1982). *Incest: Fact and Myth.* Edinburgh: Stramullion.

Ogden, T. (1979). On projective identification. *International Journal of Psychoanalysis, 60*: 357–373.

Pinchbeck, I. and Hewitt, M. (1973). *Children in English Society,* Vol 1 and 2. London: Routledge and Kegan Paul.

Royal College of Psychiatrists (1988). Report of a working group of the child and adolescent psychiatry section on 'Child Psychiatric Perspectives on the Assessment and Management of Sexually Mistreated Children'. London: Royal College of Psychiatrists.

Russell, D.E.H. (1984). *Sexual Exploitation, Rape, Child Sexual Abuse and Work Place Harassment.* Beverley Hills, Cal.: Sage.

Russell, D.E.H. (1986). *The Secret Trauma: Incest in the Lives of Girls and Women.* New York: Basic Books.

Ryan, G. (1986). Annotated bibliography: adolescent perpetrators of sexual molestation of children. *Child Abuse and Neglect, 10*: 125–131.

Scott, P.D. (1977). Non-accidental injury in children: memorandum of evidence for the Parliamentary Select Committee on violence in the family. *British Journal of Psychiatry, 131*, 366–80.

Steele, B.B. and Pollock, D. (1968). A psychiatric study of parents who abuse small children. In Kempe, C.H. and Helfer, R.E. (eds.) *The Battered Child.* Chicago: Chicago University Press.

Tate, T. (1990). *Child Pornography: an investigation.* London: Methuen.

Vandir Mey, B.J. (1988). The sexual victimisation of male children: a review of previous research. *Child Abuse and Neglect, 12*: 61–72.

Vargo, B., Stavrakaki, C., Ellis, J., and Williams, E. (1988). Child sexual abuse: its impact and treatment. *Canadian Journal of Psychiatry, 33*: 468–473.

Vermeulen, M. (1981). Turning kids into sex symbols. *Parade* (March 8) pp.4–6.

Virkkunen., M. (1974). Incest offenses and alcoholism. *Med. Sci. Law, 14*: 124–128.

Welldon, E.V. (1988). *Mother, Madonna, Whore.* London: Free Association Books.

Welldon, E.V. (1991). Psychology and Psychopathology in women – a psychoanalytic perspective. *British Journal of Psychiatry,* 158 (supplement 10):85–92.

von Bertalanffy, L. (1968). *General Systems Theory: foundation, development, application.* New York: George Braziller.

CHAPTER 5

Hatred Between Children

Neil Frude

Introduction

'I hate you, I hate you'. Although many children use the word 'hate' rather frequently, in most cases they use it simply for effect and it would be a mistake to interpret their statement literally. In a similar way a child who is a little hungry may use the expression 'I'm starving'. Thus children's statements about who, or what, they hate, especially when uttered in the heat of the moment, do not provide us with good evidence that they really do have resolute feelings of intense loathing towards the object or person who attracts their momentary vituperation.

The subject of this chapter, hatred between children, has attracted only limited interest by psychologists and educationalists. With some notable exceptions from the psychoanalytic field, there are few direct references in the psychological literature to such hatred, and a computer-based bibliographic search using 'children' and 'hatred' as the key words, for example, does not produce a rich harvest.

However, several well-researched areas of developmental psychology are relevant to our concerns. Among these areas are: peer rejection; children's aggression; bullying; and sibling rivalry. There is clearly *some* association between each of these and the topic of hatred between children, but none of these areas is closely parallel to that topic. Our exploration of these related fields therefore needs to be selective, but such enquiry may help us to identify concepts and themes within the existing knowledge base which would aid our understanding of hatred between children.

The need for careful selectivity can be illustrated using the example of fighting. Of course, some children attack and fight children whom they hate. But in many cases hatred leads to avoidance and disdain, rather than to a fight, and *most* fighting does not reflect hatred. Quite apart from the phenomenon of 'play fighting', even a fight that is 'real' or 'aggressive' may be no more than a fleeting tussle between children who are normally friends and will soon be seen playing together harmoniously.

Various definitions of hatred have been offered, and almost all include a criterion of an intense loathing which is more than momentary. If we were to accept this as our definition of hate, how would we 'diagnose' or recognize a 'case'? In other words, how can we tell whether one child hates another? Clearly, hearing a child shout 'I hate you' is not sufficient for making such a diagnosis, and neither is the sight of two children wrestling on the ground. Given the fact that many of the same behaviours are directed towards hated children and towards those who are temporarily out of favour, diagnosing hatred on the basis of explicit behaviours alone is bound to be difficult. We can describe a range of behaviours that *might* be expressions of hatred, but in every case the behaviour could be an expression of some quite different disposition towards the other child.

Behaviours that indicate hatred may be subtle and adults often underestimate the degree to which even young children are capable of communicating their feelings in a sophisticated, strategic and crafty way. Thus profound dislike may be communicated by ignoring the other child, by pretending not to hear their requests, or by failing to offer help. From an early age children know how to use selective inaction to communicate dislike, and children who are ignored recognize the deliberate snub and may be disturbed and upset as a result.

In most cases, however, hatred is communicated by overt action rather than by non-action, and the visible action may be physical or verbal. The range of verbal behaviours that can communicate dislike or aversion include teasing, mocking, deriding, jeering, ridiculing, sneering, taunting, belittling, accusing, blaming, criticising and scolding. An even longer list could be provided for the physical behaviours that might be directed towards a hated peer. Aside from the pushing, shoving and hair pulling that are very common in children's attacks on one another, several cases have been reported in which extreme acts of aggression have been perpetrated by one child against a young victim. In the literature on inter-sibling aggression, for example, we find examples of babies being thrown down the toilet, attacked with knives and scissors, and being tipped out of prams and pushchairs (for example, Orbach 1991).

Even in such extreme cases the action in itself does not allow us to infer hatred. Children respond more spontaneously, more erratically, and in a more volatile way than adults. They may attack another child in what appears to be a very determined and cruel way and yet be playing happily with that same child just a few minutes later. Thus although there is some association between hatred and aggression, it is difficult to delineate the precise nature of the relationship. Children may or may not be aggressive towards those whom they hate, and aggression may or may not be a sign of hatred.

In his book *Human Aggression*, Anthony Storr (1968) suggested that: 'Aggression turns to hatred when it comes to contain an admixture of revenge; and the tendency to persecute those who are already defeated, or who are obviously weaker than the aggressor, can only be explained by the latter's need to revenge himself for past humiliations' (p.92). In fact a number of alternative explanations of 'kicking the feeble' are possible. The weak scapegoat may be a convenient sponge used to soak up anger, for example, or may simply be a safe target for indulging in 'enjoyable' violence. Storr also suggests that '... a show of weakness on the part of the defeated is as likely to increase hatred as to restrain it. Perhaps our most unpleasant proclivity as a species is our proclivity for bullying the helpless' (pp.91–92).

In the end, Storr fails to provide an adequate analysis of the relationship between hatred and aggression, and his contribution may be more mystifying than helpful. The same is also true of the contribution of the ethologist Konrad Lorenz. In his book *On Aggression* (1966) Lorenz suggests that '... hate probably presupposes the presence of love: one can really hate only where one has loved and, even if one denies it, still does' (p.186). If we were to accept this it would clearly have important consequences for our understanding of hatred between children. However, it seems reasonable to reject the notion that hate must *always* be preceded by love, or must co-exist with it. Others have dismissed this hypothesis, too. Thus Fromm (1977) takes Lorenz to task on this point by asking 'Does the oppressed hate the oppressor... does the tortured hate the torturer because they once loved him or still do?' (p. 52).

In this chapter we will first consider the nature of peer rejection, identifying certain characteristics that increase the risk that a particular child will be rejected by his or her peers. We then examine two sharply contrasting aspects of peer-relationships in childhood – bullying and comforting. We then consider, briefly, inter-sibling antagonism before examining ways in which in might be possible for teachers, parents and others to prevent peer rejection or to lessen the trauma that may result from it. Throughout the chapter we need to be mindful of the distinction between those aspects of social relationships in childhood (such as rejection and aggression) that are amenable to direct examination and the more shadowy phenomenon – hatred between children – that is our ultimate concern.

The nature of peer rejection

Within an hour of a group of children meeting together for the first time, some will be playing together while others will be playing alone. It may already be possible to identify certain children as being 'popular' among their peers while others will appear to be ignored, and some may be recognized as having become the focus of active dislike. 'Being disliked' is clearly more than the absence of 'being liked', just as 'being rejected' is more than the absence of 'being accepted'.

Since the 1970s researchers have repeatedly demonstrated the existence of relatively stable social structures even within groups of children as young as one to three years old (for example, Sluckin and Smith 1978, Strayer *et al.* 1983). Chase (1981) showed that, within pre-school groups, linear dominance hierarchies largely reflect conflict during periods of group formation and group stabilization. Once established, the social structure is reflected in and maintained by particular peer alliances and rejections.

The social structure of a group of peers, and the sociometric status of individual children within that structure, can be determined using a number of different procedures. 'Sociometry' is the name given to one approach. In the 'peer nomination' procedure, children are asked to nominate other children within the group whom 'everybody likes', 'I like most', or 'has lots of friends', and so on. Other methods, including 'teacher nomination' and behavioural observation, also provide reliable indicators of group structure and individual status. For example, Milich *et al.* (1982) interviewed over 150 pre-school boys and girls and were able to obtain reliable categorizations in terms of popularity, rejection, and aggression on the basis of peer nominations and teacher ratings. In this, as in many other studies, there was a high level of agreement between the nominations of children and of teachers, and between the nominations provided by boys and by girls.

Thus it appears from many studies that rejected children are recognized as such by their peers (i.e., there is a general consensus about who is 'not liked very much') and by teachers. Furthermore, rejected children usually recognize themselves as unpopular and as disliked by their peers. Peretti and McNair (1987) identified social isolates (some, but not all, of whom were rejected) among sixth grade children, using a sociometric method. They then examined how these children judged themselves psychologically and socially. When interviewed, many indicated that they felt their social interactions to be superficial. Many were self-deprecating and portrayed themselves as emotionally bland, depressed and suspicious. Many of the children had pronounced fears of social rejection and it was clear that a number had become severely socially withdrawn.

Several studies indicate that there is relatively little change over time in the sociometric structure of groups which remain stable in their composition. Thus in a longitudinal study of the sociometric status of groups of eight- and eleven-year-old children over a four year period, Coie and Dodge (1983) found a high level of stability. The status of individual children within the group had generally been maintained over this period, with the status stability of 'rejected' children being particularly high.

Thus within groups of children, even of very young children, there is a sociometric structure which tends to be fairly stable, which can be observed and measured, and which marks particular children as 'popular', others as 'neglected', and some as 'rejected'. Which children will be rejected depends to some extent upon their individual characteristics and to some extent upon the nature of the group by which they are being rejected. Children rejected by one group might not be rejected by another group and aspects of the wider social context, such as the prejudices regarding particular religious and ethnic groups, also play a part in determining which children will be subjected to rejection and hatred by their peers. Before considering some of these social aspects, we first examine some of the individual characteristics known to be associated with a relatively high risk that a child will be rejected by his or her peers.

Characteristics of rejected children

In recent years a considerable amount of research has identified a number of characteristics associated with a high risk of peer rejection. These characteristics depend to some degree on the age of the children but they generally include low sociability, lack of social skills, high aggressiveness, low maturity, 'offensive' behaviour and identification with other rejected children. Most of the studies in this area are of a 'correlational' nature, so the precise nature of the association between rejection and the other variables is not clear. Thus, although it is tempting to assume that a limited repertoire of social skills is partly responsible for rejection by peers, it is possible that such rejection and subsequent low rates of social interaction might have restricted the development of the individual's social skills.

In a study involving the playground observation of eight- and nine-year-olds, Ladd (1983) found that rejected children spent less time than other children in cooperative play and social conversation, but more time in arguing and fighting. They also tended to play with younger and less popular companions. Rubin *et al.* (1982) also found that unpopular children (of kindergarten age) engaged in less mature forms of play and interacted less with other children than their more popular age-mates.

Many authors suggest that rejected children lack particular social skills. One such skill is 'breaking in' to the current social play of two or more peers, so joining the peers and enlarging the interacting group. Dodge *et al.* (1983) studied the ways in which five-year-olds attempted to join two peers who were playing together. They found that whereas popular children watched and waited, and were then gradually accepted as a result of making group-oriented statements, rejected children tended to engage in interruptive and disruptive actions which often led to their continued rejection.

In another study (Hazen *et al.* 1984) a large group of preschool children were divided into four social status groups (popular, controversial, rejected, and neglected) on the basis of sociometric choice, and the children were then observed in dyadic and triadic interactions. 'Popular' children directed their communications clearly to others and employed a wide range of social initiation strategies. They were also very responsive to other children's social initiatives. 'Rejected' children made as many social initiations as the popular children but had a more limited repertoire of initiation gambits. They also showed a lack of attention to other children. The authors suggested that such 'deficits' in social skills may explain why the rejected children received fewer initiations than any of the other groups.

Rejected children may also differ from other children in their social perception. Earn and Sobol (1990) suggested that many of those who are rejected lack sophistication in their attributional style. They showed that fourth and fifth grade children (nine- and ten-year-olds) with high acceptance and low rejection scores cited more 'controllable' causes of social behaviour than did other children. Popular children appeared to employ a more sophisticated attributional analysis, using a range of different types of social explanation, and tending to externalize failures in a more complex way than rejected children.

Aggressiveness

Thus one characteristic frequently cited as typical of rejected children is social ineptness or lack of social skills. Another is aggressiveness. A high level of aggression, especially if it is judged by peers to be used 'unfairly' and unskillfully, is a frequent cause of rejection. However, the relationship between aggression and rejection is by no means simple.

Some studies have reported a direct association between measures of aggressiveness and the likelihood of being rejected. With a sample of kindergarten and pre-school children, for example, Rubin et al. (1982) determined the sociometric popularity of the children and then recorded the level of social and cognitive play and the affective quality of the children's social interchanges. Social competence (as rated by teachers) and social problem-solving ability were also assessed. The results showed that rejection was consistently related to aggressive behaviour. Similarly, in their sample of 150 pre-school boys and girls, Milich et al. (1982) found that teacher and peer ratings of hyperactivity, aggression and peer problems were related to peer nominations of popularity and rejection. Boys nominated as aggressive were more often rejected by their classmates, whereas some of those nominated as hyperactive were popular and some were rejected.

Other studies have provided much less clear-cut results. Milich and Landau (1984) collected data on groups of six- and seven-year-old boys, including teacher rankings and ratings. They also used a peer nomination technique and observed social behaviour during free-play activity. 'Aggressive' and 'aggressive / withdrawn' groups were high on peer-nominated rejection, but some children in the 'aggressive' group were high on peer-nominated popularity. Thus it appeared that some forms of aggression may polarize opinion within the peer group.

Cairns et al. (1988) emphasised the point that an aggressive child may be popular with other aggressive children. They studied two large groups (approaching 700 children) of boys and girls in the fourth and seventh grades (nine- and ten-year-olds), examining their social networks and their aggressive behaviour. Highly aggressive subjects did not differ from matched controls in terms of isolation or rejection within the social network, although peer cluster analysis and reciprocal 'best friend' selections indicated that aggressive subjects tended to affiliate with aggressive peers. The highly aggressive children and adolescents were less popular than control subjects in the social network at large, but many were identified as nuclear members of particular social clusters.

Bierman (1986) also found that whereas some aggressive children were rejected, others were well-accepted by peers and showed no other signs of social maladjustment. Thus, although some rejected children are highly aggressive, we must be wary of overstating the degree to which aggression leads to rejection. Some aggressive children are not rejected; equally, many rejected children are not aggressive. Hodgens and McCoy (1989) distinguished between rejected-aggressive (RA) and rejected-nonaggressive (RN) on the basis of peer-nominations. Observing these children interacting in small heterogeneous groups they found that the RN children engaged in the lowest rates of initiation attempts, received the fewest initiation attempts from peers and engaged in the shortest periods of sustained interaction. The aggressive rejected children, however, were highly active socially, displaying very high rates of initiating behaviour and sustained interaction. The marked differences found between the two groups of rejected children indicate, once again, that important subgroups exist within the rejected category.

It is important, when considering the rather complex relationship between aggressiveness and rejection, to make distinctions between different types of aggression. The major distinction between hostile aggression and 'play fighting' was discussed earlier in this chapter. Other important distinctions are between 'proactive' and 'reactive' aggression, and between 'justified' and 'unjustified' aggression (i.e., as judged by a peer).

Dodge and Coie (1987) found that both reactive and proactive aggression in children's peer groups were related to social rejection, but found that proactively aggressive boys (not girls) were viewed as leaders and as having a sense of humour. These authors also found that reactive aggression (but not proactive aggression) reflected hostile attributional biases. Boys who were socially rejected and reactively aggressive were shown to interpret the intentions of 'provocateurs' in videotaped vignettes of peer interactions with hostile biases.

'Offensive behaviour'

Some aggression is seen as 'acceptable' whereas other aggression is seen as 'offensive'. From a very early age children have a keen sense of fairness and justice and are likely to reject teachers or peers who are judged as regularly engaging in 'unfair practices' (Marsh et al. 1978). There is a very large and impressive literature on the moral judgment of the child, but children do not simply judge whether something is right or wrong: they also respond emotionally and behaviourally. A child's awareness of a transgression such as another child 'pinching a toy', 'not taking turns', or 'not sharing', especially if they lose out or are put at a disadvantage as a result of the transgression, is likely to produce anger and rejection. Thus children who transgress and break rules, either because they are not sufficiently aware of the rules or because they choose not to obey them, are in danger of being rejected by their peers.

Coie et al. (1982) found that children who were 'least liked' among 300 children aged eight to fourteen years were seen as committing a number of 'offences', including disrupting group activities, starting fights and 'acting snobbish'. They were also judged as uncooperative, unsupportive and unattractive. Other studies report such offences as 'being big-headed', 'showing off', 'sucking up to a teacher', breaking a game rule and 'telling on someone'. Dygdon *et al.* (1987) asked peers to describe the behaviour of children who had previously been identified as liked, rejected, or neglected. Children who were rejected were said to behave aggressively, refuse invitations to play, exhibit non-normative behaviour and speak in an 'offensive' manner (for example using a 'posh accent').

Thus a number of characteristics of the individual child are related to high risk of rejection. Children who lack social skills, have 'impaired' or limited social perception, and who commit 'offences' are likely to be rejected. The relationship between aggression and rejection, however, is rather complex. Other characteristics that might be regarded as features of the individual are also related to social structure and social identity and will be considered later. Before discussing the broad area of social group factors, one further characteristic that may be associated with rejection will be considered – that of a child's handicap. The issue of peer rejection of those children who suffer from a disability is clearly germane to the controversial issue of 'mainstreaming' in schools.

Rejection and handicap

In a review of research, Bierman (1987) found that many rejected children have behavioural problems. In some cases these problems merely reflect the child's current rejection and subsequent isolation, but in many cases the child's problem will be chronic and evident across many situations. Sabornie (1987) studied the sociometric status of behaviourally disordered and non-handicapped elementary school pupils (second to sixth graders, seven- to eleven-year-olds) and found that the behaviourally disordered children (compared to matched controls) were far less often accepted and much more often rejected by their peers.

Handicapped children, whether the handicap be physical or intellectual, are likely to strike other children as 'different'. Some handicapped children will behave in ways that non-handicapped children find unpredictable, and a number will lack social skills. Some will be low in confidence or self-esteem, and those with a physical handicap will not be able to join in the full range of children's games.

There are a number of reasons, therefore, why we might expect handicapped children to be more at risk of rejection than other children. Such a phenomenon would clearly have important implications for the practice of educational 'mainstreaming', where handicapped and non-handicapped children are educated together. Indeed an avoidance of rejection of the handicapped by non-handicapped peers is one of the arguments offered in support of the mainstreaming strategy. A number of assumptions lie behind the thinking that mainstreaming will be beneficial. It is assumed that integration will provide the handicapped child with greater experience in social interaction with non-handicapped peers, for example, and that attendance at a normal school will result in less stigmatization than attendance at a special school. A further argument is that integrating the disabled will serve to reduce the prejudices of non-handicapped children and make them more accepting of people with limited intellectual ability or physical competence.

A number of sociometric and other studies, however, have shown that there can be a social cost, as well as social benefits, of such an attempt at 'normalization'. Thus Ray (1985) examined the sociometric status of mainstreamed handicapped children at the elementary school level. Over 600 non-handicapped and 60 handicapped (behaviour disordered, learning disabled, mentally handicapped, and physically handicapped) third to sixth graders (eight- to eleven-year-olds) completed a sociometric peer nomination instrument, while their 28 teachers completed a number of rating scales relating to social competence and popularity. The results indicated that handicapped mainstreamed children, when compared to their non-handicapped peers, are significantly more likely to be identified by their teachers as experiencing difficulty with social interaction. When sociometric measures are applied they are found to be selected only rarely, and are very often rejected.

While a number of studies do show some advantages of integrated education, other studies point to a number of other disadvantages. Harvey and Greenway (1984) examined the self-concepts of physically handicapped children who attended integrated or special schools and found that those who attended normal schools had lower self-esteem. These authors suggested that continuous comparison with normal peers leads handicapped children to evaluate themselves negatively. The claim that the integration of the handicapped into normal schools will have the effect of reducing other children's prejudices against the disabled has also been challenged. Several studies indicate that children's attitudes to the handicapped can be positively influenced as a result of their meeting disabled children (for example, Newberry and Parish 1987), but although there may be a sharp gain in positive evaluation after a limited number of meetings some residual antipathy often remains and the initial gain may not be maintained if the children continue to interact over a longer time-span.

Taylor et al. (1987) found that mainstreamed retarded children were often rejected by their non-handicapped classmates and that they were often highly anxious about their classroom interactions. Teachers judged their handicapped pupils as more socially anxious than most other children. Thus the integrated classroom does not necessarily embody the spirit of high tolerance, cordiality and co-operation between handicapped and non-handicapped children that was hoped for and expected by those who first advocated the mainstreaming approach. Handicap is a characteristic which tends to increase, rather than decrease, the chances that a child will be rejected by non- handicapped peers.

Social group factors

Some children are rejected by their peers not because of their individual characteristics but because of their identification with particular groups – either primary groups (peer groups and gangs within the classroom and playground) or secondary groups (such as ethnic or religious minorities). Wright et al. (1986) proposed that social status is a function of both individual and group characteristics and argued that two factors are necessary to predict peer popularity and peer rejection: prosocial interaction and person-group similarity. Data collected from 217 boys (average age ten years) at a summer programme for children with behavioural and social problems supported the proposed model both for peer acceptance and peer rejection.

Many researchers, many of them using an ethnographic approach, have studied the structure of peer groups within schools (for example, Meyenn 1980, Pollard 1980, Willis 1977). Teachers and pupils appreciate that there is a sociometric structure within the classroom. Each class evolves as a 'mini-society' with its key figures – its 'heroes', its 'scape-goats', its 'stars' and its 'isolates', and the presence of such identifiable and stable sub-groups can lead to strong inter-group rivalries and in-group solidarities.

Individual pupils may belong to one or more groups or 'gangs' within the class and will be highly influenced by their membership of such peer-groups. Membership depends on a number of characteristics such as ability, interests and attitude to authority, and once a pupil identifies with a group there will be strong pressures on him or her to adopt the consensus attitudes and the behavioural 'norms' of the group. Classroom sub-groups can often be differentiated by their general orientation to school and to the authority of the teacher, for there is often a polarization around this pro- or anti-school orientation. Willis (1977) found that pupils distinguished between the anti-school 'lads' and the pro-school 'ear 'oles', and Pollard (1980) found that conforming pupils were referred to by rebel groups as 'puffs', 'goody-good-ies' and 'teacher's pets'.

The use of such names indicates how membership of the 'wrong' group can lead an individual child to be rejected. However, some pupils will feel rejected and isolated precisely because they do not belong to any of the groups. Indeed, in an attempt to gain acceptance and membership they may make desperate bids for recognition and acceptance, or their frustration and loneliness may produce withdrawn or disturbed behaviour.

There is a strong and basic human tendency to divide people into in-groups and out-groups, into 'them' and 'us' (Tajfel 1982). People tend to turn to their in-group for help and for consensual validation of their attitudes and opinions. They may be aggressive towards an out-group, however, and the cognitive and affective counterparts of such aggression are prejudice and hatred. This phenomenon extends far beyond primary groups, of course. At one level, the phenomenon of inter-group rivalry (between racial, political or religious groups, for example) can be used to explain socio-historical movements. At another level it can be used to explain the rejection of individual children by their peers.

Some children are rejected because they are members of particular minority groups. Within a particular school such a minority (which may be an ethnic minority, a religious minority or any other social group minority, such as those who live on a particular housing estate) may be the subject of intense prejudice. Those children who are identified as belonging to specific minorities are likely to suffer rejection by their peers. Many examples of such prejudice are detailed in other chapters of this book. Siann et al. (1990) found that most girls from Muslim families, now living in Scotland, recognized a racist element in bullying at school, and many other authors (for example, La Fontaine 1991) have documented the fact that teasing, harassment, bullying and rejection are all related to ethnic group identification. Rejection may also be related to other kinds of social prejudice; thus an awareness or suspicion of an adolescent's homosexual orientation is sometimes the basis for rejection (Hunter and Schaecher 1987).

Children are keenly aware of 'differences'. A number of classic studies in developmental psychology show how readily children identify with others who resemble them in the slightest way (wearing a red badge, for example), thus forming a group which may enter into bitter rivalry with a group identified by the slightest difference (such as the wearing of a green badge). Since the study by Sherif et al. (1961) of a boys' summer camp, there have been numerous demonstrations of how easy it is to engender group formation and inter-group rivalry. Such groupings and conflicts do develop spontaneously within classrooms, but much of the group identification and out-group prejudice that occurs reflects the wider social prejudice against particular minority groups. There can be no doubt that much of this type of prejudice is imported into the classroom and playground from the home environment. A child who learns a prejudiced attitude in the home may carry it to school and then 'infect' others with the same attitude.

Some children are rejected, not because of their membership of a minority group or because of their individual characteristics, but because of some stigma attached to their family. Thus the notoriety of the parent or another relative may be visited on the child. A local newspaper report of a parent's or a brother's involvement in a court case may lead to the child being harassed or rejected at school. Similarly, some special fame or success gained by a relative may lead to rejection, perhaps as a result of other children's envy leading to the accusation that the child is guilty of the 'offence' of 'thinking that he or she is better than us'. Thus rejection by peers not only reflects the physical, behavioural and personality characteristics of the individual child, but also their membership of both primary and secondary groups.

Rejection and victimization

A child who is rejected by peers may be treated in a passive but disdainful way or may be subjected to active victimization. The relationship between physical and verbal abuse, on the one hand, and rejection on the other was investigated by Perry *et al.* (1988). They used a peer nomination scale to assess the degree to which children were subjected to direct physical and verbal abuse by peers. Of the 165 boys and girls in the study (third to sixth grades) 10 per cent were classified as 'extremely victimized', and this small group of children were found to serve consistently as targets of peer aggression. Victimization was not significantly related to age, sex or the victim's own level of aggression (as assessed by peer nominations), but there was a significant positive correlation between victimization and peer rejection. Victimization and aggression scores were independent predictors of rejection and together accounted for over half of the variance in peer rejection.

Some children, often referred to as 'whipping boys' (the term can apply equally to girls), attract far more than their fair share of victimization and are targets for one or more bullies. According to extensive research by Olweus (1978, 1984) and others, the victims of bullying are usually non-aggressive in their attitude and their behaviour; they also tend to be anxious, insecure and unpopular, with low self-esteem and a negative self-image. In many cases their parents are over-anxious and tend to over-protect the child. In a longitudinal study, Olweus (1984) found that, over a three year period, these victims maintained their low status within the peer group. They remained unpopular despite change of class, teacher and class-mates. Olweus concludes that: 'whipping boys possess certain characteristics that tend to make them unpopular in a variety of groups and situations... sensitivity and anxiousness, lack of assertiveness and self-esteem... directly contributed to their being rejected by their peers. At the same time, the peer-rejection is likely to have increased the anxiousness and lack of self-esteem' (Olweus 1984, p.68).

So far, we have considered the characteristics of children who are targets for peer rejection or bullying. But it is also important to examine the characteristics of children who reject other children, are aggressive towards them, or bully them. Bearing in mind the central issue of this chapter, we must avoid the assumption that bullies 'hate' their victims. Similarly, not all of the children who hate or reject other children, or are aggressive towards them, are appropriately described as 'bullies'. It is likely that most children occasionally reject one or more of their peers, and a child may be very hostile at one time and caring at another. However, there is evidence that some children are rarely positive in their response to other children, their general orientation towards their peers being callous, malicious, resentful, hostile, ruthless, vicious or 'spiteful'. Thus Reid *et al.* (1981) identified a number of children who constantly displayed both very aversive behaviours (including hitting others and issuing verbal threats) and 'mildly obnoxious' behaviours such as whining and teasing.

The study by Reid and his colleagues included a number of children who had been subjected to serious aggression by their parents, and an association between physical abuse victimization and aggressiveness is by now well-established. One of the most frequently reported characteristics of abused children is their high level of aggression. They tend to fight more with siblings, they often show aggression at school, and in home- and clinic-based observational studies they have been found to exhibit high levels of aggression towards their parents and other children (Frude 1991).

This picture of widespread and generalized aggression differs somewhat from the image of the 'bully' that has emerged from the extensive research on that topic. Olweus (1978, 1984) found in a long series of studies that bullies are distinguished by strong aggressive tendencies and weak control of these tendencies. They possess strong self-assertion and dominance needs. Most bullies have a generally positive view of themselves and are confident, tough, and non-anxious. Furthermore they are no less popular than the average child in their social group. Thus it is the bully's victim, rather than the bully, who is rejected by the wider peer group. Some bullies are rejected by peers because of their bullying, but in many cases the victim has few supporters and the bully's behaviour appears to be unrecognized, ignored or forgiven. Indeed, it is clear that bullies select particular children as their victims largely because they lack popularity within the group. The victims, being weak and unpopular, are relatively safe targets for the bully's aggression, both physically and socially.

Incidentally, recent research on children's views of bullying suggests that most children are less concerned about the brief violent episodes that are often central to adults' concepts of bullying and are much more concerned about the 'psychological' aspects of bullying – the longer-term rejection, menacing and intimidation of the victim (La Fontaine 1991). Similarly, victims are more likely to be distressed by the rejection and name calling than by physical attacks. La Fontaine (1991) found that many incidents of bullying were in fact 'demonstrations of the norms of children's social groups... Bullying outlaws and punishes those who do not conform'. Thus bullying is closely related to rejection of the victim, but the crucial rejection involved seems to be the rejection by the peer group rather than the rejection by the bully.

Children's response to peers' distress

Children are sensitive to the emotions of others from an early age. There is a wealth of evidence showing that even very young infants are 'tuned in' to their mother's responses and respond 'in sympathy'. In the second year of life children can begin to interact with other children and with adults, with the clear intention of comforting them, or of hurting them. Most children respond to the evident distress of other children with some show of concern. They may show evident distress themselves, as they empathize with the child's suffering, or they may offer comfort in the form of verbal sympathy ('Never mind') or a physical gesture (an arm around the child's shoulders, for example). In some cases a toy may be offered, or the child may be asked to participate in a game, in a bid to 'compensate' or distract them. In response to another's distress a child will often desist from any action that is helping to maintain the distress, or which might add to it. Thus Camras (1977) showed that children often refrain from taking a toy from another child when they see the other child looking sad. Even a slight change in facial expression may be sufficient to change another child's action. In many cases evident distress also curtails aggression, so that if a child's victim appears hurt, falls over, or starts to cry, there is likely to be an abrupt end to the aggression.

It is clear that many children, even from a very early age, skillfully interpret slight behavioural cues in order to assess another's emotional state. In many cases they respond sensitively and directly to any indication of worry or annoyance, but many aspects of the social context also affect the nature of their response. Thus whether they offer comfort or not depends to a some degree on who is witnessing the interaction, and adults often provide a prompt in order to spur a child to offer support or nurturance. Zahn-Waxler *et al.* (1979) demonstrated that mothers' reactions greatly influenced their children's response to distressed peers. Some mothers were more active than others in encouraging compassionate behaviours and they had a greater effect in promoting positive responses.

A number of observational studies of peer interactions show that some children respond in markedly different ways to the evident distress of their peers. Some, indeed, respond in an aggressive way and seem intent on exacerbating the troubled child's distress. Working with a sample of children who had been physically abused by their parents, George and Main (1979) found that, in response to another child becoming distressed, many abused children failed to show the usual concern or sadness. They tended to respond instead with fear or anger, and in some cases they actually hit the child who was distressed. In a later study Main and George (1985) studied two groups of children, aged between one and three years. One group had been physically maltreated and the other had not. The children were observed playing with others during day-care sessions, and particular attention was paid to situations in which another child became distressed. In response to such distress, none of the abused children responded with a clear comforting response to the disturbed child. In many cases they did show concern, but this took the form of fear or distress or a combination of these responses. In many other cases the abused children became aggressive towards the disturbed child, either making verbal or non-verbal threats or directly attacking the crying child. None of the non-abused children ever showed hostility to the distressed child, and many showed an obvious concern.

Sibling rivalry and antagonism

'Sibling rivalry' is familiar to all of those who have brothers and sisters, and to parents of two or more children. Even when the relationship between siblings is positive overall there is usually some element of comparison and competition. In adulthood, a brother or sister may provide a kind of yardstick against which one can measure one's own success and failures, strengths and weaknesses, and degree of popularity. In childhood, siblings are often in competition over such limited resources as space, possessions, power, and, particularly, the parents' love and attention.

Following the birth of a brother or sister, over 90 per cent of previously single children are seen by their parents as becoming 'more demanding' and 'more naughty', and the behaviour disturbance which occurs around this time sometimes takes the form of aggressive actions directed against the new baby (Dunn and Kendrick 1982). In one case reported by Dunn and Kendrick, a toddler reached into the baby's cot, pulled the bottle from the baby's mouth, drank the milk and then hit the baby with the empty bottle. It appears that children are more jealous when the new child is of the opposite sex, and this may be related to the fact that mothers apparently give more attention to their second baby if it is of a different sex to their firstborn than if it is of the same sex.

In order to study of the interaction between older siblings, mothers have been asked to keep diaries recording the occasions on which one sibling hits, upsets, comforts, or consoles the other. Siblings appear to upset one another as frequently as they give comfort to the other, and antagonistic responses are more often given by the older sibling, with the younger child as the target for the unfriendly action (Dunn and Kendrick 1982). Some children appear gleeful in response to their sibling's discomfort. Some frequently act to cause their sibling distress, and such children rarely provide comfort or consolation when the brother or sister shows anxiety or sadness.

Chronic hatred between siblings, at least during childhood, is fortunately rare, but there are cases in which the intensity of aggressive responses to a brother or sister is so high that the action can properly by labelled 'sibling (physical) abuse'. In a paper entitled 'Child abuse by siblings', Green (1984) provides case histories of a number of children between the ages of four- and twelve-years-old who inflicted serious injuries on their younger siblings. A number of common factors marked the history and current situation of the children who perpetrated the abuse. All of them had been physically abused themselves; their families were currently 'in crisis'; they were burdened with excessive caretaking for the target sibling; and the target was perceived as the parents' favourite. Green suggested that such serious sibling abuse represents an intensification of 'normal' sibling rivalry due to the abuser's own maltreatment and deprivation and that the abusers identified with the parents who had aggressed towards them. The attacks on siblings were also seen as functional for the abusers in a number of ways: they provided retribution against the more highly valued sibling rival; they represented a displacement of aggression originally directed against the abusing parent; they gained attention from the parent; and they enabled the child to gain a sense of mastery over the trauma of their own abuse.

A process model of the development of deviancy was devised by Patterson *et al.* (1984). This focuses on family interaction in general and on interactions between siblings in particular. The model examines the reciprocal influence of disruptions in parent discipline practices on irritable exchanges between the target child and other family members. Disrupted parent discipline and irritable exchanges within the family were hypothesized to provide a basic training for aggression that generalizes to other settings such that the child is identified by peers, teachers, and parents as physically aggressive.

Assessments including interviews, questionnaires, laboratory studies and home observations were carried out with the families of 91 fourth, seventh, and tenth grade boys (nine-, twelve- and fifteen-year-olds). Indicators from the assessment battery were used to define the constructs of inept parental discipline, negative exchanges, physical fighting and poor peer relations. Structural equations were used to describe the relations among the constructs. Findings supported the hypothesis that, under certain circumstances, family interaction may serve as basic training for aggression. In particular, it was found that interactions with siblings in the home appeared to have a pivotal role in subsequent aggressive behaviour.

Intervention – helping the rejected child

Parents and teachers are often in a powerful position to intervene in the social structure of peer groups and their interventions may help to reduce victimization, bullying and rejection. Such interruption in the 'natural' social processes of child groups is important for the alleviation of distress in those children who are victimized, bullied or rejected. It may do more than merely remedy immediate distress, however, for there is evidence of a fairly strong link between peer rejection in childhood and later problems. Ladd (1984) reviewed the evidence of associations between problematic peer relations during childhood and interpersonal disorders in later life and found strong support for the view that many problems of adolescence and adulthood are anticipated by disturbances of social relations in childhood.

Thus there is evidence to suggest that early interventions for such problems as social isolation, peer neglect and rejection, and friendlessness might prevent the development of certain long-term difficulties. This is not to say that problems are initiated at the peer level, however, because peer rejection itself may be an effect of specific antecedents. One model which places peer rejection in such an intermediate position is that put forward by Patterson *et al.* (1989). They outline a developmental model of antisocial behaviour, following evidence of a longitudinal course of antisocial behaviour from early childhood through adolescence. The model suggests that the route to chronic delinquency follows a reliable developmental sequence of experiences. Ineffective parenting practices and disturbed family interaction processes are viewed as determinants for childhood conduct disorders which may then lead to academic failure and peer rejection. These, in turn, may increase the risk of the child becoming depressed and becoming involved in a deviant peer group. It is assumed that children following this developmental sequence are at high risk for engaging in chronic delinquent behaviour.

There are two types of approach to helping the rejected child. One focuses on reducing the extent to which the child is rejected; the other attempts to help the child come to terms with his or her rejection and to reduce the trauma that may be associated with it. Reducing the extent to which a child is rejected may involve interventions at the individual level or at the group level. One obvious and important strategy is for the teacher to deal directly with issues of prejudice, discrimination and bullying by placing these issues for discussion on the classroom agenda, and by devising strict rules as to which behaviours are 'tolerable' and which are 'intolerable' in the classroom, in the playground and outside the school. Particular cases of victimization, name-calling and bullying need to be dealt with on an individual basis. Although there are a number of useful guidelines for teachers for dealing with racism, sexism and prejudiced attitudes towards the handicapped, and there are practical guides relating to the management of bullying (for example, Tattum and Lane 1991), it is clear that appropriate action is not always taken, or is not always successful.

In some cases the principal task is to help a child who is isolated and rejected to gain entry to a social group. Again a teacher or parent may help, for example by encouraging a group of peers in a sensitive way (without labelling or stigmatizing the lone child further) to accept the previously rejected child into their games and activities. In some cases, once the barrier of initial acceptance has been overcome, the child will become a *bona fide* member of the group (in other cases he or she will simply be tolerated). Other strategies for helping the rejected child to gain acceptance include 'appointing' him or her to a position of some power or responsibility within the group, or encouraging one popular member of the group to befriend the rejected child – to act as a 'buddy'. This child, chosen because of his or her own powerful position within the peer group (and identified, perhaps, as an 'opinion leader') may sway the group into accepting the formerly unpopular child.

The other approach to increasing a child's acceptability to the group involves broadening their range of skills. For example, there have been several attempts to help rejected children by training them in social skills. Thus Furman *et al.* (1979) introduced rejected four- and five-year-olds to play sessions with a younger partner, and this appeared to give them more social confidence. With older children, modelling techniques have been used. Oden and Asher (1977) instructed eight- and nine-year-old rejected or neglected children in such skills as how to participate in groups and how to communicate with peers. This coaching, together with role plays involving peers, was found to produce significant improvements in the children's sociometric status. Indirect approaches aimed at raising the child's achievement level and self-esteem can also prove effective. Thus Coie and Krehbiel (1984) demonstrated that children's acceptability to their peers increased when they took part in a programme aimed at improving their academic skills.

A detailed case report of a multi-factor assessment and intervention programme with a socially rejected child has been given by Petersen and Moe (1984). The authors describe a nine-year-old girl whose attempts to control other children led to negative peer interactions, social rejection and isolation. Significant improvements were achieved through a wide-ranging intervention that combined structured teaching sessions, role playing and feedback, observation of a social model, supervised and unsupervised play, and a number of generalization exercises.

Rejected children recognize their rejection to varying degrees. Although it would be easy to underestimate the trauma precipitated by peer rejection, it is also possible to over-estimate the degree to which children are stressed by being unpopular. Some children might be described as 'thick-skinned'. They are in some way resilient to the stress of being rejected. It would be interesting to know whether they use particular coping strategies to minimize the adverse emotional impact of their rejection; some for example, might be able to 'write off' the opinions of peers, perhaps choosing to focus instead on the more positive feedback gained from adults (teachers or parents) or from separate groups of peers (children from the neighbourhood or from Sunday school, for example, rather than their peers at school). Other children may have such a highly developed sense of self-worth that their peers' opinions of them simply do not cause them concern. Boldizar et al. (1989) showed that some aggressive children actually cared little about rejection by their peers. Compared to non-aggressive children in their class at school, aggressive boys and girls placed little value on peer rejection.

But while some children are blissfully unaware of their unpopularity, or are relatively unperturbed by it, others are painfully aware of being rejected by their peers (and, it should be added, some children feel rejected when in fact they are popular with all but a few of their peers). A number of strategies might be used by parents and teachers to reduce the trauma of children who are upset by peer rejection. Pastoral care within the school, for example, might be geared towards providing the rejected student with a range of coping or emotional survival skills. Children can be helped, even at an early age, to reframe and redefine their experience so that the traumatic effects are limited.

There are well-developed intervention programmes aimed at reducing the adverse psychological effects of bereavement, chronic illness and parental divorce, for example, and many of the intervention strategies used in these programmes could doubtless be adapted to reduce the emotional effects of peer rejection. Such strategies might involve the use of structured play sessions, stories, art work, puppetry and role-play. Children might also be helped to build their vocabulary so that they are better able to express their feelings and to explain their current situation to peers and adults, and to deal with fears of rejection. Such intervention programmes may evoke high anxiety and they therefore need to be structured so that the relevant issues are tackled indirectly. Thus a story character might be used as a 'carrier' of emotions, and feelings may be identified by the use of masks and pictures. Similar work focusing on the prevention and treatment of adverse effects following parental divorce has been documented by, for example, Ceborello *et al.* (1986) Pedro-Carroll and Cowen (1985) and Rossiter (1988).

References

Bierman, K.L. (1986) The relation between social aggression and peer rejection in middle childhood. *Advances in Behavioral Assessment of Children and Families, 2,* 151–78.

Bierman, K.L. (1987) The clinical significance and assessment of poor peer relations: Peer neglect versus peer rejection. *Journal of Developmental and Behavioral Pediatrics, 8,* 233–40.

Boldizar, J.P., Perry, D.G. and Perry, L.C. (1989) Outcome values and aggression. *Child Development, 60,* 571–9.

Cairns, R.B., Cairns, B.D., Neckerman, H.J. and Gest, S.D. (1988) Social networks and aggressive behavior: Peer support or peer rejection? *Developmental Psychology, 24,* 815–23.

Camras, L.A. (1977) Facial expressions used by children in a conflict situation. *Child Development, 48,* 1431–5.

Cebollero, A.M., Cruise, K. and Stollak, G. (1986) The long-term effects of divorce: Mothers and children in concurrent support groups. *Journal of Divorce, 10,* 219–28.

Chase, I.D. (1981) Social interaction: The missing link in evolutionary models. *The Behavioural and Brain Sciences, 4,* 237–8.

Coie, J.D., Dodge, K.A. and Coppotelli, H. (1982) Dimensions and types of social status: A cross-age perspective. *Developmental Psychology, 18,* 557–70.

Coie, J.D. and Dodge, K.A. (1983) Continuities and changes in children's social status: A five-year longitudinal study. *Merrill-Palmer Quarterly, 29,* 261–82.

Coie, J.D. and Krehbiel, G. (1984) Effects of academic tutoring on the social status of low- achieving, socially rejecting children. *Child Development, 55,* 1465–78.

Dodge, K.A., Schlundt, D.C., Shocken, I. and Delugach, J.D. (1983) Social competence and children's sociometric status: The role of peer group entry strategies. *Merrill-Palmer Quarterly, 29,* 309–36.

Dodge, K.A. and Coie, J.D. (1987) Social-information-processing factors in reactive and proactive aggression in children's peer groups. *Journal of Personality and Social Psychology, 53,* 1146–58.

Dunn, J. and Kendrick, C. (1982) *Siblings: Love, Envy and Understanding.* Massachusetts: Harvard University Press.

Dygdon, J.A., Conger, A.J. and Keane, S.P. (1987) Children's perceptions of the behavioral correlates of social acceptance, rejection, and neglect in their peers. *Journal of Clinical Child Psychology, 16,* 2–8.

Earn, B.M. and Sobol, M.P. (1990) A categorical analysis of children's attributions for social success and failure. *Psychological Record, 40,* 173–85.

Fromm, E. (1977) *The Anatomy of Human Destructiveness.* Harmondsworth: Penguin.

Frude, N. (1991) *Understanding Family Problems: A Psychological Analysis.* Chichester: Wiley.

Furman, W., Rahe, D.F. and Hartup, W.W. (1979) Rehabilitation of socially withdrawn preschool children through mixed-age and same-age socialization. *Child Development, 50,* 915–22.

George, C. and Main, M. (1979) Social interactions of young abused children: approach, avoidance and aggression. *Child Development, 50,* 306–18.

Green, A.H. (1984) Child abuse by siblings. *Child Abuse and Neglect, 8,* 311–7.

Harvey, D.H.P. and Greenway, A.P. (1984) The self-concept of physically handicapped children and their non-handicapped siblings: An empirical investigation. *Journal of Child Psychology and Psychiatry, 25,* 273–84.

Hazen, N.L., Black, B. and Fleming-Johnson, F.(1984) Social acceptance: Strategies children use and how teachers can help children learn them. *Young Children, 39,* 26–36.

Hodgens, J.B. and McCoy, J.F. (1989) Distinctions among rejected children on the basis of peer-nominated aggression. *Journal of Clinical Child Psychology, 18,* 121–8.

Hunter, J. and Schaecher, R. (1987) Stresses on lesbian and gay adolescents in schools. *Social Work in Education, 9,* 180–90.

Ladd, G.W. (1983) Effectiveness of a social learning method for enhancing children's social interaction and peer acceptance. *Child Development, 52,* 171–8.

Ladd, G.W. (1984) Social skill training with children: Issues in research and practice. *Clinical Psychology Review, 4,* 317–37.

La Fontaine, J. (1991) *Bullying – The Child's View.* London: Gulbenkian Foundation.

Lorenz, K. (1966) *On Aggression.* London: Methuen.

Macmillan, D., Jones, R. and Meyers, C. (1976) Mainstreaming the mentally retarded: Some questions, cautions and guidelines. *Mental Retardation, 14,* 3–13.

Main, M. and George, C. (1985) Responses of abused and disadvantaged toddlers to distress in agemates: A study in the day care setting. *Developmental Psychology, 21,* 407–12.

Marsh, P., Rosser, E. and Harre, R. (1978). *The Rules of Disorder.* London: Routledge and Kegan Paul.

Meyenn, R.J. (1980). School girls' peer groups, in Woods, P. (ed.), *Pupil Strategies: Explorations in the Sociology of the School.* London: Croom Helm.

Milich, R., Landau, S., Kilby, G. and Whitten, P. (1982) Preschool peer perceptions of the behavior of hyperactive and aggressive children. *Journal of Abnormal Child Psychology, 10,* 497–510.

Milich, R. and Landau, S. (1984) A comparison of the social status and social behavior of aggressive and aggressive/withdrawn boys. *Journal of Abnormal Child Psychology, 12,* 277–88.

Newberry, M.K. and Parish, T.S. (1987) Enhancement of attitudes towards handicapped children through social interactions. *Journal of Social Psychology, 127,* 59–62.

Oden, S. and Asher, S.R. (1977) Coaching children in social skills for friendship making. *Child Development, 48,* 495–506.

Olweus, D. (1978). *Aggression in the Schools: Bullies and Whipping Boys.* Washington D.C.: Hemisphere.

Olweus, D. (1984). Aggressors and their victims: Bullying at school, in Frude, N. and Gault, H. (eds.), *Disruptive Behaviour in Schools.* Chichester: John Wiley and Son.

Orbach, S. (1991) Strife in the family. *Guardian,* August 10th.

Patterson, G.R., DeBaryshe, B.D. and Ramsey, E. (1989) A developmental perspective on antisocial behavior. *American Psychologist, 44,* 329–35

Patterson, G.R., Dishion, T.J. and Bank, L. (1984) Family interaction: A process model of deviancy training. *Aggressive Behavior, 10,* 253–67.

Pedro-Carroll, J. and Cowen, E. (1985) The children of divorce intervention project: An investigation of the efficacy of a school-based prevention program. *Journal of Consulting and Clinical Psychology, 53,* 603–11.

Peretti, P.O. and McNair, A. (1987) Self-perceived psychological and social characteristics of the sociometric isolate. *Education, 107,* 310–1(4).

Perry, D.G., Kusel, S.J. and Perry, L.C. (1988) Victims of peer aggression. *Developmental Psychology, 24,* 807–14.

Petersen, N.J. and Moe, G.L. (1984) A multimethod assessment and intervention with a socially rejected child. *School Psychology Review, 13,* 391–6.

Pollard, A. (1980). Teacher interests and changing situations of survival threat in primary school classrooms, in Woods, P. (ed.), *Pupil Strategies: Explorations in the Sociology of the School.* London: Croom Helm.

Ray, B.M. (1985) Measuring the social position of the mainstreamed handicapped child. *Exceptional Children, 52,* 57–62.

Reid, J.B., Taplin, P.S., and Lorber, R. (1981) An interactional approach to the treatment of abusive families. In R. Stuart, (ed.) *Violent Behaviour: Social*

Learning Approaches to Prediction, Management and Treatment. New York: Brunner/Mazel.

Rossiter, A.B. (1988) A model for group intervention with preschool children experiencing separation and divorce. *American Journal of Orthopsychiatry, 58,* 387–96.

Rubin, K.H., Daniels-Beirness, T. and Hayvren, M. (1982) Social and social-cognitive correlates of sociometric status in preschool and kindergarten children. *Canadian Journal of Behavioural Science, 14,* 338–49.

Sabornie, E.J. (1987) Bi-directional social status of behaviorally disordered and nonhandicapped elementary school pupils. *Behavioral Disorders, 13,* 45–57.

Sherif, M., Harvey, O.J., White, B.J., Hood, W.R. and Sherif, C.W. (1961) *Intergroup Conflict and Cooperation: The Robbers' Cave Experiment.* Norman, OK: University of Oklahoma.

Siann, G., Macdonald, M., Macleod, M. and Glissov, P. (1990) Gender and aggression: Gender stereotyping with respect to aggression and experience of bullying – A cross-cultural comparison. Presented paper: 'Workshop on Gender and Aggression', Ambleside, Cumbria, September, 1990.

Sluckin, A. and Smith, P. (1978) Two approaches to the concept of dominance in preschool children. *Child Development, 48,* 917–23.

Storr, A. (1968) *Human Aggression.* London: Allen Lane – The Penguin Press.

Strayer, F.F., Jacques, M. and Gauthier, R. (1983) L'evolution du conflit social et des rapports de force chez les jeunes enfants. *Recherches en Psychologie Sociale.*

Tajfel, H. (1982) Intergroup relations, in Rozenzweig, M.M. and Porter, L.W. (eds.) *Annual Review of Psychology.* Palo Alto: Annual Reviews.

Tattum, D. and Lane, D. (1991) *Bullying in Schools.* Stoke-on-Trent: Trentham Books.

Taylor, A.R., Asher, S.R. and Williams, G.A. (1987) The social adaptation of mainstreamed mildly retarded children. *Child Development, 58,* 1321–34.

Willis, P. (1977) *Learning to Labour.* Farnborough: Saxon House.

Wright, J.C., Giammarino, M. and Parad, H.W. (1986) Social status in small groups: Individual-group similarity and the social 'misfit'. *Journal of Personality and Social Psychology, 50,* 523–36.

Zahn-Waxler, C., Radke-Yarrow, M. and King, R.A. (1979) Child rearing and children's prosocial dispositions towards victims of distress. *Child Development, 50,* 319–30.

CHAPTER 6

The Therapeutic Importance of Racial Identity in Working with Black Children Who Hate

Jocelyn Emama Maxime'

'I hate me! I am ugly! I am like them... Black People... all ugly!' Mary shouts as she wraps her arms with healing radiator-induced sores around her body and folds herself into a ball. Her attempts at removing her skin colour on the radiator were not successful and she is thoroughly disappointed. (From the case of 10-year-old Mary, 1991)

'I attempted suicide' she offered untruthfully as I looked at her arms. Sue has laceration marks from her elbow down to her wrists; from afar one would mistake her arms to be adorned with bracelets, on approach however, you realise that they are all healed marks from razor cuts. Sue lacerated herself and tried to destroy the skin she carries. (From the case of Sue, a teenager, October 1991)

Sadly, the above cases are dated 1991 instead of 1961. It remains unfortunate that the area of Race has been viewed and studied primarily under 'a political umbrella'. The result is that the important ethnographic aspect of race, as it is embedded in the child development process with its wealth of contributions to the 'theories of child development', and toward enhancing the skills of child practitioners to name but a few, is virtually lost. It is now legally imperative, due to the requirements of the Children Act 1989, that we commit ourselves to exploring the many dimensions of 'Race', aiming at a greater understanding and service toward Black children.

One of the major areas of child development is the formation of Identity. Unfortunately the research and practice implications in this field, although numerous, have been mainly researched in the following areas:

- Self-concept
- Self-esteem
- Self-confidence
- Pride
- Positive feelings

- Racial awareness (less researched)
- Racial evaluation (less researched).

What this clearly demonstrates is a current problem in the area of identity research at large. In fact the area of racial identity in children is gravely under-researched in Britain, especially in the therapeutic field. All the above areas are combined, used interchangeably and often referred to as 'Identity'. This fusion underlies the essence of this chapter, which encourages all to clearly distinguish the aspects of identity if we are to provide true quality and equality of service. Figure 6.1 dismantles this notion in a diagram of 'The self' and illustrates two differing aspects of identity, derived from the above categories.

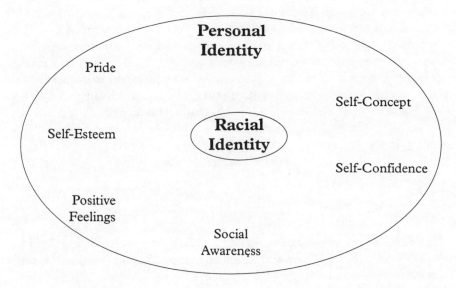

Figure 6.1 *The Self*

In the outer circle Pride, Self-Concept, Self-Esteem, Social Awareness, Positive Feelings, and Self-Confidence are all located within the aspect of *Personal Identity*. It is important to note, as Cross (1987) pointed out, that Personal Identity consists of universal components of psychological functioning which are inherent in all human beings regardless of race, gender or culture, whereas in the smaller circle *Racial Identity* represents the ethnographic dimension of the self. Professor Cross, in a comprehensive treatise on Racial Identity (or as it is sometimes called Reference Group Orientation) explained the following:

> In this light, studies of racial attitudes... racial self-esteem, racial evaluation, racial preference, or racial self-identification are subcate-

gories of the domain, reference group orientation (RGO). (Cross 1987, p.124)

I have previously (Maxime' 1989) discussed many of the conceptual and methodological problems inherent in researching 'Personal and Racial Identity' in detail. However, the focus in this chapter will be on enhancing one's understanding of the importance of 'Racial Identity' and how it interplays with the issue of self-hatred. Toward this goal the subject of nurturance is of utmost importance.

Nurturance

Interestingly, if one examines the above list of the Personal Identity components, what stands out is the fact that each area requires 'Nurturance' toward sound psychological development and health. No one will expect a baby of one month old to run across a room. Everyone understands that a certain maturation period of motor development is necessary before such a feat. Similarly the notion of nurturance is fully acknowledged in the enhancement of self-confidence. Nevertheless, for many parents, carers and workers the idea of nurturance is often forgotten as regards 'Racial Identity'.

I have argued (Maxime' 1983, 1986) that nurturance of Black children's development of racial identity is fundamental to sound psychological well-being. It seems essential at this point to reflect briefly on the way in which 'identity' or the 'self' is portrayed in the literature via some of the popular approaches.

The self

In one of the most thorough books on Black self-concept, Banks and Grambs (1972) stressed in a review of research on identity that the 'ideal self' is seen as synonymous with caucasian, and particularly middle class, white identity. They concluded that in the quest for a positive sense of racial identity, many Blacks, including young children, have to reject their old identity with its correlative inferiority. Clark (1965), in a study focusing on the development of Black children, stressed that:

> Children who are consistently rejected understandably begin to question and doubt whether they, their family and their group really deserve no more respect from the larger society than they receive. (Clark 1965, p.3)

This is even more transparent if one briefly examines some of the child developmental approaches. It is important to point out that the following approaches presented are on the basis of their contribution toward understanding the complex area of racial identity, and not for comparative purposes.

The Eriksonian Approach

Erikson (1968), like Goldstein (1939), Maslow (1954), and Rogers(1962) maintained that identity formation is a continuing process of 'progressive differentiations and crystallisations which expand self awareness' (Burns 1979). In fact, Erikson (1968) stressed the importance of the cultural context in which identity evolves. He defined identity formation in the following way.

> In psychological terms, identity formation employs a process of simultaneous reflection and observation, a process taking place on all levels of mental functioning by which the individual judges himself in the light of what he perceives to be the way in which others judge him in comparison of themselves and to a typology significant to them; while he judges their way of judging him in the light of how he perceives himself in comparison to them and to types that have been relevant to him. (Erikson 1968, p.22)

Eriksonian psychology propounds that identity is a construct that denotes both individual uniqueness and a striving for continuity and group solidarity. Hauser and Kasendorf (1983) further suggested that the 'continuity' often referred to actually implies temporal stability, which refers to the constancy of one's self-image over a period of time. According to Goodman (1972), Erikson further defines 'identity' as being a psychoanalytic term as well as a psychosocial one. Erikson (1959) maintained that identity covered more than what was commonly accepted as 'self'; he argued that it included the 'ego synthesizing functions which are concerned with the genetic continuity of self-representation'. Self-identity as viewed by both Freud and Erikson evolved through successive developmental stages. Erikson, however, extended the functions of the ego beyond those of Freud's to a wider social setting. He also focused more on healthy development, which according to Erikson was contingent upon the successful resolution of eight developmental stages.

Part of the attraction, as well as the difficulty in adopting an Eriksonian model, according to Rosenthal (1987), is the fact that each of the eight stages of development is systematically related and dependent on the previous stage, and one stage must be successfully resolved before it can be integrated into the person's identity. Thus all experiences throughout one's life span, especially those in adolescence, contribute to the process of identity formation. According to Rotheram and Phinney (1987), the Eriksonian approach does point to the importance of ethnic group membership via its emphasis on social relationships. However, as Ciaccio (1978) concluded, this approach has not been used widely in understanding the process of racial identity development in young children.

The Piagetian Structural Approach

Piaget's work as a psychologist dates from 1921, and his account of development is set within a biological framework. According to Piaget, each organism must be able to adapt to its environment for survival, and adaptation involves psychological structural changes. Piaget identified a series of stages and substages, the order of which he regarded as fixed since each presupposed the level of adaptation reached in the previous stage. The stages themselves are thus structurally distinct and the four main stages are named in accordance with the dominant cognitive structure, as follows: sensori-motor (birth to about two years), pre-operational (two to seven years), concrete operations (seven to eleven years), and formal operations (upwards of eleven years).

Of particular interest to this chapter is the 'concrete operational stage'. This is the period between seven and twelve years old in which, it is argued, clarity of thought develops with an acute awareness of separateness from others. Interestingly and importantly, I have found from my clinical case load that the vast majority of children experiencing 'racial identity confusion' or displaying various acts of 'self-hatred' fall within this age group. Thus, although there are various criticisms leveled at Piaget's work for its lack of acknowledgement of social and emotional factors, his work – especially the area of conservation – does contribute to our understanding in the complex area of racial identity.

The Behavioural Approach

In an earlier work (1986), I examined two basic aspects of the behavioural approach – rewards and observation/modelling – which seem to assist in understanding how racial identification is 'shaped' in Black children.

Work by Bandura (1969), has shown that mere observation is sufficient for the acquisition of behaviours. Baer and colleagues even demonstrated how they established generalized imitation in young children via simple social reinforcement from a puppet. Three years later Baer et al. (1967) showed how imitative behaviours could be even more quickly acquired when significant social models were used. There is a strong element of dependency by young children who are vulnerable to the prevailing attitudes and behaviours in their environment. Powerful influencers like the media and society in general, by their persistent lack and de-emphasis of positive Black models, do affect how some Black children perceived their racial identity. The result is that some Black children, especially those who might not be in receipt of the positive nurturing influence of the family (Boykin and Toms 1985), may try to imitate and adopt behaviours of significant others in their environment which are self-destructive to themselves.

Most Black children in white dominated societies are reinforced positively when they show signs of adjustment and acceptance to society and its values, even when the said society is so often hostile and rejecting to them as Black people. Maxime' (1986), highlighted the case of five-year-old Morris who had already developed survival skills and was into some complex psychological manoeuvring. Maxime' (1991) also shared the case of Chris, aged six, who had already become an obsessional washer. Little Chris, whenever he held his hands out for inspection after washing them at lunch-times, was told by staff from the age of four, 'Chris we have no way of knowing if your hands are dirty or clean'. By the age of six Christopher was engaged in obsessional washing to make his hands 'clean like the other children' i.e. white.

The Psychodynamic Approach

Of particular interest is the Object Relations theory, as described in the work of Melanie Klein (1932) and Fairbairn (1958). This psychodynamic theory postulates that the child not only reacts to the objects in its environment but is constituted by its object-relationships. Fairbairn stressed that early mental internalisation of the environment and its reproduction in the unconscious mind determines personality, while Klein emphasised that a young child's perception of external reality and external objects is perpetually influenced and coloured by his or her experiences. She stressed that it was impossible to separate the outer and the inner realities completely as they overlapped. The area of Klein's work which is of importance is that in which she highlights a child's inexperience of a certain negative external reality and the frustration the child experiences as it is beyond his or her comprehension. Thus a child's inexperience in integrating the outer and inner realities stands unprotected against this interaction and projects that rage onto his or her external objects while internalizing the same object in all its terror and fearfulness.

The above is interesting and on close examination does assist in the understanding of racial identity development in young children. In fact, the object relations theory goes further in offering a possible explanation for the incidence of identity crisis and self-hatred. Of relevance is the case-work in England of Small (1982), Divine (1984) and Maxime' (1983, 1986) who found that some Black children in Britain – many being cared for by white carers both in local authority care and in foster and/or adoptive homes – harbour very negative attitudes either towards Black people in general or to what they imagine Black people to be like. Due to these young children's inexperience in dealing with Black people and the often negative views received about 'Blackness', the physical realization of self as 'Black', which is often not perceived to be good or right, then becomes frustrating to these Black children. What results from this, as Klein pointed out, is rage toward others in the environment, so that aggression is expressed especially to negative objects, in this case Black people. Small (1986) highlighted many incidences from his case-work in which Black social workers have experienced this rage from Black children in this predicament.

Thus, Klein's explanation of the interactive process of the outer and inner realities in the formation of identity development is useful in understanding the consequences which could result due to the lack of nurturance of some Black children's racial identity development. It seems very plausible in the light of what this theory states, coupled with the reality of many Black children, that there is no mystery in the findings of numerous researchers who have found some Black children to have a very poor racial concept of self and often claim to hate themselves.

The Symbolic Interaction Approach

Cooley (1902) and Mead (1934) are cited by Nobles (1973) as the researchers who originally conceived the symbolic interaction approach to the study of self-concept. According to this approach, one's self-concept is a continual product of social interaction with others. Cooley (1902) postulated that an essential unity existed between mind and society. He then developed the 'looking-glass theory of self' which stated that what an organism internalized as its own was based on information received from others. Mead (1934), in support of Cooley's theory, criticised the behaviourist notion (as he perceived it) of the passivity of individuals as they respond to stimuli and contended that organisms determine their own environments to a great extent. He suggested two analytically distinguishable phases – the 'I' and the 'Me' – as references for awareness of self. Mead viewed the 'I' as the perception of oneself as reflected by the shared meanings and values of others, while the 'Me' was constituted by the incorporated attitudes of others. Thus, according to Nobles (1973), Mead felt 'that the way one perceived the "me" constituted the "I"; and that both combined constituted the nature of self' (Nobles 1973).

On close examination of both Cooley's and Mead's theories, neither seems to put forward a very adequate account of the relationship between one's 'I', 'Me' and society; the feeling or perception of being defined as a member of a particular group, referred to by Nobles (1973) as 'We-ness' or as Cross (1987) stressed, one's reference group orientation. Thus Nobles has argued that an

> expansion of Mead's analytically distinguishable phases... to a combined 'I', 'Me' and 'We'... is important for a clear understanding of Black self-conceptions... which defines the self. (Nobles 1973, p.16)

Therefore Nobles (1973, 1976, 1978) as well as Mbiti (1970) and Semaj (1978) have all contended that the relationship between the 'I', 'Me' and 'We' gives rise to the dynamic character of the cognitive-self structure. In fact, Nobles (1972) postulated that one's racial identity is an 'extended identity or one's extended self'. He argued that since consistency between the 'I' and 'Me' is necessary if a person is to maintain a particular image then due to the importance of the group (the 'We') in relation to self-identity, consistency between the three self-referents ('I', 'Me', and 'We') is also of significance to the individual's conception of self. Nobles (1972) additionally concluded that a true understanding of Black identity is dependent on an understanding of the African concept of self which incorporates the three referential aspects 'I', 'Me', and 'We'.

The above paragraphs attempt to demonstrate the contributions from the different perspectives. One of the approaches not mentioned in detail, which Maxime' (1989) has compiled and researched, is the Socio-Cognitive Developmental Approach. This uniquely describes an age-related progression in the ability to perceive, process, and interpret racial cues, which leads to the acquisition of racial identity. This approach, which hopefully will be soon published, calls for a paradigmatic revolution in the areas of race and identity as they affect education also.

Nevertheless, for the purposes of this chapter, the above raises therapeutic issues which if not understood could actually go unnoticed, to the detriment of many Black children. A short personal experience that clarified my approach and commitment in this area will be offered, followed by examples from my Clinical work.

On reflection, my concerns about the psychological and academic well-being of Black children in Britain relate closely to my childhood and racial identity development, which fortunately was nurtured constantly and purposefully by my mother in particular. I have realised, as I have grown older, that this actually shaped not only my psychological and academic perspective in life, but also my therapeutic approach. A brief experience will be mentioned as it contributes to the discussion presently.

A personal childhood experience

I remember asking myself a profound question at the age of four in 'post-colonial' Trinidad when I first started to read. My pride in reading aloud to my teacher was always marred by the puzzling question of 'why do these children look like that?'. I could not understand why Dick and Dora had this strange paint on their skin and hair, and stemless apples on their cheeks. We were all Black children learning to read from the 'Dick and Dora happy venture series', experiencing our first intimate contact with children being reflected on pages. Yet these children were all white with blue eyes and blonde hair. I remained puzzled, especially since I felt none of my teachers offered me a suitable explanation.

Eventually, as I reached the age of five, I turned to my mother who seemed to be the only one who not only offered me an explanation but engaged me in an ongoing discussion which, on reflection, was surely the foundation stone for my identity. From the age of five my mother progressively introduced me to history and a variety of cultures through poetry and literature. As she explained slavery, she helped me in understanding why all our school books were white-oriented. By the age of seven my perception of self was not limited because of my racial or economic grouping, but was continually nurtured by my mother whose phrase was 'Remember child, the sky is the limit'. Thus at the age of nine, when my primary school was called to assembly and we were told about our country gaining 'Independence', I was jubilant; I thought at last *'Goodbye Dick and Dora'*.

I did not realize that the process was to be a long and drawn out one which would even require my contribution, however small. By 1970, many of us young people felt that we had experienced and waited long enough; changes were slow and we were impatient. A group of us were approaching our O- Level Exams and we were adamant in our protest. This time we demanded answers from the Minister of Education. We refused to study only Wordsworth, Browning and Shakespeare while being debarred from being examined on Niapaul, Lamming and Eric Williams to name but a few. Our Caribbean History and Economic Geography were also being left in abeyance. Our curriculum was such that with closed eyes we could draw the maps of England and the United States and talk about their economic power with only a mere mention that the raw materials like sugar cane and bauxite that they used came from the West Indies. It was a costly exercise, but most of us refused to sit our examinations that year. Importantly, we got many parents, teachers and primary schools to join us in lobbying the Ministry of Education.

Two important changes took place which, however briefly, deserve to be mentioned. The first change was on the personal level for many of us taking part in the protest. Collectively, we realised how important our own history was in securing our personal identities. As we read more about Uriah Butler and others, we felt strengthened in our plea to the Government that each child should have the opportunity to grow up secured in their racial identity via exposure to positive and informative aspects of one's race.

The second change was that the Minister of Education met with us and not only promised changes, but revealed that plans were afoot to negotiate with the Examining Boards in England for the introduction of West Indian Geography, Literature and History as major O- and A-Level subjects. These changes outweighed the personal cost that some of us endured in having to sit our exams a year late.

Nevertheless, that experience taught me that the true essence of one's identity formation, as discussed, really relied on 'a process of simultaneous reflection and observation' (Erikson 1968); a process which Klein in 1932 postulated as a reaction not only to the objects in one's environment, but in effect being actually constituted by one's object-relationships. The die was cast, the importance of the interaction between one's perception of self and that of the environment and how each influenced and shaped each other was understood. I knew then from that experience in 1970, even though the clarity of my conceptualizations were not as sophisticated at the time, that it was vital for elements of self to be reflected and portrayed in the environment. On reflection years later I realised that this semblance and portrayal of self in one's environment was essential in the development of a positive sense of identity. This childhood experience positively influenced my teaching and clinical approaches years later in the United Kingdom.

A teaching experience

On my arrival in England in the seventies I found a genuine concern within the Black communities. Many Black young persons were leaving comprehensive schools without what could be considered as basic academic skills. This problem was so widespread in the inner cities that, in 1981, some Black professionals, including myself, decided to work part-time to teach on the then Youth Opportunities Programme (YOP). Personally, I felt impelled to teach even part-time by my conscience, political perspective, and a sense of frustration that I encountered with many Black teenagers in therapy. I found far too many were expressing a sad sense of hopelessness, a lack of zeal which was accompanied by a very poor self-image, and for some a display of what could only be described as 'self-hatred'.

At a South London college of further education in which I taught, the young people complained bitterly about the racism within the educational system and their teacher's low expectations of them, which quite sadly I was witnessing in their self-fulfilling prophecy. Interestingly, what most of the youngsters had in common was a very poor image of 'self'. Many of the young people explained that although they were born in England they were treated and looked upon as 'nobodies' and as such why should they bother with anything. The statement one sixteen-year-old girl made to me in front of three teachers in a Black organisation in 1981 epitomized the reason for our concern. So profound was her statement that permission was sought to use the recording.

> Well, I was once interested, I was even doing well, so well that I even wanted to be a vet until my teacher and the career adviser found out. They reminded me about my family's poverty and my race. Strange, that was the only time they both spent some time talking about Black people and what we can do. Anyhow I was advised to aim for the domestic Arts College in the town centre if I wanted to make it to college. I gave up, they had to be right, I have never seen a Black vet in England. They even switched me from the O-Level class to the CSE one, I couldn't be any good. I just wanted to fail, to hang my hat where my hand could never reach, as my teacher said. I don't care now, I can't be bothered, so what if I'm a bum. (Recorded from a conversation with J.C.of Birmingham, 1981 and shared at 'Black parents and teachers bridging the gap' meeting in Birmingham,1981.)

Towards a solution

I started experimenting with transferring a few of the psycho-historical methods (for example, the use of relevant historical information for psychological purposes) from my therapeutic work to a class of young people to whom I was teaching mathematics on a Youth Opportunity Programme. They were attached to an engineering firm and as such were exposed to practical engineering at a very basic level. When I met the boys they were a close group of Black boys with one white colleague, who were disinterested in school work of any kind. All fifteen lads including the white youngster claimed that they were content to be either 'aides to mechanics or a car sprayer or welder'. They could not see the usefulness of mathematics, English or any other subject which they were being taught at City and Guilds Level. In brief, most of the Black boys viewed themselves so poorly that some remained in the nearby shop with an amusement machine while classes were in progress with the remark that nothing we were doing will make a difference. It was around this time that I decided to introduce the class to a Black pioneer in the engineering field as a form of 'positive self-reference material'.

The effect was startling: apart from captivating their interests the boys were genuinely impressed with Elijah McCoy's life story. We used the story in three parts: in engineering; as the life experience of a Black person in 1865; and to compare McCoy's experiences with that of the 1980s and various opportunities of that era in that field. The boys started attending classes, and in June they all attempted their exams.

Highlights from clinical work

Working with Black children in the therapeutic setting further clarified the importance of the area of racial identity, especially for one's psychological well-being. Therapeutic work with some Black children in residential, transracially fostered and adoptive care settings illustrated an extremely destructive process being displayed by some of the Black children I was working with, which could best be described as 'self-hatred' or, as it is more commonly called, racial identity confusion/crisis, or negromachy.

The phenomenon of racial identity confusion was called 'negromachy' by Thomas (1970) who described it as being characterized by devalued self-worth and dependence on white society for self-definition. Excerpts from two case-studies are provided to further explain this phenomenon.

Peter Weinreich (1979) highlighted the case of a teenage Black boy called John, who rejected his own skin colour and expressed hostile evaluations of Black people. John was actually born in Jamaica and came to England at age nine, with an over-riding desire to identify more closely with white people. His role models were white, while he perceived that any identification with Blacks:

... of which he felt himself to be one in the past, is a threat to his stability of mind and to what he has achieved in establishing a more favourable self concept... He wishes to be white. (Weinreich 1979, pp.70–7)

Maxime' (1985) described the case of a twelve-year-old Black boy called Henry, who from the age of six lived with white foster parents in a very middle-class area on the outskirts of London. Henry was an intelligent and handsome child who was already in receipt of various prizes for dancing, and was commonly referred to by neighbours as 'our own dancer'. A racial identity assessment, however, revealed that Henry viewed Black people very negatively. His response to a particular card stimulus depicting an identifiable Black man standing in front of a group, looking as if he is teaching or describing something, was:

A man is disrupting a social evening of friends and the others phoned the police for him.

Henry made similar negative remarks about Black people throughout the assessment. However, his racial identity confusion was prominently displayed when I asked him how did he perceive himself:

I see myself as a spastic in a wheelchair, you expect people to watch at you, to laugh at you, to call you names. The only difference is that one day a doctor might come along, find a cure, and the spastic could get better. But I can't, I'm trapped in my skin, it just stays. (From H.A. Therapeutic Recordings, 28.8.84.)

The above were two examples of this phenomenon which Nobles (1973), after an extensive review of similar case studies, describes as follows:

... the self-hatred research did in fact demonstrate that some Black people hated themselves and that this hatred was reflected in a denial or rejection of group membership. (Nobles 1973, p.22)

At this stage it seems pertinent to mention that the seriousness of racial identity confusion/crisis is one which requires therapeutic help and, as Cross (1978) demonstrated, proceeds along various stages toward resolution. Cross (1971) developed a five-stage model of what he called 'Nigrescence' which refers to the process some individuals go through toward a secure and confident Black identity. Maxime' (1986, 1991) provided a summary of Cross's five stages which characterize a demoralized Black person in the process of positive change. The five stages will be summarized below and excerpts from the author's clinical cases will be offered to further highlight and explain each stage, in the hope that careers and workers will be assisted in recognizing where some children are, and where they are struggling toward.

1. The Pre-Encounter Stage

At this level, the person's world view is white orientated (eurocentric). He or she will even deny that racism exists. Interestingly, this stage transcends class distinctions. An example of this stage could be seen from the case of Mary: Mary knew that she was referred to a clinical psychologist; however, she did not realise nor was she told by the referring agency that I was Black. On meeting me for the first time these were Mary's reactions. She snarled, *'Go away, I'm not talking to you, I have nothing to say to you'*, before grabbing three big floor cushions and wrapping them around herself. She proceeded to roll within the cushions across the room, finally to lodge behind a sofa from which she continued her abusive discourse.

In this stage, which parallels the conformity stage of Sue and Sue (1990), the child usually makes a request for a white psychologist/therapist. There is also a clear display of the difficulty Klein highlighted in a child inexperienced in integrating the outer and inner realities, especially when the outer reality is perceived as negative and the reality of one's racial self has not been nurtured.

2. The Encounter Stage

The person now experiences or observes a situation that brings him or her face to face with racism. The experience is so shattering that it forces the individual to reinterpret his or her world. The case of Charles, discussed through the stages in Maxime' (1986, 1991) provides a vivid example of how shattering the encounter stage can be, as there could be the onset of various 'psychiatric and psychological disturbances'.

Young Mary (discussed above) stood unprotected against the interaction of meeting a Black psychologist. She projected her rage onto me as I represented that negative extension of self, while sadly she internalized or encountered 'herself' within that same experience in all its terror and fearfulness. Later, Mary became so frightened of 'herself' in therapy, as I gently brought her to a stage of looking at herself as she really was – a Black child – that she projected that fear in abuse to every Black person she came into contact with. Although painful to observe, the experience was a necessary one for Mary. When brought to London by two white social workers, police had to intervene nearly twice as a result of her inappropriate behaviour. She literally ran up to Black people at the bus stop and started abusing them.

The sensitivity of the therapist/counsellor/worker/parent cannot be overemphasised at this stage. An understanding of the child's experience is vital so that the overt behaviours can be placed in context, because experience in this area has shown that the focus at this stage must be on the internal turmoil that the child is experiencing. In fact, White and Parham (1990) pointed out from their work that this stage seems to involve two phases, the first being a realization that the old frame of reference is inappropriate, and the second involving a decision toward developing a positive Black identity. Little Mary is presently at the point of realization that her old frame of reference is inappropriate; she is slowly moving toward her decision.

3. The Immersion-Emersion Stage

'This stage encompasses the most sensational aspects of Black identity development' (Cross 1971). This is undoubtedly the most sensitive of the stages as outlined by Cross. Within this phase the person struggles to remove all semblance of the old identity, while intensifying 'Blackness'. Unfortunately, because the identity process is not positively founded, typical behaviours sometimes includes the disparagement of white people while deifying Black people. This could be especially painful for white parents of Black children or dutiful and consistent white workers who suddenly find themselves under attack, verbally and emotionally.

One teenager, who will be referred to as 'Tina', provides a classic example of some behaviours at this stage. When Tina (of Asian and African decent) first came into therapy she wore her hair combed over her face, her eyes were hardly visible (especially due to the way she hung her head), and her clothes were purposefully pulled covering all fingers. After taking Tina through the two previous stages, when she entered this stage it was surely sensational. To the amazement of white carers, Tina reduced her communication to them and got up one morning and proceeded to paint her entire room black, including the furniture. Her carers, as well as a sensitive psychiatrist, were understandably anxious, but trusted me to continue the programme.

Once more, understanding the period the child is going through is essential if we are to aid the young person through this phase. Work in this area has shown that individuals at this stage can be encouraged through therapy to emerge gradually from this heavily ego-involved state to a more rational position. However, there are some hidden complications that can and do arise, as will be mentioned at the end of the stages.

4. The Internalisation Stage

The individual has now managed to separate the old identified self and the new self, thus moving towards a positive Black identity. In this stage, the child has been assisted to explore race, its impact, its influence and how it relates to him or her. Care should be taken at this stage to ascertain that the young person is not equating a positive Black identity with mistrust of white people and friends. In the case of Paul, a mixed-parentage child who was rejected by his white foster mother after her Black husband left her, he painfully worked through the stages and his pain but felt he could not trust white people again. He even wanted to leave the youth club he was in as he felt he could no longer trust his white friends there. In this case Paul was assisted to review the reality of his situation and place people and incidents clearly in their perspective. As this focus developed, Paul was able to accept that he did have some caring and sound white friends who he valued and appreciated. What he found most significant at this time was that he could for the first time love his white friends without feeling 'bad' about being Black and hating his skin colour. He reported that he was now comfortable and liked himself for the first time as he was.

5. The Internalisation – Commitment Stage

Here the individual advances on the previous stage by involving him or herself in Black groups or community issues. Paul now extended his network of groups and lost the deep-seated fear that areas where there were many Black people should be avoided at all costs.

Importantly, my clinical work to date supports Parham's (1989) findings that identity resolution can occur in at least three ways:

1. *Stagnation.* This refers to the child's failure to move beyond his or her initial identity state. In fact some young people stagnate at various stages, especially the 'immersion' stage, and could be there for some time unless help is given to assist the young person to move onwards toward identity resolution.

2. *Stage-wise linear progression.* As is the case of many clients, wherein there is a sequential movement from one identity stage to another.

3. *Recycling.* Here the child or young person may move back through a stage already completed. There have been some Black children who have found the encounter stage so shattering, especially in vicarious learning situations, that they attempt to revert back to the pre-encounter stage. In the case of Tina above, when Tina realized that she was in the immersion stage and what was taking place she attempted to revert back to the pre-encounter stage. Thus, vigilance during process is extremely important.

It is sometimes felt that the format described above is unsuitable in fully understanding and categorising racial identity confusion in young children. However, Professor Gay (1982), after careful analysis of the stages, advocated their usefulness once some minor modifications were made so as to accommodate the developmental levels of young children. Gay (1982) proposed that the first pre-encounter stage had to be sub-divided into two dimensions, due to the process of racial identity development in young children. According to Gay (1985) the first stage is described in the following way:

> Thus, two dimensions of pre-encounter ethnicity are apparent. One dimension can be described as pre-consciousness, pre-cognitive, or pre-conceptual ethnic identification. This is the time in one's life when knowledge of ethnicity has not been systematically incorporated into his or her reasoning, valuing, and feeling structures. It does not shape attitudes and behaviours in conscious and deliberate ways. This is the

kind of ethnic identity that is most evident among pre-school and early elementary-age children. Developmentally, they are too immature cognitively and emotionally to understand the experiential, ideological, existential, and philosophical meanings of their ethnicity... This 'ethnic innocence', or naivete, is short-lived. Before long, many of these youngsters begin to experience true denigrative pre-encounter feelings and values as they begin to hear, know, and respond to the negative beliefs and attitudes assigned to their ethnic identity by others.

The second dimension or level of pre-encounter ethnic identity is far more devastating than the first. It is what Thomas calls 'negromachy' (a form of psychological illness characterized by self-ethnic denigration and denial) and Banks describes as 'psychological captivity'. (Gay 1982, p.70)

Gay (1982, 1985) demonstrated in her work that when the 'ethnic innocence' or pre-conceptual view of racial identity is dislodged, young children do experience the encounter stage. Two short examples of her description of Black children in the encounter stage seem relevant here.

... Thus, when denied membership on a playground team by her second grade white friend 'because she is too brown', Deidre is crushed! So is ten-year-old Maurine when she realizes that only whites are in attendance at a birthday party to which she was not invited. (Gay 1985, p.46)

Clinical work to date has shown that after this experience, which introduces the child to the encounter stage, the other stages followed a very similar progression to that described for older children and adults, once nurturance to one's racial identity is absent.

While utilizing the stages as a framework in therapy, three therapeutic strategies emerged. These three approaches repeatedly proved useful and are widely used now in my therapeutic intervention (See extended case histories, Maxime' 1986):

1. The cognitive aspect
2. The socio-historical aspect
3. The behavioural aspect

Another important dimension to emerge from my therapeutic work, especially in the area of fostering and adoption, was that the Black children in my caseload experiencing problems with their identity were children in the seven to twelve years age group. This is an important age group in the acquisition of identity development as was discussed in relation to the Piagetian concrete operational stage. My task then involved simplifying the techniques derived from the above three approaches to be useful to the group of children experiencing each stage. What made the task more difficult was that 'ethnobibliotherapy', which refers to the therapeutic use of literature that provides behavioural models and strategies for resolving racial identity problems, hardly existed in the United Kingdom, especially for children under twelve years old. Toward this end I (Maxime' 1991) developed two 'Black Like Me: Identity Workbooks' for children within the seven to twelve age group which are widely being used to help young Black children enhance their racial identity and cease the detrimental aspects of self-hatred.

In conclusion, what is apparent from work in this area thus far is that racial identity clearly needs to be understood by practitioners as well as parents. Not only is this a developmental issue which needs to be acknowledged but evidence beyond the scope of this chapter provides documented proof that it affects one's health, education and psychological well-being. *As therapists/workers/parents, we must remember that we are the custodians of the Health, Education, and Well-being of this and future generations of Black children.*

References

Baer, D.M., Peterson, R.F., and Sherman, J.A. (1967) The development of imitation by reinforcing behavioral similarity to a model. *Journal of the Experimental Analysis of Behavior, 10, 405–16.*

Bandura, A. (1969) *Principles of behaviour modification.* New York: Holt, Rinehart and Winston.

Banks, J. and Grambs, J. (1972) *Black Self Concept,* New York: McGraw Hill.

Boykin, A.W. and Toms, F.D. (1985) Black Child Socialization: A Conceptual Framework, in McAdoo and McAdoo (eds.) *Black Children.* London: Sage Publications.

Burns, R.B. (1979) *The Self Concept: Theory, Measurement, Development and Behaviour.* Harlow: Longman.

Cooley, C.H. (1902) *Human Nature and the Social Order.* New York: Scribner's.

Clark, K. (1965) *Dark Ghetto.* New York: Harper and Row.

Cross, W.E. (1971) The negro-to-black conversion experience: towards a psychology of black liberation. *Black World, Vol. 2.*

Cross, W.E. (1978) The Thomas and Cross Model of Psychological Nogrescence: A review. *Journal of Black Psychology 5,* 13–31.

Cross, W.E. (1987) A two-factor theory of Black identity: Implications for the study of Identity Development in Minority Children, in Phinney, J. and Rotherham, J. *Children's Ethnic Socialisation: Pluralism and Development.* London: Sage.

Divine, D. (1984) Black children in care positive action needed. *Caribbean Times, 5.3.*

Erikson, E.H. (1968) *Identity, Use and Crisis.* New York: Norton.

Fairbairn, W.R.D. (1958) On the nature and aims of psycho-analytical treatment. *Journal of Psycho-Analysis, Vol. 29, no. 5,* pp. 374–85.

Gay, G. (1982) Developmental prerequisites for multicultural education in the social studies, in Rosenzweig, L. (ed.), *Developmental perspectives on the Social Studies,* Washington DC: National Council for the Social Studies, 67–81.

Gay, G. (1985) Implications of selected models of ethnic identity development for educators. *Journal of Negro Education, 54, 1,* 43–55.

Goldstein, K. (1939) *The Organism.* New York: American Book Company.

Hauser, S. and Kassendorf, E. (1983) *Black and White Identity Foundations.* Robert E. Kreiger Publishing Co.

Klein, M. (1932) *The Psycho-Analysis of Children,* London: Hogarth.

Maslow, A.H. (1954) *Motivation and Personality.* New York: Harper and Wolf.

Maxime', J.E. (1983) *Psychological Aspects in Caring for Black Children,* paper presented at the Commonwealth Institute Training Day for Residential Workers.

Maxime', J.E. (1986) Some psychological models of black self-concept. In Ahmed, S., Cheetham, J. and Small, J. (eds.) *Social Work with Black Children and their Families.* London: Batsford, pp.100–16.

Maxime', J.E. (1991) *Black Identity: Workbook One of Black Like Me Series.* (2nd ed.) Emani Publications.

Maxime', J.E. (1991) *Black Pioneers: Workbook Two of Black Like Me Series.* (2nd ed.) Emani Publications.

Maxime', J.E. (1989) *The Effects of Positive Self Reference Material on Seven to Twelve Year Old Children of The African Diaspora.* Unpublished Ph.D.Thesis: University of London.

Maxime', J.E. (1991) Identity and consciousness. In *To Overcome Is To Undertake:* Report of the first Connexional Conference of Young Black Methodists.

Mbiti, J.S. (1970) *African religions and philosophy.* New York: Anchor.

Mead, G.H. (1934) *The Social Psychology of George Herbert Mead.* Strauss, A. (ed.) Chicago: University of Chicago Press.

Nobles, W. (1972) African philosophy: foundations for black psychology, in Jones, R.L. (ed.), *Black Psychology.* New York: Harper and Row.

Nobles, W.W. (1973) Psychological research and the black self concept: a critical review. *Journal of Social Issues, no. 29, 1,* pp.11–31.

Nobles, W.W. (1976) Extended self: rethinking the so-called negro self- concept. *Journal of Black Psychology, no. 2, 2,* pp.15–24.

Nobles, W.W. (1978) African consciousness and liberation struggles: implications for the development and construction of scientific paradigms. In Williams, R.L. (ed.), *Selected Papers. Beyond Survival: The Practical Role of Black Psychology in Enhancing Black Life.* Washington: Association of Black Psychologists.

Parham, T. (1989) Cycles of psychological nigrescence. *The Counseling Psychologist, 17(2)* 187–226.

Phinney, J.S. and Rotheram, M.J. (1987) *Children's Ethnic Socialization: Puralism and Development.* London: Sage.

Rogers, C.F. (1962) *Client-Centred Therapy.* Boston: Haughton and Mefflin

Rosenthal, D.A. (1987) Ethnic identity development in adolescents. In Phinney, J.S. and Rotheram, M.J. (eds.), *Children's Ethnic Socialization: Puralism and Development.* London: Sage.

Semaj, L. (1978) *Racial Identification and Preference in Children: A Cognitive Developmental Approach*. Ph.D. thesis: State University of New Jersey.

Small, J. (1982) *Black Children in Care: Good Practice Guide (Transracial Placements)*, Paper presented to New Black Families Unit.

Small, J. (1986) Black children in Care. Transvacial Placement: Conflicts and Contradictions. In Ahmed, S., Cheetham, J. and Small, J. (eds) *Social Work with Black Children and their Families*. London: Batsford.

Sue, D.W. and Sue, D. (1990) *Counseling The Culturally Different: Theory and Practice*. Chichester: John Wiley and Sons.

Thomas, C. (1970) Different Strokes for Different Folks. *Psychology Today*, Vol. 4, no. 4., pp.48–53, 78–80.

Weinreich, P. (1979) Cross-ethnic identification and self-rejection in a black adolescent. In Verma, G.K. and Bagley, C. (eds.), *Race, Education and Identity*. London: Macmillan.

White, J. and Parham, T. (1990) *The Psychology of Blacks: An African-American Perspective*, (2nd ed). New Jersey: Prentice Hall.

CHAPTER 7

Children and Hate
Hostility Caused by Racial Prejudice

Nandini Mane

Can young children be prejudiced? Can they feel hostility and even hatred for people on the basis of racial differences? Research conducted over the past two decades certainly points to the fact that children as young as four can be prejudiced towards those who are racially and ethnically different from themselves.

Let us begin with a definition of prejudice in this context. 'The most salient characteristic of prejudice is its negative hateful quality. This negativity defines prejudice. More precisely, prejudice refers to an organised predisposition to respond in an unfavourable manner towards people from an ethnic group because of their ethnic affiliation' (Aboud 1989, p.4). In other words, the main features of racial prejudice seem to be the following:

1. Making an unfavourable or negative judgement about people from an out-group. Evaluating people from another ethnic group negatively. This can be manifested in the form of dislike for a person or a whole group and can result in describing people in negative terms such as 'bad, ugly, mean or dirty' (Aboud 1989, p.3). This evaluation is based predominantly on negative stereotypes assigned to the whole group as well as individual members of it. According to Milner (1983), essentially prejudiced attitudes are irrational, unjust or intolerant dispositions towards other groups.

2. This negativity is particularly directed towards persons on the basis of their *ethnic* or *racial* group membership, particularly when the main feature of the group is dark skin colour.

An important feature of racial prejudice appears to be that it is entirely learnt. Although there are those who claim that a child is born with a disposition to be aggressive and hateful towards those who are different, this is not borne out by the research conducted in this area. For instance, it is well documented that in white majority societies, white children as young as three have expressed negative attitudes towards black people. By the time they are four, prejudices are considerably more prevalent (Asher and Allen 1969, Kircher and Furby 1971, Milner 1983). When black children were tested in those same areas, although they appear to form attitudes around the same age as the white children, i.e. by three to four years, the pattern of 'in-group attachment and out-group rejection is not found among them' (Aboud 1989, p.37). In other words, there is no evidence that in a white majority society black children develop prejudice for those who are different from themselves, particularly if they are white. On the contrary, there is evidence that many black children identify with pictures of white children and show preference for white peers rather than black. This leads us to believe that prejudice and hostility is expressed by children belonging to the visibly powerful majority group towards the visibly less powerful, minority groups.

It also leads us to believe that this prejudice is learnt from attitudes reflected in society; attitudes that are reinforced by various institutions as well as by the structures and systems devised to maintain and promote the *status quo*. Racial prejudice is based on the value attached to various groups by that society. Children get the message from adults that certain groups of people are important and of value and others are not. Children also pick up the ideology which says to them that in this society, it is generally the white group that is important and of value; the black group of people is of less value and is therefore not as important. When this hierarchy of value attached to skin colour is reflected in the environment in which children live and learn and reinforced by the media, the education system, culture books, toys etc. then children learn to become racially prejudiced and develop hostility towards the group seen as less important and negative. When this ideology of 'white superior – black inferior' pervades society, it promotes and reinforces prejudice, hostility and discrimination.

History of racism

One of the planks that upholds racism is the belief in hierarchical order of human value. This hierarchy has lent itself to the perpetuation and reinforcement of racism in white majority areas throughout the world.

Negative attitudes towards black people have existed in Britain certainly since Elizabeth I, and perhaps even earlier – ever since the first contact between the white peoples of Europe and the black peoples of Africa, as a result of travels and voyages undertaken by Europeans to the African continent. These early contacts gave rise to a lot of exotic notions and myths about black people, which became popular in Europe and may have had an influence on how black people were later regarded. The myths created and fostered by travellers and writers almost always associated black with sinister, black with savagery, black with dirt and with ugliness, in order to sensationalise and shock the people back home. In the eighteenth and nineteenth centuries (coinciding with the slave trade) these myths were reinforced by pseudo-scientific classifications of 'human types' which place the white European 'race' at the top of the ladder and black 'races' at the bottom. The so-called scientific treatises of well-established scientists, philosophers and thinkers were systematically racist and insidious. They deeply influenced the major politicians of the day as well as institutions. These influences and racist ideology over the years have permeated the very fabric of society and are effortlessly passed on to new generations. In the next section we will examine how this process occurs.

How is racism transmitted to children?

> Attitudes are made, not born. Social attitudes do not unfold from germ plasm or inhere in particular genetic configurations; they are not innate, nor do they enter human tissue for transmission to future generations. They arise, are communicated and are sustained in human social life. (Milner 1983, p.52)

As soon as a child is born in this society, whether black or white, he or she begins to absorb the influences of their surroundings; namely, their home, locality and, later on, their playgroup/nursery and school, as well as the culture and mass media. It is from these sources that children will learn about themselves, their immediate group and the wider world. This is called the socializing process. 'In the socializing process children learn not only "what to do" but also "how things are" as "we" see them. Learning the business of living in a culture is not only a question of learning skills but also learning meanings', which can happen 'intentionally, and by accident, with or without their realisation' (Milner 1983, p.53).

The role of parents

Parents are the most significant people in the young child's life. Their values, attitudes and way of doing things are bound to shape the child's early experiences. Children will learn who is regarded as 'good' or 'bad', welcome or unwelcome, who is a desirable playmate or otherwise from the way parents organize social life for their children. Social attitudes can be conveyed to children by parents either by direct tuition or indirectly. Parents' attitudes are conveyed to children in a number of ways: what sort of books and toys are made available to children; what kind of playmates are approved of; what sort of neighbourhood is considered desirable. Everything gives children messages about 'how "we" think about things, how "we" do things and ultimately who "we" are' (Milner 1983).

In a society where in-group attachment is strong and out-group rejection is prevalent, children also pick up the message that the way 'we' do things is better because 'we' are better than the out-group.

Indirect tuition, according to Milner, includes 'processes by which children reproduce aspects of adult behaviour, in this case their attitudes, without conscious or intentional teaching on the part of the parents'. This children do by imitating their parents – modelling themselves on them.

> Children of two years and older have a tendency to act in a number of ways like their parents. They adopt parental mannerisms, play parental

roles, and in the late pre-school years seem to incorporate in their value system many of the values, restrictions and ideals of the parents. (Milner 1983, p.53)

There has been research done in order to find out how parents can directly or indirectly teach children racial attitudes. The general findings indicate that 'ethnic attitudes of children are related to the ethnic attitudes of their (parent)... the transmission of ethnic prejudice is certainly not surprising since children easily adopt prejudiced attitudes if these are displayed by parents who typically have high reinforcement value' (Milner 1983). But this is only part of the story. Prejudiced attitudes are reinforced by other institutions that children come in contact with, as well as by the media in a way that makes it almost natural or the norm.

Once racism has taken root in a particular society and permeated every social, political and cultural institution, it can then be transmitted to children by the simple process of socialisation. This is done consciously as well as unconsciously, intentionally or unintentionally, thereby upholding the false belief that being white is 'better' or superior than being black in this society. If the environment in which children grow, learn and play is permeated with racism then this is bound to affect the perceptions, values and future attitudes of children, both black and white.

How does culture transmit racism to children?

Let us look in detail at books, toys and the mass media in this section to assess how racism can be conveyed to children. Books are regarded as a source of learning and information and are vested with unquestioned significance as 'important' carriers of culture. And yet, when examined closely, books can convey racism to children in several ways. A look at some popular children's books will help to understand how books can convey to children the message that 'white' is the norm and that skin' is associated with 'subservience', 'evil', 'savage', 'unimportant', 'ugly', 'dirty' etc. *Robinson Crusoe*, still around and often the only book in large popular book stores representing any black characters at all, is a typical example of how the idea of a powerful and resourceful white person is juxtaposed with the subservient black person, and interwoven into an exciting adventure tale. What about the perennially popular *Charlie and the Chocolate Factory*, by Roald Dahl, first published in 1967 and now revamped due to pressure from the anti-racist lobby, but still conveying some insidious, racist messages to children – not only in book form but as a film, which is often televised in the school holidays. This is the story of Mr Wonka who has a chocolate factory and is looking for an heir to run it. He invites five children to his factory and intends to choose one. No black child is a contender, although the 'Oompa Loompas' or little people who are the work force sound suspiciously like representations of black people. In the original version Mr Wonka has found his work force in the form of a tribe of 'miniature pygmies' in the 'very deepest and darkest part of the African jungle where no white man had ever been before'. These people are called 'Oompa Loompas', which again seems like a vulgar attempt at making fun of African language sounds. Moreover, the Oompa Loompas are 'practically starving to death' in the jungle until rescued by Wonka who gives them worthwhile work in his chocolate factory where they are willing workers and delighted to accept 'cocoa beans instead of meals or wages'. They are depicted as simple souls, yet savage enough to do the dirty work of getting rid of unacceptable contestants; they are 'childish, dehumanised' and entirely dependent on the goodwill of Wonka.

Other classics for children which are still around and read avidly include *Dr Dolittle*, *The Water Babies*, and *Huckleberry Finn* and convey similar messages equating black with inferiority and white with superiority. All books presented to children need to be assessed in order to intervene and combat racism.

Toys must similarly be assessed. In November 1991 an organisation called Working Group Against Racism in Children's Resources conducted a nationwide survey of toys in the high street toy shops with the aim of finding out how many of these toys and their packaging reflect black children in an effective and positive way (Working Group 1991). The organization, which is a voluntary one, asked its 700 members to participate in this project in which branches of 25 leading toy shops were visited. The results of this survey are predictably grim. It shows that there is very little in the high street toy shops to indicate that black children and communities are an important part of this society. The survey indicates that the toy industry discriminates against black children on a massive scale by not representing them in a meaningful way. The survey shows that not only are there very few toys representing black children, but that there are still toys around that portray black people negatively: there are toys and games around that invoke the whole 'jungle and the great white hunter' imagery, there are numerous versions of 'cowboy and Indians' games, and toys where the 'Indians' are predictably depicted as savage and 'to be subdued'. There are umpteen 'military' toys which promote violence and equate 'black' with 'evil'. The colour black is almost always used to symbolise the 'enemy' – one that must be destroyed. 'Gollywogs' are still found in toy shops and regarded as harmless.

As a result young children can pick up negative messages about black people – messages that can have a very harmful effect on children in their crucial early years. This is precisely how white children can learn racial prejudice. They can get false messages about themselves and their place in an unjust hierarchy of colours. This will make it possible for white children to think that it is permissible to feel hostility towards black children and adults because it is allowed to be expressed in many different ways by adults.

The mass media reinforces the same negative images, by focusing on stereotypical representations of black people. They are associated with 'criminality', 'poverty', 'rioting', 'unemployment' or else with 'sport' and 'entertainment'. Children's television programmes emphasise the same imbalance. Practically all the heroes of these programmes – fantasy figures – are white – such as Superman and She-ra. There is an absence of black heroes, fantasy figures and role models with whom black children can identify. As a result of all the messages conveyed in many different ways, children learn that being black is not desirable in this society. It leads in some cases to black children denying their 'identity' as black; in other cases it can lead to a feeling of anger and frustration. In many cases it leads to a sense of alienation.

The effect on white children and young people is equally damaging. They can get the message that they are 'good', 'clean' and on the side of 'right' because they are white. Their perception of their black peers is shaped by the way in which black people are treated and represented. They are likely to draw the conclusion that black people are not to be trusted; that they are unclean, noisy and aggressive. This, combined with the message that it is permissible to treat them as inferior, can lead to rejection of black peers, abuse and harassment, and discrimination. White children perceive and observe how their black peers are treated by adults in powerful positions. The fact that more black children are excluded from school on lesser charges than white pupils is not lost on them. The fact that more black children are forced into special schools and regarded as failures by the education system is not lost on them either. As a result many white youngsters can and do develop a disregard for black people generally. This hostility and intolerance is given a boost when those in power – politically or socially – reiterate the endemic racism in society. The examples that immediately come to mind are Enoch Powell's campaign against immigration and Margaret Thatcher's infamous statement about being swamped by alien cultures which was followed by a decade that 'produced Brixton, Tottenham, Dewsbury, the Honeyford and McGoldrick disputes, rows over refugee and immigration policies, inner-city jihads, escalating racial assaults, attacks on anti-racism, the Rushdie affair and the Gulf war' (Alibhai-Brown 1992). It is clear that all this contributed to an increase in ill-feeling, increased harassment of black children and adults and increasing hostility.

In 1981 the Home Office undertook a study of thirteen selected police areas. It was found that people of Asian origin were fifty times more likely than white people to be victims of racially motivated offenses. In the case of African-Caribbeans the number of victims of racial incidents per thousand of the population was 37 times higher than that of whites. A recent report of the Inter-Department Racial Attacks Group indicates that these forms of racist violence are only the tip of the iceberg. A range of hostile events including jostling in the streets, racial abuse and daubing of racist graffiti 'create an insidious atmosphere of racial harassment and intimidation' (Home Office 1989).

In Colin Brown's 1984 study, more than half of the black people interviewed said that life had become worse for their group. On the one hand parents fear for their children, hardly daring to send their children anywhere unsupervised; on the other it is feared that black young people are more likely to be harassed by the police. A CRE report appearing in the *Times Educational Supplement* in August 1991 showed that 'where white children aged between 10 and 16 were cautioned, black children were more likely to appear in the magistrate's court or be sent to schools for the behaviourally disturbed'. In London a black child is twice as likely to be prosecuted as a white child.

Research conducted by people like Cashmore reveals the prevelance of racism among people in a north-east region where ethnic minorities form less than one percent of the overall population. Although their contact with black people is negligible, most of the young people interviewed held 'explicitly racist views, while others who claimed not be racist, frequently made racist statements' (Coffield *et al.* 1986).

Winifred Mould's study of the racial attitudes of 13-year-olds was undertaken in 1987, in order to convince the education authority to take action to combat racism in schools. Mould's aim was to uncover the fallacy of 'no problems here' attitude, usually adopted by teachers in all-white areas. Two hundred primary and secondary school pupils took part in a project where they were asked to write on the topic of black people. An analysis of the project revealed that three quarters of the pupils 'held negative attitudes about black people and one third of these held strongly hostile attitudes' (Mould 1987). This corroborates the CRE report *Learning in Terror*, which said that 'racial harassment is not uncommon in "non-contact" areas' (CRE 1988).

Shahnaz Akhtar's study of the racial attitudes of children attending primary and middle school in Norwich also points to the presence of racist understandings in young children (Akhtar and Stronach 1986). Akhtar found that 'racial name-calling and bullying started much earlier than teachers tend to assume'.

The findings of the Working Group Against Racism in Children's Resources corroborate Milner's account of the development of racial attitudes in very young children.

One of the important discoveries of these studies is that children are able to develop racial awareness very early in life. Between the ages of three and five children are able to identify their own racial group as well as racial differences. Ammons found in his study done in 1950 that 20 per cent of the two-year-olds and 50 per cent of the three-year-olds in his study were able to distinguish between skin colour and facial features between black and white dolls. What is equally clear from the findings of WGARCR, as well as others like Milner, is that the child has also 'absorbed a simple polarized evaluation of the groups involved, so that one (group) is positive, good and liked, the other negative, bad and disliked' (Milner 1983, p.110). Milner adds 'the establishment of this first, basic evaluative foundation is extremely influential in determining the course of later attitude development'. What the WGARCR research has shown is that the white children very often begin to associate 'positive' and 'good' with white skin and 'negative' or 'bad' with black skin because these are the clear messages they receive from everything around them: the books they read; the toys they play with; the way they perceive black people being treated by powerful institutions and the way they are represented in the media. The black children pick up negative messages about their identity and background which has damaging consequences for all.

The research points to ways in which racism manifests itself at different stages in children's lives. When children are at the pre-school stage, white children will demonstrate their feelings of hostility by rejecting the black children in their group or nursery. They may say 'I don't like him, he smells' or 'I won't hold his hand, he's black', but basically it is a response based on their perceptions of negative treatment of black communities, at home and/or elsewhere. Children are also known to say, 'I'll wash off your black colour if you are good'. My own daughter, who felt a bit sad at being told the story of the Ugly Duckling in class, was informed by her (white) friend, 'Don't worry, when you grow up, you will turn into a beautiful girl...look, the ugly duckling turned into a beautiful white swan!'

As children grow older and go to primary schools, the most common expression of racism becomes racist name-calling. Troyna and Hatcher have published their findings in a recently published book, *Racism in Children's Lives* (1992), in which they have researched the attitudes of children in schools in two neighbouring LEAs in England. Their findings also come to the same conclusion that for some children name-calling can be an every-day happening; for others it may be less frequent but 'for all it is in general the most hurtful form of verbal aggression from other children' (Troyna and Hatcher 1992, p.195). Many of the children in the schools also had experiences of racism outside school, for example harassment by older children. They have also experienced it in the adult world: 'disputes with neighbours, arguments in shops, conflict in the community. These experiences, and the roles taken up by black adults within them, provide a context for their experiences in school' (p.196).

A report of a study into the classroom experiences of African Caribbean and Asian primary school children in four schools in an LEA in the north of England aims to present an insight into the possibility that there are factors within the primary school experience which act as a restraint on the children's educational progress (Wright 1992). The report focuses on the children's actual, subjective experiences of daily school life, and provides information about the nature of their relationships with teachers, support staff, and peers as well as the children's academic and social progress. It also brings out the contrast between the policy on multicultural education and racial justice and the actuality.

The report found that, although the staff are caring individuals, a considerable proportion of the teaching staff held low expectations of the children's ability and behaviour. In the classroom both the African-Caribbean and Asian children were perceived by teachers as a potential threat to classroom management, but for different reasons; the Asian children's language proficiency was felt to place limitations on the teachers' ability to work effectively, whereas the African- Caribbean children were regarded as a problem because of their perceived bad behaviour. They were continually reprimanded in the classroom and other settings. They were also more likely to be physically restrained by the teacher. The most overt racism was directed against the Asian children by their white peers – a situation which was in a very complex way reinforced by 'pupil culture' in the schools. However, all black children faced considerable and continuous racist abuse from some children in school.

The researcher interviewed some children during the study. When an Asian child was asked if there were fights in the playground between 'Pakistani children and white children' he replied 'Yes, Miss'. When asked why he said, 'They call us Pakis and hit us so we get mad and hit them... for calling us names and throwing our balls away'. When asked why he did not report the incident to the teacher, he said 'the teachers don't do nothing... If we hit them, they (teachers) pick on us'. The playground for these children represents the epitome of school harassment. The teachers are aware of this and are actively involved in doing something about it, although they themselves seem to have stereotypes in their minds about 'Asian' people. For instance a teacher explained why a particular white child was consistently refusing to hold an Asian child's hand:

> She has consistently, from the time she came to school, been specific about it (not wanting to hold an Asian child's hand). But she has also been prepared to say that the child concerned is not very clean and so part of her reasoning is based on the cleanliness rather than just the racist thing...

The same teacher also felt that 'the problem with the Asian children is because they dress differently, because they eat differently... They are themselves rather a separatist group... seem to see themselves... as being Asian children... in general are not open to attempts to see themselves as part of a larger whole'. Contrast this attitude with the school's multicultural activities such as celebrating Eid. This attempt fails to impress either the Asian children (they only end up being taunted and teased even more by their peers) or the white parents, who feel it is a waste of everybody's time. There is obviously a problem of attitude towards black children which needs to be resolved by the staff themselves. This attitude is largely reflected in the behaviour of the white children as well as the black. The white children think that it is okay to harass the Asian children. The African-Caribbean children are forced into patterns of reacting to the way they are treated by the teachers and peers.

Conclusion

How can we, as adults (teachers, parents and others concerned with children's wellbeing) combat racism in the lives and environment of children?

First, by recognising that racism is an issue for all children and the implications of it for adults as well as for curriculum.

Second, to have a policy for dealing not only with racist incidents but also with creating an environment in which all children can learn and play freely, and without intimidation. Third, to examine learning materials and curriculum. 'Race' issues need to be dealt with in the curriculum, through appropriate resources, books, discussions etc. Troyna and Hatcher (1992) specify:

> In order to respond to the real meaning of 'race' in children's lives, the curriculum needs to open itself up to and engage with the full range of children's experiences... The curriculum needs to not only address the real experience that children bring with them to the classroom, it needs to offer them the conceptual tools to interpret it. (pp.201/203)

Troyna is concerned that his study indicated that many children had 'little or no understanding of how "race" was socially structured by, for example the economy and the state'. This he feels is a symptom of 'a general absence of political education in the primary curriculum'. Second, the notion of equality was not understood by all children. Troyna again emphasises that 'the curriculum can make an important contribution towards helping children to develop the principle of equality that is so important in their personal lives into a more complex and encompassing concept of social justice' (Troyna and Hatcher 1992, p.203).

The implications for training are self-evident. It also means that all training courses for teachers and childcare workers need to be evaluated and monitored, regularly.

It is true that racism is significant in white children's lives as well as black. It is also true, and has been borne out by research conducted by Troyna, that the strength of anti-racist behaviour and attitudes is a crucial factor in the lives of children who are exposed to it and one on which teachers and childcare workers can build.

References

Aboud, F. (1989) *Children and Prejudice*. Oxford: Basil Blackwell.

Akhtar, S. and Stronach, I. (1986) They call me Blacky. *Times Educational Supplement 19.9.86*.

Alibhai-Brown, Y. (1992) Race and the Single Nation. *The Guardian 29.1.92*.

Ammans, R.B. (1950) Reactions in a projective doll play interview of white males, two to six years of age, to differences in skin colour and racial features. *Journal of Genetic Psychology, 76*, 326–341.

Asher, S.R. and Allen, V.L. (1969) Racial preference and social comparison processes. *Journal of Social Issues, 25,* 157–167.

Coffield, F., Borrill, C. and Marshall, S. (1986) *Growing Up at the Margins.* Milton Keynes: Open University Press.

CRE (1992) *Cautions v. Prosecutions: Ethnic Monitoring of Juveniles by Seven Police Forces.* London: CRE.

Home Office (1989) *The Response to Racial Attacks and Harrassment.* (The Inter-departmental Racial Attacks Group.) London: HMSO.

Kircher, M. and Furby, L. (1971) Racial preferences in young children. *Child Development, 42,* 2076–2078.

Milner, D. (1983) *Children and Race: Ten Years On.* London: Ward Lock Educational.

Mould, W. (1987) 'The Swann report: An LEA response', in T.S. Chivers (ed) *Race and Culture in Education: Issues Arising from the Swann Committee Report.* Windsor: NFER-Nelson.

Troyna, B. and Hatcher, R. (1992) *Racism in Children's Lives.* London: Routledge.

Working Group Against Racism in Children's Resources, (1991) Toy Survey.

CHAPTER 8

Religion, Hatred and Children
A Freudian Sociological Analysis

Robert Bocock

Many people associate both religion and children with feelings of love and kindness rather than with hatred. However, changes in the 1980s have changed these associations. As modern social formations in the West, the Middle East and in the former Communist bloc have moved into what some writers have called *postmodernity* – a cultural situation in which belief in progress through science and reason has died away – one consequence of this process has been a challenge to Enlightenment ideas of social and moral progress being possible through the development of *modern* science and technology (Hall *et al.* 1992). 'Modern' ideas of progress, stemming from the Enlightenment, included the hypothesis that religions would be replaced by science. This would help to usher in an epoch of peace and prosperity so it was hoped and believed by those followers of the Enlightenment gods of science and technology. The notion of 'postmodernity' challenges the Enlightenment idea of religion as an institution which belongs to the past because it is mistaken, based upon false beliefs. Religions have become powerful motivators of action in some parts of the world, including the United States, the Middle East and in what was Communist Eastern Europe.

There has probably not been a more dramatic blow to the fondly held idea of the innocence of children than that of television news pictures during the 1980s – pictures which have shown children and young people involved in acts of violence towards others of a different ethnic and religious group. From the conflicts between Muslims, Christians and Jews in the Eastern Mediterranean to the conflicts between Catholics and Protestants in Northern Ireland; from the turmoil in what was once the Soviet Union and Yugoslavia to the fighting between Tamils and Buddhists in Sri Lanka; children, and young people, have been involved in violent communal conflicts. This kind of action tends to be seen by many people in the affluent western countries as being rooted in historical, national or ethnic conflicts between adults who are 'wicked enough' to involve children in their violence and warfare. Yet the feelings of hate, and the acts of violence, of the adults in such situations have their roots in their own childhood experiences. To see what this proposition means, I shall explore some of the concepts in Freudian psychoanalysis, for there, I think, can be found part of a theoretical account to help situate these feelings of hatred between peoples of different ethnic and religious groups, and the associated acts of violence.

Hatred between people of different ethnic, religious communities is not to be seen, however, simply as the result of universal childhood experience. If this were the case, there would be hatred and violence everywhere and in all historical periods. Given that this is not the case (for at some times, and in particular countries and social formations, there are people who belong to a variety of religious communities who live reasonably peaceably together) we have to explain why the potential for hatred towards others does not always manifest itself among children or adults. There needs to be an approach to this topic, therefore, which combines a psychoanalytic approach with a more sociological and anthropological one which takes account of different historical circumstances. History, in this sense of violent conflicts between ethnic groups, has not come to end, as some claim (Fukuyama 1989).

The logical place to start is with the more universal, or near-universal, theoretical account of hate in psychoanalysis, before linking this with more specific sociological and cultural variables. Freud's work with patients, both men and women, Jews and Christians, between the late 1890s and the 1930s, led him to develop a complex theory of human development and social psychological functioning. His work is certainly useful and applicable in the cultural context of Judaism and Christianity in western societies in the twentieth century (Bocock 1976, 1983). In both the theoretical realm and in his therapeutic practice, Freud's work was based upon the foundational concept of the *unconscious* (Althusser 1971). This concept marked a major break with previous conceptions of human beings as rational creatures, not only capable of mathematical and scientific thought but typified by it. This conception had been found in European philosophy among the ancient Greeks and had reappeared in the work of Aquinas in the thirteenth century, who learned of the ancient Greeks' work from the Islamic scholars of the previous century. The Freudian concept of the unconscious marked a break with the rational conception of human beings. Freud emphasised the importance of wishes, desires, symbols and emotions in human experience, drawing upon ancient Greek drama and mythology to do so. He also included a rational component in his theory of the mind: the component of the mind termed the 'ego' ('I') and a moral element too (the 'superego') (Freud 1923). However, his main importance lies in the foundational role he gave to the concept of the unconscious in producing a new human science – a unique conceptualisation of how human beings operate, which put feelings, emotions and symbols into the centre of the picture. Emotions of a complex kind are as typical of human beings as are scientific thoughts; more so in terms of the numbers of people involved, for everyone feels emotions while not everyone can think scientifically or do mathematics.

In Freud's theory, the concept of the unconscious operates in a *timeless* manner. This proposition is to be read as a basic axiom of the theoretical structure, akin to the proposition in Euclidian geometry that the shortest distance between two points is a straight line. It is, crucially, not a simple empirical *finding*; it is axiomatic (in Kantian terms it is a 'synthetic' *a priori* proposition). From this proposition, it follows that the early experiences of a baby and a child do not weaken or dissolve with the passage of time. A person of eighty may still have dreams whose symbolic content can only be interpreted fully by relating it to early experiences, especially those *before* the baby had acquired a full capacity to speak his or her cultural groups's language. A child becomes hooked into a culture – not some general culture, but a specific one – with its own language, symbols and rituals; its own expression of the religious dimension. This process of capturing a new born infant's interest so that he or she becomes motivated to gain access to language or to cultural symbols cannot itself be done through language. One of Jacques Lacan's (1901–1981) important contributions to psychoanalysis has been in this crucial area, as we shall see.

Lacan distinguished between the early phase of mental functioning, before a baby has developed the skills required to speak a language fully, which he called the 'imaginary', and the later phase, which he termed the 'symbolic'. In this later phase, the child is able to speak and understand his or her own ethnic group's language. The transition from the Imaginary to the Symbolic, from the exchange of *signs* to the ability to exchange *symbols* is critical (Langer 1951). It cannot be done within language, but has to be done outside. Lacan suggested that children begin to enter the Symbolic after the 'mirror phase', which occurs between six to eighteen months after birth. In the mirror phase an infant begins to recognise herself, or himself, in the mirror (Lacan 1977). This is not something which young animals or birds ever do. In the human species uniquely, the young can begin to 'recognise' the mirror image as the 'self'. 'That is me' in the mirror image is a profoundly important experience for a child. It is to cross the Rubicon into a specific culture.

This process may seem to be dependent upon the invention of the mirror. In one sense it could be said that this is the case but there is the possibility of an infant seeing its reflection in a pool of water, as the figure in Greek myth, the young man Narcissus, did. This experience of 'recognition' could be widened, or universalised, by treating the mirror as a metaphor for the baby's mother's eyes and face. The eyes and face of a mother always serve to hook a baby into culture, into language. The mother's gaze at her baby is critical. From this flows the capacity to be a speaking subject, to enter language, to become involved with the cultural, symbolic, life of a specific group. (The process is delayed with a baby which is born blind, but even then he or she can be hooked into a human culture. Helen Keller was born blind and deaf, and yet eventually she too was able to understand language (Langer 1951)). This process shows the profound difference that entry to a culture makes to being human. A human being is not merely an animal with a larger range of noises than a member of any other species possesses. Human babies are introduced to something *qualitatively different* from the signal exchanges between animals, birds or insects. They learn to speak, to use symbols.

This theoretical point, grounded in empirical observations but dependent upon a *philosophical* position, entails that those approaches which seek to reduce human functioning to those of other species are profoundly mistaken and morally dangerous. They are mistaken because signal exchange is not the same phenomenon as symbolic exchanges. Human beings can do both; other species can only exchange signs or signals, *not* symbols (Langer 1951, Bocock 1992). They are dangerous because the view can be used to legitimate the expression of violence in acts of hatred towards others, on the mistaken assumption that because animals fight and are violent towards intruders coming onto their territory, this entails that human beings, in particular males, cannot help being violent and fighting. This is false, because human beings are socialised as children into being members of cultural, ethnic groups in which religion plays a central role. No animal, bird or insect species, no matter how socially organised, possesses a 'culture' of the kind human groups do. No animal species has a religion in the way all human cultural groups do, even if not all individual members participate in the rituals. Animals, birds and insects do not socialize their young into a complex symbolic culture and language. This symbol–using capacity among human beings is not entirely 'a good thing', however. Humans can hate others in a way which is unique to *homo sapiens*.

Why should entry into culture – into language, into a religious symbol, belief and value system – be liable to produce hatred and violence towards others? There is, first of all, the unconscious meaning of the process of the entry into a culture. In both Freud, and even more in Lacan, the process is not seen as entirely a happy one. Freud's theory underwent a major change which has important implications for the way in which hatred is understood in theoretical terms in psychoanalysis. In the first half of his working life, between the work done on the text of *The Interpretation of Dreams* (first published in 1900) and the essay 'Beyond the Pleasure Principle' (1920), the events of World War I had affected Freud's work. Both in therapeutic practice with some male patients wounded in the war and in terms of the effects which the outbreak of trench warfare had on European assumptions about 'civilization' being rooted in that continent, Freud had to think out new psychoanalytic theories.

Before the effects of World War I had been experienced, Freud's theory had approached the conceptualization of the unconscious in terms of a duality of feelings, desires and wishes which were termed the 'sexual drives' and the 'ego, or self-preservative, drives'. (The term which Freud used in German was 'Trieb', not 'Instinkt' – a more biological term than the former.) From 1920, he began to use a second theorisation of the dualism in the desires of the unconscious – the sexual drives and the 'death drives' (translated as the 'sexual instincts' and the 'death instincts' in the standard edition in English). Here Freud retained the idea of positing two sources of desires in the workings of the unconscious, but changed the way in which they were distinguished.

The therapeutic work which led Freud to posit the 'death drives' involved the difficulties Freud had in being able to account for the dreams of soldiers who had been traumatised in World War I. These patients reported that they had dreams in which they had dreamt of other soldiers being blown apart, wounded, or killed, and that these dream images were often repeated from one week, or month, to another. This posed a theoretical puzzle to Freud (Freud 1920). In the first twenty or so years of his work, Freud had assumed that dreams were based upon wishes, desires, which could not be admitted into the consciousness of the dreamer because they were defined in the dreamer's culture as being improper desires to acknowledge. Such desires were of two main kinds – sexual desires towards culturally forbidden objects ('objects' of desire such as other people's wives or husbands, younger persons of the opposite or same gender, children, animals, or physical fetishes, like a shoe) and aggressive wishes to see some rival dead. The latter were seen as being derived from the aggression needed to preserve the organism in the environment, but the drive could be deflected towards others who might prevent the person realizing their erotic wishes too.

The theoretical problem arose when Freud thought about the dreams of the soldiers mentioned above. Their dreams were inexplicable on the first formulation of psychoanalytic theory of the interpretation of dreams. This had rested upon the assumption, the premise, that the unconscious worked according to the *pleasure principle* – that it always sought the release of some desire for the organism, the yard-stick of such pleasure being sexual orgasm. But the problem for the theory was that the soldiers were dreaming of painful scenes, of pains being inflicted upon people they did not necessarily know. Furthermore they *repeated* these painful experiences. They seemed to derive no benefit from the dream-work – the process of transformation of repressed desires into dream symbols – as was the case in the other types of dreams which Freud had interpreted. They seemed to be dreaming according to a new principle – a compulsion to repeat pain (Freud 1920).

Not only did these soldiers' dreams raise problems for the existing psychoanalytic theory of dreams; there were other examples of the compulsion to repeat painful experiences which Freud tried to handle. One example Freud discussed was that of a baby who kept throwing an object, such as a cotton reel, out of its bed. This simple action was also puzzling to Freud because again the infant seemed to repeat an action which produced pain – being parted from an object. However, the baby was pleased when the object was returned. Why did the baby keep throwing the object away, and experiencing distress as a result? (Freud 1920). Some principle of mental functioning was involved in this simple action which went 'beyond the pleasure principle'. There must be some other principle of mental functioning which sought to repeat painful experiences. This became one of the reasons why Freud posited the new concept of the death drives from which the new principle of the workings of the unconscious could be derived. Freud played with the idea of 'the Nirvana principle' to try to accommodate this type of phenomenon, but this concept never became as fully established in his work as one might have expected since it would have provided a balance to the pleasure principle and the sexual instincts within the theory (Bocock 1976).

From the basis of the post-1920 theory of Freudian psychoanalysis it is possible to assert that, as a postulate in the theoretical structure, babies are predisposed towards finding some release for both their infantile sexual desires (first in the oral, anal and phallic, phases, later for latency and geniality wishes) and for the desires of the death drives. The latter are a source of hate and of a desire to kill. If we read Freud retrospectively, that is, if we read the early theory up to 1920 in the light of the post-1920 theory which included the death drive theory, then it is possible to re-read Oedipus. We can re-present Freud's theory of the desires of infants and children in the early stages of development as being a mixture of desires rooted in the infantile sexual desires and desires derived from the death drive. The anger which babies express is not simply that they desire to be fed, which is derived from the idea of the self-preservative drives in the theory up to 1920 and is congruent with common-sense notions. In the second theoretical structure, the anger and rage, the hatred expressed towards parent figures by infants and children is seen as being derived from a quite distinct source of feelings and desires which seek some outward expression, namely from the death drive.

The concept of the death drive may seem an extraordinary idea to posit. We may not like to think that infants and children are little devils as well as little angels. It is not being asserted that we *know* that babies, infants and children are monsters as well as angels, but that Freud's post-1920 theory is a *useful* one for understanding both children's actions and those of adults. The complex of feelings experienced by children around the phallic stage (from between two and five), the Oedipal complex of emotions, contain both the sexual desire for the parent of the opposite gender and the desire for the death of the competing parent. Not only is this second parent a competitor, a rival, in the sphere of sexual desires, but he or she may also be the one who disciplines the child or who is perceived by the child as the main agent of social control.

As Lacan pointed out, the child has to be introduced to the 'Law of the Father'. This is done by religion in the Name of the Father. Lacan played on the sounds and meanings of the French words 'non' (no) and 'nom' (name) when giving his oral seminars. The French phrase 'the name of the father' can sound the same as 'the no of the father': 'le non/nom du pere'. The Law of the Father says that a boy may not have sexual relations with his mother and that a girl may not have sexual relations with her father (Lacan 1977).

Given the bisexual nature of infantile desires, the Law of the Father also implies that the son may not have, nor admit to desiring, sexual relations with his father, and that the daughter may not admit to a desire for sexual relations with her mother. It is also important to allow, in theoretical terms, for either parent to be the one who may concretely act as the upholder of the Law of the Father. This Law is a cultural, religiously grounded set of rules, as in Judaism, Christianity and Islam. The love and hate the child experiences may be toward either parent or toward the same figure in one-parent families. These feelings may also be projected onto the symbolic father – the god figure – of the child's own religious group or that of another group, so fuelling atheism, or religious hatred towards those outside the person's own religious culture.

At some point, all good enough parenting involves introducing the child to the Law of the Father which governs the expression of desire in their culture – crucially, that mothers and fathers are forbidden objects of desire to children (the incest taboo). This point is particularly important in British culture at the end of the twentieth century, because there are periodic moral panics about child abuse. A situation involving child abuse, ideal typically, involves a new male living in a household as the partner of a young girl's mother, but who is not the biological father of the young girl. Incest by biological fathers towards their own daughters is what the incest taboo condemns, but it does also include incest between step fathers and daughters.

Equally, the incest taboo is a taboo against sexual relations between mothers and sons. Indeed, this is the ideal typical case in Freud writings. Oedipus, the son, made love to his mother, having killed his father. He was not consciously aware of what he was doing in either of these actions. In any case, the emphasis about 'incest' in the moral panic in the British media and cultural institutions generally (including the law, religious groups and politicians, as well as journalists) has been far removed from what Freud was theorising in his writings. Freud was concerned with mother–son incest, as theoretically prior to father–daughter incest (Freud 1912/1913). The reasons for this priority were theoretically significant and involve the idea that daughters are introduced to the Law of the Father – the move into culture, into language, and into the religions of the Western and near-Eastern culture zone is, therefore, in this sense, a gendered one. Women are able to represent the 'symbolic father' to children of both genders, so the point is not that Freud was an apologist for patriarchal cultures but that he was an analyst of this depth structure in occidental religions (Mitchell 1974).

The second important point about Freud's theorisation of Oedipal feelings is that the direction of feeling runs from the children towards their parents not, as in the British media's version of incest, from a parent (always fathers/husbands/men) to children (nearly always daughters, not sons). British culture, ás represented by the media and major institutions, claims that children are always victims of adult assault. While not wishing to deny that this does happen, it is essential for academic study of these phenomena to include Freud's attention to the desires of children. Adults who commit 'incest' were once children who had incestuous desires. Children, in Freud's theory, do have infantile desires for what to them represents sexual relations with a parent. These are at a very elementary level – cuddles, being stroked, fondled, or held, but *not* a form of sexual intercourse. There has been some controversy about whether or not some of Freud's early patients had been seduced by a parent, again typically a daughter by a father. Whatever the reality may have been among some of Freud's first patients – something which is very difficult to establish a century after the events – the crucial point Freud made is that children do experience forms of what Freud called 'sexual desire' too. The central case in Freud's theory was the desire of sons towards mothers and sisters; the desire of daughters towards fathers and brothers was included too. These desires are defined as taboo: they are culturally forbidden and hence they are repressed; they are pushed into the unconscious, from where they still operate in a distorted, but culturally acceptable, form. The theory is not primarily about adults' desires towards children: it is addressing the issue of how desires are formed in human beings, *before being able to speak a language.*

The flow of desire does not run in one direction only, from adult parent to child; nor is it gendered in such a way that it runs only from fathers to daughters or daughters in law. It may be from mothers to sons; from fathers to sons; from daughters to fathers, fathers-in-law, or mothers; from sons to mother, father, or father in law. All logical permutations must be allowed for in any adequate theory of incestuous desires. Furthermore, it is not only sexual desires which are involved, whether infantile desires of an oral, anal, phallic or latent kind; desires derived from the death drive are involved too.

Love and hate are very strong layers of desire in the unconscious, according to psycho-analytic theory, after the introduction of the death drives. Hate is derived from the destructive aggressive drives which are part of the 'death instinct'. In Freudian theory love and hate can exist side by side in the unconscious, even towards the same figure in the external world. They do not cancel one another out at the unconscious level. Only at the conscious level are they combined to form socially and culturally acceptable emotions – at least among the middle classes of Europe and North America – which appear as affection or irritation towards someone.

The formation of the 'super-ego', the internal critic of our desires as well as of our actions, involves learning to turn the destructive aggressive energy from external objects or people onto the self. Freud wrote, for instance, about severely depressed persons: 'Following our view of sadism, we should say that the destructive component had entrenched itself in the super-ego and turned against the ego. What is now holding sway in the super-ego is, as it were, a pure culture of the death instincts...' (Freud 1923, p.43). Such patients had turned the destructive energy of the death drives onto themselves. More normal law abiding citizens do this in milder·forms too. Those without this capacity, without a super-ego structure of any strength at all, become delinquent, criminal, ruthless and aggressive towards others.

Religions have in the past provided, and for some groups in contemporary social formations still do provide, a key means of reinforcing a process which begins in the family – the development of a strong enough super-ego. Both families and religious organisations may help to form what Freud regarded as an 'over-severe super-ego'; that is, one which is very critical of the self. Perhaps surprisingly to some, it is more likely to be lenient parents whose children develop a severe super-ego, which in turn leads to them experiencing *guilt*, rather than those with stricter parents. 'Guilt' is the word used in western culture for the emotion produced by the energy of the death drive being turned upon the self and not on external objects, including people. It is the children of parents who were lenient, kind and understanding towards their offspring who have most difficulty in articulating, and actively or verbally expressing, feelings of hostility towards their mother and/or father. The feelings of anger and hostility which they feel towards those who introduced them to the rules, norms, values and laws of their sociocultural group – angry feelings which are an inevitable part of this process and which aid emotional growth – cannot be easily expressed to parents who are 'so understanding'. The anger and hostile feelings are turned inwards, onto the self, the 'ego', rather than onto an external person, thus increasing the energy available for guilt.

Religions vary in the way they handle these issues concerning the super-ego. Some religious movements do not expect all their members to live by the very strictest moral code; this expectation may be limited to an elite group of priests, nuns and monks rather than applying to all laity. This has been the typical pattern in Roman Catholicism and in most forms of Anglicanism, for example. On the other hand, both Protestant denominations which operate fairly strict entry requirements for membership and some sects with rigourous entry standards do expect laity to live up to a high standard of keeping the moral rules of the religious community. They may have some mechanisms for expelling those who are thought to have failed to keep to the rules. In either case, however, there is frequently a heightened awareness of boundaries – of those who are to be counted as 'one of us', and those who are outside the fold.

Religions operate by linking people ritually into a sociocultural group with a very powerful sense of belonging. The cost of this may be a heightened sense of 'difference'. This is typically linked with a sense of national, or ethnic, group membership. It makes for a powerful sense of group membership internally, within the ethnic religious group. Under some conditions it can also lead to hostility, to strong feelings of hate, towards those who are not members of the same ethnic religious communal group.

Religions, by definition, link these powerful group emotions to what the French sociologist Emile Durkheim called 'the sacred' – that which is *set apart* from the everyday world of profane activities (Durkheim 1961). The sense of belonging to a religious community, or social group, can become interlinked with this sense of the sacred and with belonging to a specific ethnic group. Under stable economic and military conditions, a plurality of different ethnic groups – each with its own religious community, its own rituals and symbols concerned with the sacred – may be able to live together relatively peaceably in the same social, political, economic formation. The various ethnic groups must all share the value of not aiming to convert others who belong to different religious traditions – at least not by the use of force and the threat of violence or no amount of economic prosperity will be sufficient to maintain peace.

If the economic or the military situation in a social formation changes for the worse, and/or major groups in the society feel economically insecure or a war develops, then these same hitherto prosperous groups may come to feel themselves threatened. Under these conditions hatred towards other ethnic or religious groups may develop and be expressed. Both children and adults may become involved in this process which may begin with social exclusion and expressions of dislike towards the 'out-group', but may turn violent. The latter outcome is likely if arms are fairly easily obtainable, as they have been in the last two or three decades in many parts of the world outside of Britain and most of Western Europe.

If such a conflict situation arises then children are likely to pick up a very simplified view of the world – a world divided into 'them' and 'us'. Once learned, such patterns of dividing up the world are likely to last a long time, if indeed they ever disappear in the thought processes of such a person. The more positive social contacts that a child or young person has with religious and ethnic groups other than the one into which they were born, the more likely they are to become tolerant, though such tolerance will not be enough to overcome deep conflicts between religious-ethnic groups under conditions of major change or stress. In any case, there is a special set of problems for males, given the way that boys are socialized in many cultures, not only in the West. Males, in particular, are prone to become the bearers, the carriers, of ethnic religious intolerance.

At this point, psychoanalytic theory becomes relevant again. It is because of the specific way in which the male gender role has been defined in the main cultures, at least in the Occident and it would seem in the Orient too, that hatred and violence continues towards those who are 'different'. Those groups of people who are different in their religion, and consequently in their definition of what constitutes 'civilization', come to represent a threat to the 'home ethnic group' of a person (Elias 1978).

Males are defined in patriarchal cultures as those who will fight if necessary. Females are defined as those who mother (see Chodorow 1978). The thrust of much social scientific work in recent years has been to show that these are, indeed, *social roles*. They are not the direct product of nature. Theoretically speaking, it needs only one tribe to be found which does not define gender roles as strongly in this way as the dominant cultures of the

Occident and the Orient have done for the point to be established, in logic, that the gender roles of these societies are *produced* culturally and historically. They are not the direct products of nature or of human biology, as the ideology of patriarchal cultures maintain. Things could be different. They are different in some tribes (Mead 1962). It is here that Freud's work, seen as an analysis of western patriarchal culture, is important.

The theory, or myth, that Freud outlined in *Totem and Taboo* (1912/1913) concerned the killing of the primal father by the band of brothers, which inaugurated patriarchal culture. The 'evidence' for this mythic theory is to be found in the rituals, symbols and scriptures of some of the world religions – especially in Judaism, Christianity and Islam, for they are especially concerned with relations between humanity and a male deity (YHVH in Judaism; the Triune God of Christianity; Allah in Islam). Freud concentrated upon the relations between Judaism and Christianity in some of his later work (Freud 1930, 1939). The roots of anti-semitism lay in this complex religious history. Freud held that anti-semitism was not the same kind of racism as other kinds in what was still, in Freud's own lifetime, a colonialist Europe. He argued that anti-semitism had unique features because in Christianity the Jews had been made to appear as the murderers of Jesus (see also Reich 1953).

The complexities of Freud's argument cannot be entered into here, except to say that the band of brothers, having killed the primal father who had prevented the sons from having sexual intercourse with the women (their sisters or mothers) in the primal horde, were filled with remorse, with guilt. They instituted religious rituals and sacrifices of animals, or later on of human beings, to assuage the guilt they felt. It seems that this myth is just that – a myth Freud devised to try to conceptualise the roots of western patriarchal culture, a culture which had grown out of a sect which began within Judaism (the early Christians were all Jews). Jesus was a practising Jew – a major problem for anti-semites in Christian cultures. However, this simple point was hidden, disguised and repressed in the collective uncon-scious of Christian cultures. The repressed has returned to haunt European culture in the form of anti-semitism and nationalism. The later fed the war-makers' need for an ideology to support killing people who wore other countries' uniforms; the former produced the gas chambers of the early 1940s.

Can we move away from this complex, unconscious, patriarchal, cultural 'archaic heritage', as Freud called it? Can male roles, in particular, be changed? Unless male role definitions do change, women will not be able to change their roles as wives, mothers, sisters, prostitutes, or as potential or real victims of male violence.

The main hope lies in the needs of western capitalism to develop more consumers, among men of all ages. This will produce profits for investors as well as more environmental problems, but it is the one chance we have now, at a realistic level, to hook young males, boys and young men at puberty into being consumers rather than fighters (see Bocock 1993). Consumers desire peace, controlled expressions of violent impulses in consumer sports, and men may be able to define masculinity as centred around sexual pleasures, not around a capacity for physical fighting in school playgrounds, in streets, in soccer stadia, on beaches, in gangs, or in the armed forces of their ethnic-religious group. Religions will have to come to terms with this social-psychological necessity to focus definitions of masculinity around sensual, pleasure-oriented consumption if we are to break the cycle of children, girls and boys being socialized into believing that 'real men' hate, fight and will kill if necessary.

References

Althusser, L. (1971) 'Freud and Lacan', Appendix to, *Lenin and Philosophy and Other Essays*, translated by B. Brewster, London: New Left Books.

Bocock, R. (1976) *Freud and Modern Society.* London: Nelson.

Bocock, R. (1983) *Sigmund Freud.* London: Routledge.

Bocock, R. (1993) *Consumption.* London: Routledge.

Chodorow, N. (1978) *The Reproduction of Mothering: Psychoanalysis and the Sociology of Gender.* Berkeley, Cal.: University of California Press.

Durkheim, E. (1961) *The Elementary Forms of the Religious Life.* New York: Collier Books.

Elias, N. (1978) *The Civilizing Process.* Oxford: Blackwell.

Freud, S. (1912/1913) *Totem and Taboo.* London: Routledge.

Freud, S. (1920) *Beyond the Pleasure Principle.* References to 1967 edition, New York: Bantam Books.

Freud, S. (1923) *The Ego and the Id.* References to 1960, James Strachey edition, New York: W.W. Norton and Company.

Freud, S. (1930) *Civilization and its Discontents.* London: Hogarth Press.

Freud, S. (1939) *Moses and Monotheism.* London: Hogarth Press.

Fukuyama, F. (1989) The End of History? *The National Interest.* In Hall, S., Held, D. and McGrew, A. (1992) (eds) *Modernity and its Futures.* Cambridge: Polity Press.

Lacan, J. (1977) *Ecrits. A Selection.* London: Tavistock.

Langer, S. (1951) *Philosophy in a New Key.* New York: Mentor Books.

Mead, M. (1962) *Male and Female.* Harmondsworth: Penguin Books.

Mitchell, J. (1974) *Psychoanalysis and Feminism.* Harmondsworth: Penguin Books.

Reich, W. (1953) *The Murder of Christ.* New York: Noonday Press.

CHAPTER 9

Authority and Hatred

Kevin Epps and Clive R. Hollin

What is hatred? In order to gain some understanding of the relationship between authority and hatred we think it is necessary to consider the meaning of this word. In seeking meaning, it is undoubtedly true that the eventual definition one favours will be determined by one's own theoretical leanings. The theory favoured in this chapter is cognitive-behavioural theory, which suggests that we must look to *cognition* – that is, the attitudes and beliefs that underpin hatred – as well as to the *actions* of people who hate. Furthermore, as this chapter is about young people, these cognitive-behavioural factors must be placed in a *developmental* context, which includes the associated social and environmental conditions.

In order to consider young people, authority, and hatred from our chosen position we first look at research on the topic of authority and young people; then at what is known of the development of attitudes, cognition, and moral values with respect to authority. The blending of these concepts with regard to individual differences is discussed in an attempt to describe the amalgam of factors that produces hatred towards authority. In the final section we consider two areas, delinquency and extreme political beliefs, which exemplify young people's hatred of authority.

Authority and young people

Much of the early literature and thinking regarding the development of attitudes towards authority among children and adolescents has its origins in the psychoanalytic tradition. Within this school of thought the concept of authority was generally considered to be a destructive and controlling force. Freud (1960) has influenced much of the thinking in this area with his view that all 'submission' to authority is a generalisation of unconscious respect for the father. Thus the common theme from Freud onwards is that compliance with authority is unhealthy, immature, and morally suspect (Hogan 1975). Later, in the same tradition, Adorno *et al.* (1950) in *The Authoritarian Personality* made a case for the destructive effects of 'deference' to authority. The basis of their argument was that racial intolerance can be attributed to a specific personality syndrome in which preoccupation with relations of authority has achieved pathological proportions. Milgram's (1974) studies of adult obedience to authority figures adopted a similar stance, but proposed that the potential for 'destructive' obedience to authority is rooted in human biology and is therefore universal.

With regard to childhood, the period of adolescence has for some time been considered as particularly important with regard to the development of attitudes to authority. Traditionally, psychiatrists and psychologists supposed that adolescence is a period of psychological upheaval and disturbance. Adolescence is characterised as a time of 'identity crisis', as young people struggle both for increased autonomy and independence from their family, striving to achieve their own distinct personality. Over time the position has been constructed of adolescents as a group becoming increasingly distanced and estranged from their parents, as they form a separate culture that has little in common with the rest of society (Coleman 1961, Modell and Goodman 1990). Indeed, the notion of a 'generation gap' has seized the popular imagination and adolescents are popularly portrayed as a group that holds negative, hateful views of adult authority figures (Muncie 1984). These negative views of the adult world act, in turn, to disqualify young people from fully participating in adult society. Haigh (1976), for example, argues that a breakdown in society's hierarchical structure has occurred – consequently there are no firm and unambiguous guidelines as to what constitutes appropriate behaviour for young people. He cites as examples the blurring of class boundaries by the introduction of comprehensive schools and the abolition of National Service. However, Conger (1973) suggests that while 'the values of the average contemporary adolescent do appear to be changing in a number of respects, the extent of these changes does not begin to approach current popular stereotypes, either in extent or quality' (p.471). It is worth noting that this perceived decline in adolescent attitudes to authority as a result of societal changes was certainly not a new one (Averill 1935).

The development of cognitive-behavioural theories within mainstream psychology saw the emergence of a more favourable outlook on the concept of authority. For example, Kohlberg (1976) adopted a developmental perspective, maintaining that the negative effects of authority can be contained by the development of an autonomous and rational conscience, which is not fully elaborated until adolescence or early adulthood. Kohlberg identified normal maturity as the capacity to choose what is right on the basis of justice alone, and to oppose authority if it contradicts this choice.

Another impact of cognitive-behavioural theory was to stress the importance of the social environment upon the learning of attitudes and behaviours (for example, Bandura and Walters 1963). Organisational psychologists pointed out that respect for established authority in a group is necessary for the survival and effective functioning of any social unit (for example, Katz and Kahn 1978). Further, empirical research began to challenge the idea of a generation gap and appeared to indicate, contrary to popular belief, close *positive* relationships between certain authority figures and adolescents

(Coleman and Coleman 1984, Conger 1973, Lesser and Kandel 1969, Murray and Thompson 1985, Rigby et al. 1987, Rutter et al. 1976). For example, in a study of attitudes towards different types of authority in over 300 young people, Rigby et al. (1987) came to the conclusion that adolescents are not uniformly negative and hostile towards adult authority. A similar conclusion was reached by Murray and Thompson (1985) in a study of over 2000 adolescents: they not only found little support for the idea that young people in general are anti-authority, but also that attitudes towards authority figures such as parents, teachers and the police were, on the whole, positive. Murray and Thompson stress, however, that they are referring 'To the views of mainstream adolescents, not those who may have particular problems of a transient or more permanent kind' (p.228). Rigby (1988) makes the important point that it is entirely rational to accept authority based on competence; it is only the unthinking acceptance of authority based solely on power that is irrational and suggestive of psychopathology.

If we accept, then, that attitudes can be specific to different manifestations of authority, then to understand hatred of authority we need to understand the various guises that authority can assume.

Types of authority

The concept of authority is an abstract one and has been defined in various ways. For example, Weber's (1947) analysis of bureaucracy argued that in any social group authority is accepted to the degree that it is perceived by group members to be legitimate. Weber proposed that there are three basic types of legitimacy of authority: these he called *charismatic, traditional,* and *legal-rational.* The first of these, charismatic legitimacy, is based on the 'special character' of an extraordinary individual, typically acclaimed as heroic or holding divine power. In the case of traditional legitimacy, obedience is owed to what is customary and to those sanctioned to speak in the name of tradition. It is the third type, however, that Weber believed to be most significant in the modern world. In the case of legal-rational legitimacy, 'Obedience is owed to the legally established impersonal order. It extends to the persons exercising the authority of office under it only by virtue of the formal legality of their commands and only within the scope of authority of the office' (Weber 1947, p.328). Weber argued that legal-rational authority is the defining characteristic of all formal organisations, such as the government and public administration.

The traditional view has been of a 'generalised attitude' towards all forms of authority; that is, an attitude that is a stable part of the individual's personality, independent of specific situational variables (Adorno et al. 1950, Freud 1949). As noted above, the trend in the psychological literature has been towards identifying specific types of authority and examining attitudes towards these different aspects of authority. For example, the distinction has been drawn between 'personal' and 'impersonal' types of authority. This distinction hinges on the degree to which an authority is normally a close, familiar one, as with parents and children; or is relatively remote and formal, as in the case with a government. Such a distinction is clearly relative rather than absolute. Johnson *et al.* (1981), in a study of college students, found that this group distinguished private, personal authority, giving as examples one's parents, boss and teacher; and public, informal authority such as the police, the government, the church and the law courts. Johnson *et al.* suggest that the quality of the interpersonal relationship normally existing between young people and these two types of authority is so different as to give rise to dissimilar attitudes to these two manifestations of authority.

More recently, Rigby (1982, 1984) and Rigby and Rump (1979, 1981) have provided strong evidence for the existence of a specific attitude to *institutional* authority. Rigby and Rump (1979), for example, report positive correlations among the attitudes of students to such authorities as the police, the army, the law, and teachers. Further, certain young people appear to hold negative attitudes to certain specific manifestations of authority, such as the police (Gibson 1967), the law (Brown 1974), and school (Hargreaves 1967). Meanwhile, Rump *et al.* (1985) have produced cross-cultural evidence for the generality of attitudes toward various institutional authorities in their studies of Italian college students and Sri-Lankan school-children. On the other hand, Rigby *et al.* (1987) found little support for a separation of attitudes towards personal and impersonal types of authority. They found, for example, that favourable attitudes towards the police were associated with positive behaviours towards parents.

While it remains to be finally established whether or not a generalised attitude to authority exists, there are certainly marked individual differences in attitudes towards authority among young people. Wide variations in attitudes towards such authorities as teachers, parents, the police, and the school have been reported among adolescent school children in several recent studies (Emler and Reicher 1987, Murray and Thompson 1985, Reicher and Emler 1985, Schibeci 1984). The issue that arises from these studies lies in identifying the factors that influence the young person's attitudes towards authority.

The development of attitudes towards authority

Parental and family influences

There can be little doubt that parents exert considerable influence over the development of attitudes and behaviours in their children. Cognitive-behavioural theorists, like many other commentators, view the family as crucially important in the child's social and moral development. It is the family, especially the parents, that largely determines the social environment to which the child is exposed; the family that reinforces the types of behaviours and attitudes which it considers desirable or good; and the family that punishes what it considers to be undesirable or bad. Thus by rewarding and punishing what they consider to be good and bad, parents act as a source of authority, probably the first that a child will encounter.

It has often been assumed that attitudes, either favourable or hateful, towards impersonal or institutional authority, such as the police, are partly determined by attitudes towards one's parents, especially one's father (Freud 1949, Piaget 1951). However, evidence supporting this proposition is sparse and studies of both adolescents and adults have produced mixed findings (Marsten and Colemen 1961,Tuma and Livson 1960, Wright 1962). There can be little doubt, however, that the way in which parents exert authority over their children acts as an important influence upon children's attitudes and behaviour outside the home. Elder (1975), for example, defined three types of parental power which he called *authoritarian, democratic,* and *permissive.* He showed differences in children's attitudes and behaviour according to which of these types of authority were used by their parents. For example, it is held that homes characterized by authoritarian control (high control together with low democracy) produce quiet, well behaved, nonresistant children who were socially aggressive. In contrast, the democratic home is characterized by a general permissiveness, avoidance of arbitrary decisions, and a high level of verbal exchange between parents and children: children from such homes are more active, creative, original, and outgoing.

The attributes of an 'ideal' parent have been described by Baumrind (1971) in what she calls the 'authoritative' parent. This kind of parent appreciates both independent self-will and disciplined conformity, and exerts firm control when they and the child have different points of view. Parenting styles that substantially deviate from the 'ideal' are, generally speaking, regarded as undesirable, although there is little in the way of empirical research to provide solid evidence. Becker (1964), however, has summarised the kinds of behaviour problems found among children that are associated with particular combinations of parental attitudes and behaviours. For example, the most serious consequences tend to result from punitive methods persistently used against a background of rejecting, hostile parental attitudes. The methods are often referred to as power-assertive, in which the adult asserts dominant and authoritarian control through physical punishment, harsh verbal abuse, and deprivation of privileges. Becker (1964) has identified a positive relationship between the extensive use of physical punishment in the home by parents and high levels of aggression in their offspring outside the home. Physical violence, it would appear, is the least effective form of discipline when it comes to moulding a child's behaviour (Johnson and Medinnus 1968). However, the debate about the effects of physical punishment remains very much alive (Kurz 1991, Loseke 1991, McCord 1991, Straus 1991a, b). Delinquent youngsters, for example, are more likely to have been the victims of adult assaults than non-delinquents (Hotaling *et al.* 1989, Lewis *et al.* 1989) although it would be premature to assume direct linear causality between harsh parenting and later antisocial behaviour (Patterson 1986, Widom 1989).

It is generally recognised that parental authority declines as the child ages, particularly during adolescence, and as the salience of the peer group increases. This decline in parental authority can be a source of conflict: as Coleman (1980) notes, 'It is true to say that at some level all adolescents are involved in a process whereby adult standards are questioned, adult authority is challenged, and the emotional dependence on the parents formed in early childhood is gradually weakened' (p.409).

The period of adolescence, therefore, is associated with a negotiation of family roles and Baranouski (1981) has shown that the adolescent is more likely to effect this change through the mother than the father. In a longitudinal study of family interaction patterns, Steinberg (1981) found that by middle-adolescence, conflict is intensified between the adolescent and his or her mother. During the latter part of adolescence, however, this conflict diminishes. The way in which parents use their positions of authority and control to manage and resolve such conflicts can determine the extent to which adolescents are more, or less, susceptible to peer group influences (Baumrind 1971, Bronfenbrenner 1967, Dornbusch et al. 1985, Patterson and Southamer-Loeber 1984). In their analysis, for example, Dornbusch et al. found that the degree of autonomy granted to adolescents by their parents is significantly and positively related to the adolescents' involvement in deviant activities.

Parental authority should not however be treated as a global construct (Youniss and Smollar 1985); while adolescents may consider parental authority legitimate in specific domains, they will question the legitimacy of parental authority in other areas. Contemporary adolescents appear to view an increasing range of issues that were once viewed as legitimately subject to parental control as now under personal jurisdiction. In particular, the work of Youniss and Smollar (1985) in the USA suggests that children become less accepting of parental jurisdiction over issues such as styles of dress, choice of friends, or attendance at social events. Similarly, Smetana (1988) indicates that children's and parent's conceptions of parental authority shift in the transition to adolescence, and these conceptions are differentiated according to conceptual domain.

Coleman and Coleman (1984) carried out a similar study in England. They found that three main areas of parental conflict were identified by their sample of 14- and 15-year-olds: these were *time to be home, leisure activities,* and *money.* The rank order of these conflicts for boys remained almost identical from 14 to 15 years of age: for girls, however, there was a marked change, with different issues assuming prominence at the two ages. They also looked at the adolescents' views on the means by which such conflicts should be resolved in the home. A 'democratic' resolution was the most popular overall; although the number of boys choosing a 'permissive' resolution increases sharply between the ages of 14 and 15 years.

In order to understand the reasons for these age-related changes, in terms of expectations and attitudes towards authority figures, it is necessary to examine some of the cognitive changes that are associated with this period of development.

COGNITIVE DEVELOPMENT AND MORAL REASONING

The extent to which a particular form of authority is considered by an individual to be a 'good thing', and therefore liked and obeyed, or a bad thing, and hence disliked, hated and disobeyed, depends to a large extent on whether the source of authority is perceived to be just and fair. As might be expected, perceptions of justice begin to develop at a very early age. For example, Bandura *et al.* (1963) presented findings in which nursery school children devalued a victim of aggression if the aggression was successful. Piaget (1948) studied 167 children aged from 6 to 12 years of age who were told stories in which a child steals and disobeys and then accidentally falls into the water while trying to escape punishment. It was hypothesised that very young children would associate falling into the water with the transgression so that the accident would be considered a payment for wrongdoing. This automatic link between misbehaviour and just consequences was labelled as immanent justice and Piaget suggested that the younger the child, the greater the belief in immanent justice. As predicted, 86 per cent of six-year-olds believed that the accident would not have occurred if the boy had not transgressed, whilst only 34 per cent of the 11- and 12-year-olds held this view.

Table 9.1: Levels and stages of moral judgement in Kohlberg's theory

Level 1: Pre-morality

| Stage 1. | Punishment and Obedience: Obeys rules to avoid punishment |
| Stage 2. | Hedonism: Concern with own needs and having favours returned |

Level 2: Conventional Conformity

| Stage 3. | Interpersonal Concordance: Conforms to avoid social disapproval and gain social approval |
| Stage 4. | Law and Order: Conforms to avoid censure by legitimate authorities |

Level 3: Autonomous Principles

| Stage 5. | Social Contract: Acknowledgement of individual rights and democratic principles |
| Stage 6. | Universal Ethical Principles: Importance of conscience so that moral judgement may transcend legal dictates |

As shown in Table 1, Kohlberg (1967) proposed that the development of moral judgements progresses through sequential stages, and implied that such judgements stem from the child's interaction with the social environment. According to Kohlberg (1976), orientation to authority is dependent upon cognitive development, and this is not fully elaborated until adolescence or early adulthood. Acceptance of authority is treated as part of the more general development of moral reasoning which itself proceeds through a sequence of six qualitatively distinct stages.

As pointed out by Emler and Reicher (1987), Kohlberg's analysis of the growth of moral reasoning suggests 'a progressive emancipation of the autonomous conscience, first from the constraint of authority that is based on power, and then from authority based on tradition, collective opinion, or the political status quo' (p.109). Kohlberg identifies moral maturity with the capacity to choose what is right on the basis of justice alone, and to oppose authority if it contradicts this choice. Kohlberg's (1976) definitions suggest that only by the fourth stage would a young person appreciate the nature and legitimacy of legal-rational authority in the terms spelled out by Weber (1947). According to Kohlberg this stage is not normally reached until mid- to late-adolescence.

The research evidence does, in fact, support the idea that attitude to authority changes in relation to age, particularly during adolescence. Perhaps the most comprehensive study examining the development of attitude toward authority in adolescence was conducted by Rigby and Rump (1981). They compared the attitudes of 13-, 15-, and 17-year-olds toward parental and institutional authority and found that while the attitudes toward these sources of authority were significantly and positively correlated, there were age differences. In particular, the oldest adolescents indicated more favourable attitudes toward authority but less favourable attitudes toward their own parents. Similarly, in a study of 96 adolescents, Lapsley et al. (1984) found that younger adolescents were more favourably disposed to authority than older adolescents.

There appear, however, to be a number of difficulties in using growth in the ability to reason and think hypothetically as the sole explanation to account for changes in attitudes toward authority during adolescence. To begin with, Kohlberg's model makes little allowance for the cultural context in which development occurs. Other theorists have defined moral development as the learning or internalisation of cultural values (Aronfeed 1968, Maccoby 1968). Tests of 'moral knowledge' have generally shown that children do have an awareness of the values of their society at an early age. Further, Motta and Tiegerman (1979) produced evidence supporting the view that perceptions of justice formed in early childhood (Piaget 1932, 1948) may not undergo major changes, despite the subsequent growth of rational thought. Emler and Reicher (1987) similarly suggest that variations in attitude toward authority among adolescents can be better explained by differences in *beliefs* about the legitimacy of authority, rather than by the ability to *understand* moral issues raised by relations with authority.

Sex differences

Early studies suggested that sex differences need to be taken into account in studies of attitudes towards authority among young people. For example, Coleman (1974) noted that:

> For boys, the relationship to authority involves confrontation. Authority, whether it be in the form of parents or policemen, represents a challenge, and it is expected that an attempt will be made to stand up for it. For girls, on the other hand, the conflict is very much less direct, in fact quite often there is no conflict at all. (p.129)

The implication of this perspective is that attitudes towards authority may have different behavioural consequences for the sexes, with females being less likely to show anti-authority behaviour. However, the results of recent research studies have not been entirely consistent regarding sex differences in attitudes towards authority. Several British studies have found that female adolescents were significantly more pro-authority than male adolescents (Emler and Reicher 1987, Murray and Thompson 1985, Reicher and Emler 1985) and similar findings have been reported by Rigby and Densley (1985) in a study of Australian high schools. However, Rump *et al.* (1985) reported that in a Sri Lankan high school male adolescents were *more* in favour of authority. More recently, Rigby *et al.* (1987) found only slight sex differences in their sample of Australian adolescents, and concluded that: 'It is not safe to assume that male adolescent attitudes are generally more anti-authority than those of females' (p.252). They suggest that with the growing influence of feminist views in the western world, patterns of socialisation may be changing rapidly.

Personality differences

Generally speaking, when psychologists refer to the concept of personality they are referring to an individual's *style* of behaviour. Research into the relationship between personality and attitudes toward authority has identified a number of personality characteristics that help to determine whether or not an individual opposes or conforms to authority. Three main clusters of personality characteristics in particular have been described: these are *authoritarianism, conservatism,* and *criminality.*

AUTHORITARIANISM

The concept of authoritarianism is embodied in the classic formulation of Adorno *et al.* (1950) who were concerned with the question of why some individuals appear more submissive to authority than others. They evolved a portrait of the prejudiced personality, which they called the 'authoritarian personality'. Such people see the world as divided into the weak and the strong, and are power-oriented in their personal relationships. That is to say, they are submissive and obedient to those they consider their superiors but contemptuous, hateful and authoritarian toward those they consider inferior. Authoritarians find it difficult to tolerate ambiguity and tend to hold highly conventional values. Authoritarian individuals, according to Adorno *et al.* are the sort of people who would be particularly susceptible to the kind of fascist ideology that was promoted in Nazi Germany.

Eysenck (1954) proposed that the essential element of authoritarianism was toughmindedness; later, Eysenck and Eysenck (1976) proposed that toughmindedness could be indexed more appropriately by the personality dimension of Psychoticism (P); and later still Eysenck and Wilson (1978) added that inheritance of a particular personality configuration, involving a mixture of Extraversion (E) and P, defined the authoritarian personality. Research, however, has failed to confirm predictions based upon Eysenck's model of authoritarianism (for example, Ray and Bozek 1981). Similarly, studies with school children have failed to find a positive correlation between pro-attitudes and behaviour towards authority and P and E (Rigby and Slee 1987).

CONSERVATISM

According to Wilson (1973), conservatism is 'A general factor underlying the entire field of social attitudes [this factor] is presumed to reflect a dimension of personality similar to that which has similarly been described in the semi-scientific literature in terms of a variety of labels such as fascism, authoritarianism, rigidity, and dogmatism' (p.3–4). Anderson (1962) reported a progressive decline in conservative attitudes over the course of adolescence. Similarly, Pannes (1963) found significant decreases in dogmatism from lower to higher grade levels in high school: this accords with the view, discussed earlier, that younger adolescents are more favourably disposed to authority than older adolescents. However, Rigby and Slee (1987) tested the conservative personality model among school children and found little support for the assumption that a favourable attitude toward authority reflects conservatism.

CRIMINALITY

A number of personality characteristics have been associated with anti-social behaviour and criminality, and some of these have also been used to explain negative attitudes and behaviour toward authority among delinquents – an association that has been demonstrated in several studies (for example, Gibson 1967, Reicher and Emler 1985). Eysenck's (1977) view was that anti-social behaviour was associated with high scores on E, P, and Neuroticism (N). Evidence regarding E and N has been somewhat inconsistent (Hollin 1989), but the relationship between P and criminality among school children has received support in a number of studies (for example, Powell and Stewart 1983).

Rigby and Slee (1987) tested the relationship between Eysenck's personality factors and orientation towards authority among school children. They found a significant negative correlation between pro-authority attitudes and P for both boys and girls, concluding that P is a factor underlying school children's orientation toward authority.

Thus far we have examined those factors that appear to be important determinants of young people's attitudes, beliefs, and behaviour towards authority. We have seen that the concept of authority is a complex one and that most young people conform to authority most of the time, although there may be times during the course of development that young people come into conflict with particular forms of authority. This, however, can be considered part of normal adolescent development. However, a number of factors have been identified which could lead to the development of long standing hostile and negative, hateful relationships with authority, or at least certain types of authority. Given that authority, in its various forms, is such a common feature in the lives of most people, particularly in modern industrialized societies, it is not difficult to understand how an individual with an anti-authority disposition could encounter a variety of difficulties. The next section of this chapter examines two possible outcomes of hatred of authority: these are delinquency and extreme socio-political attitudes.

Delinquency

A number of researchers have found an association among young people between delinquent behaviour and negative attitudes towards authority (for example, Emler and Reicher 1987, Gibson 1967, Ray 1984, Rigby et al. 1989). The suggestion has been made that this association may be a causal one, in that the presence of anti-authoritarian attitudes may contribute to the development of delinquent and anti-social behaviour in children and adolescents. Emler and Reicher (1987) argue that young people with negative attitudes towards authority tend to view the official systems as biased and discriminatory, and have a desire to 'Redress grievances and ensure self-protection, problems for which delinquency could appear to provide solutions' (p.15).

Empirical tests of control theory of delinquency have shown that *attachment* to family, school and conventional others, *commitment* to conventional lines of action, and *belief* in the validity and legitimacy of the legal order are elements of a social bond to conventional society which inhibits delinquent behaviour (for example, Hindelang 1973). Clearly, young people with negative, hostile attitudes towards authority, particularly institutional and traditional forms of authority such as teachers and the police, could find it difficult to participate in mainstream society and hence find themselves at odds with the law. Failure to participate in any useful or meaningful way in mainstream society may also result in young people looking elsewhere for sources of attachment and reinforcement, particularly to other young people who find themselves in a similar position (Agnew 1991). This is particularly likely to occur when parents allow their children too much freedom and autonomy in early adolescence. Dornbusch *et al.* (1985), for example, found that the degree of autonomy granted to adolescents by their parents is significantly and positively related to the young person's involvement in deviant activity.

Extreme social-political attitudes

Adolescence is an important time in the development of political views. Adelson (1971) saw the years of early adolescence (ages 12–16 years) as 'A watershed era in the emergence of political thought. Ordinarily the youngster begins adolescence incapable of complex political discourse... By the time this period is at an end, a dramatic change is evident; the youngster's grasp of the political world is now recognisably adult' (p.1013). It seems inevitable that the political socialisation of a young person will be affected by the extent to which he or she is able to participate in and feel part of mainstream society. If, as has been argued above, young people who hate authority are excluded from mainstream society and feel unable to exert control over their lives, one could predict that this would in some way influence their political orientation.

Billig (1985, 1986) has studied the development of political beliefs in young people. He has argued for a rhetorical approach to the analysis of the development of political beliefs, proposing that rather than political beliefs being handed down from generation to generation, young people form their beliefs based on their own experiences. Billig has particularly been interested in modern-day British Nazism, as evident in extreme right-wing parties such as the National Front (NF), the National Constitutional Movement and the British Movement. Such groups, by their very words and actions, are clear manifestations of hatred directed towards certain members of society. A number of public opinion surveys have indicated that potential support for parties such as the NF is to be found disproportionately amongst adolescents (Harrop *et al.* 1980). In their national survey of support for the NF, Harrop *et al.* have shown that NF supporters tend to be younger than would be expected by chance. Over 20 per cent of supporters were aged between 15 and 20, and a further 16 per cent were between 21 and 24. They also describe the typical NF voter as a young, white, urban working-class male; while Weir (1978) found that those committed to the NF were likely to have left school at 16 with the minimum of qualifications. Similarly, the majority of NF sympathizers in a study carried out by Billig and Cochrane (1981) indicated that they would not be staying on at school after the fifth year, and had lower career expectations than those whose sympathies lay with other parties. Cochrane and Billig (1982) have also shown that supporters of the NF and other fascist parties are more likely to express the view that violence is sometimes justified in achieving political ends, and are strongly anti-authority and anti-establishment.

Billig and Cochrane (1981) found that most NF supporters lack both a knowledge of and interest in politics. They suggest that NF support reflects a certain cultural style rather than a defined political commitment, a style described by Willis (1978) in his book *Learning to Labour*. This cultural style involves the rejection of a conventional school ethos; an admiration of toughness, together with a corresponding contempt of weakness; and deep-rooted xenophobic and sexist attitudes. In many ways, this is similar to the authoritarian personality described by Adorno *et al.* (1950), which social psychologists have long associated with support for fascist parties; although without the exaggerated respect for authority. Unlike classic authoritarians, the young people in Willis's study reject the conventional symbols of law and order and respond with aggressively anarchic rebelliousness. Cochrane and Billig (1982) suggest that NF support is to some extent an expression of an aggressively masculine stereotype, and that the appeal to some youngsters lies more in its aggressive style than any specific ideological attraction. The anti-authoritarian tone is reflected in the NF party propaganda, such as the National Front News, with accusations of the police being 'bully boys' and 'running riot'.

However, it would appear that some individuals attracted to Nazism do, in fact, resemble more closely the classic authoritarian personality profile. Not all supporters of the fascist parties support the use of aggression and violence, and some are more interested in authoritarianism, discipline, and strong leadership, with the aim of establishing an elitist party which embodies strictly enforced standards of dress and conduct. The formation of the New National Front in Britain in 1980, whilst having similar ideological principles to the NF, is an attempt to achieve this goal. Party propaganda reminds members of the 'important sacrifices' they must make and of the necessity to 'cultivate a healthy attitude towards authority' (see Billig and Cochrane 1981). It is probably the case that authority within such groups is dependent upon Weber's (1947) idea of 'charismatic' leadership, rather than traditional or legal-rational authority.

There is some evidence to suggest that support for such parties increases during times of economic and social difficulties. Thus hatred of institutional authority in this context may, in part at least, be a response to the perceived lack of effectiveness of traditional parties. This, in turn results in the adoption of simple, often nationalist or authoritarian solutions to economic problems, such as the expulsion of non-whites as a solution to the problem of unemployment. Cochrane and Billig (1990) found, for example, that over a three-year period during the early 1980s the 'louts' and 'skinheads' were joined in their support for the NF by a more 'respectable' type of youth – a trend which appeared to reflect the youngsters' despair with conventional politics and its inability to regain control over the economic and social situation that prevailed during this time.

Summary

In this chapter we have suggested that hatred of authority is not, contrary to popular belief, a normal part of a child's development. We maintain that to understand why children hate authority, we must understand both the child and his or her world. While there may be times during development that a child comes into conflict with authority, specifically with their parents, it would be a mistake to conceive of this conflict in terms of hatred. We suggest that when hatred towards authority does occur, it should be understood in very specific terms: that is, the object of the hatred and the individual characteristics of the child concerned must be clearly defined. In terms of types of authority we suggest that a distinction is most usefully made between *personal* and *institutional* manifestations of authority, while with regard to the child, there are a number of individual and developmental factors to consider, including the moral development and attitudes. Furthermore, these individual factors do not function in isolation from the world: we suggest that certain environmental conditions, primarily styles of family functioning and social and economic deprivation, provide the settings that nurture a child's hatred of parts of his or her world.

References

Adelson, J. (1971) The political imagination of the young adolescent. *Daedalus,* Fall, 1,013–1049.

Adorno, T., Frenkel-Brunswick, E., Levinson, D., and Sandford, N. (1950) *The Authoritarian Personality.* New York: Harper

Agnew, R. (1991) The interactive effects of peer variables on delinquency. *Criminology, 29,* 47–72.

Anderson, C. (1962) A developmental study of dogmatism during adolescence with reference to sex differences. *Journal of Abnormal and Social Psychology, 54,* 132–5.

Aronfeed, J. (1968) *Conduct and Conscience: The Socialization of Internalized Control Over Behaviour.* New York: Academic Press.

Averill, R. A. (1935) *Adolescence.* London: Harrap.

Bandura, A., Ross, D., and Ross, S. A. (1963) Vicarious reinforcement and imitative learning. *Journal of Abnormal and Social Psychology, 67,* 601–7.

Bandura, A. and Walters, R. M. (1963) *Social Learning and Personality Development.* New York: Holt, Rinehart and Winston.

Baranouski, M. (1981) Adolescents' attempted influence on parental behaviours. *Adolescence, 13,* 585–603.

Baumrind, D. (1971) Current patterns of parental authority. *Developmental Psychology Monograph, 4,* Pt. 2, 1–103.

Becker, W. C. (1964) Consequences of different kinds of parental discipline, in Hoffman, M. L., Hoffman, L. W. (eds.) *Review of Child Development Research*, Vol. 1. New York: Russell Sage Foundation.

Billig, M. (1985) Prejudice, categorization and particularization: from a perceptual to a rhetorical account. *European Journal of Social Psychology, 15*, 79–103.

Billig, M. (1986) *Arguing and thinking: a rhetorical approach to social psychology.* Cambridge: Cambridge University Press.

Billig, M. and Cochrane, R. (1981) The National Front and Youth. *Patterns of Prejudice, 15*, 3–15.

Bronfenbrenner, U. (1967) Some familial antecedents of responsibility and leadership in adolescents. In Petrullo, L. Bass, B. M. (eds.) *Leadership and Interpersonal Behaviour.* New York: Holt, Rinehart and Winston.

Brown, D. (1974) Adolescent attitudes and lawful behaviour. *Public Opinion Quarterly, 38*, 98–106.

Cochrane, R. and Billig, M. (1982) Youth and the SDP – breaking the mould? *New Society, 60*, 291–292.

Cochrane, R. and Billig, M. (1990) The political and social beliefs of adolescents, in Fraser, C. and Gaskell, G. (eds.) *The Social Psychological Study of Widespread Beliefs.* Oxford: Clarendon Press.

Coleman, J. S. (1961) *The Adolescent Society.* London: Collier-Macmillan.

Coleman, J. (1974) *Relationships in Adolescence.* London and Boston: Routledge and Kegan Paul.

Coleman, J. C. (1980) Friendship and the peer group in adolescence. In Adelson, J. (ed.) *Handbook of Adolescent Psychology.* New York: John Wiley and Sons.

Coleman, J. C. and Coleman, E. Z. (1984) Adolescent attitudes to authority. *Journal of Adolescence, 7*, 131–43.

Conger, J. J. (1973) *Adolescence and Youth.* New York: Harper and Row.

Dornbusch, S., Carlsmith, J., Bushwall, S., Ritter, P., Leiderman, H., Hastorf, A. and Gross, R. (1985) Single parents, extended households, and the control of adolescents. *Child Development, 56*, 326–41.

Elder, G. (1975) Parental power legitimation and its affect on the adolescent. In Conger, J. (ed.) *Contemporary Issues in Adolescent Development.* London and New York: Harper and Row.

Emler, N. and Reicher, S. (1987) Orientations to institutional authority in adolescence. *Journal of Moral Education, 16*, 108–16.

Eysenck, H. J. (1954) *The Psychology of Politics.* London: Routledge.

Eysenck, H. J. (1977) *Crime and Personality.* (revised edition) London: Paladin.

Eysenck, H. J. and Eysenck, S. B. G. (1976) *Psychoticism as a Dimension of Personality.* London: Hodder and Stoughton.

Eysenck, H. J. and Wilson, G. D. (1978) *The Psychological Basis of Ideology.* College Park MD: University of Maryland Press.

Freud, S. (1949) *An Outline of Psychoanalysis.* New York: Norton.

Freud, S. (1960) *Civilization and its Discontents*. New York: Norton. (Originally published 1922).

Gibson, H. B. (1967) Self-reported delinquency among schoolboys and their attitudes to the police. *British Journal of Social and Clinical Psychology, 6,* 168–73.

Haigh, G. (1976) *The Reluctant Adolescent*. London: Temple Smith.

Hargreaves, D. (1967) *Social Relations in the Secondary School*. London: Routledge and Kegan Paul.

Harrop, M., England, J. and Husbands, C. T. (1980) The bases of National Front support. *Political Studies, 28,* 271–83.

Hindelang, M. J. (1973) Causes of delinquency: A partial replication and extension. *Social Problems, 20,* 471–87.

Hogan, R. (1975) Theoretical egocentrism and the problem of compliance. *American Psychologist, 30,* 533–40.

Hollin, C. R. (1989) *Psychology and Crime: An Introduction to Criminological Psychology*. London: Routledge.

Hotaling, G. T., Straus, M. A., and Lincoln, A. J. (1989) Intrafamily violence and crime and violence outside the family. In Ohlin, L. and Tonry, M. (eds.) *Family Violence*. Chicago: University of Chicago Press.

Johnson, J. A., Hogan, R., Zonderman, A. B., Callens, C. and Rogolsky, S. (1981) Moral judgement, personality and attitudes to authority. *Journal of Personality and Social Psychology, 40,* 370–3.

Johnson, R. C. and Medinnus, G. R. (1968) *Child Psychology: Behaviour and Development*. New York: John Wiley and Sons.

Katz, D. and Kahn, R. L. (1978) *Social Psychology of Organization*. (2nd edn.) New York: John Wiley and Sons.

Kohlberg, L. (1967) Moral and religious education and the public schools: A developmental view, in Sizer, T. (ed.) *Religion and Public Education*. Boston: Houghton Mifflin.

Kohlberg, L. (1976) Moral stages and moralization: the cognitive development approach. In Lickona, T. (ed.) *Moral Development and Behaviour: Theory, Research and Social Issues*. New York: Holt, Rinehart and Winston.

Kurz, D. (1991) Corporal punishment and adult use of violence: A critique of 'discipline and deviance'. *Social Problems, 38,* 155–61.

Lapsley, D. K., Harwell, M. R., Olson, L. M., Flannery, D., and Quintana, S. M. (1984) Moral judgement, personality, and attitude to authority in early and late adolescence. *Journal of Youth and Adolescence, 13,* 527–42.

Lesser, G. and Kandel, D. (1969) Parent-adolescent relationships. *Journal of Marriage and the Family, 31,* 348–58.

Lewis, D. O., Mallouh, C., and Webb, V. (1989) Child abuse, delinquency, and violent criminality. In Cicchetti, D. and Carlson, V. (eds,) *Child Maltreatment*. New York: Cambridge University Press.

Loseke, D. R. (1991) Reply to Murray A. Straus: Readings on 'discipline and deviance'. *Social Problems, 38,* 162–6.

Maccoby, E. E. (1968) The development of moral values and behaviour in childhood. In Clausen, J. (ed.) *Socialization and Society.* Boston: Little, Brown and Co.

Marsten, B. H. and Coleman, J. C. (1961) Specificity of attitudes toward parental and non-parental authority figures. *Journal of Individual Psychology, 17,* 96–101.

Milgram, S. (1974) *Obedience to Authority: An Experimental View.* New York: Harper and Row.

McCord, J. (1991) Questioning the value of punishment. *Social Problems, 38,* 167, 179.

Modell, J., and Goodman, M. (1990) Historical perspectives. In Feldman, S.S. and Elliott, G.R. (eds.) *At the Threshold: The Developing Adolescent.* Cambridge, MA: Harvard University Press.

Motta, R. W. and Tiegerman (1979) Perceptions of justice: An adolescent view. *Journal of Community Psychology, 7,* 151–7.

Muncie, R. (1984) *The Trouble with Kids Today.* London: Hutchinson.

Murray, C. and Thompson, F. (1985) The representation of authority: An adolescent viewpoint. *Journal of Adolescence, 8,* 217–29.

Pannes, E. (1963) The relationship between self-acceptance and dogmatism on junior-senior high school students. *Journal of Education and Sociology, 36,* 419–26.

Patterson, G. R. (1986) Performance models for antisocial boys. *American Psychologist, 41,* 432–44.

Patterson, G. and Southamer-Leober, M. (1984) The correlation of family management practices and delinquency. *Child Development, 55,* 1299–307.

Piaget, J. (1932) *The Moral Judgement of the Child.* New York: Harcourt, Brace.

Piaget, J. (1948) *The Moral Judgement of the Child.* Glencoe, IL: Free Press.

Piaget, J. (1951) *Play, Dreams and Imitation in Childhood.* New York: Norton.

Powell, G. E. and Stewart, R. A. (1983) The relationship of personality to anti-social and neurotic behaviours as observed by teachers. *Personality and Individual Differences, 4,* 97–100.

Ray, J. J. (1984) Authoritarian attitudes and authoritarian personality among recidivist prisoners. *Personality and Individual Differences, 5,* 265–72.

Ray, J. J. and Bozek, R. S. (1981) Authoritarianism and Eysenck's P Scale. *Journal of Social Psychology, 113,* 231–4.

Reicher, S. and Emler, M. (1985) Delinquent behaviour and attitudes to formal authority. *British Journal of Social Psychology, 24,* 161–8.

Rigby, K. (1982) A concise scale for the measurement of attitudes towards institutional authority. *Australian Journal of Psychology, 34,* 195–204.

Rigby, K. (1984) The attitudes of English and Australian college students toward institutional authority. *Journal of Social Psychology, 122,* 41–8.

Rigby, K. (1988) Relationships among three concepts of authoritarianism in adolescent school children. *Journal of Social Psychology, 128,* 825–32.

Rigby, K. and Densley, T. R. (1985) Religiosity and attitude toward institutional authority among adolescents. *Journal of Social Psychology, 125,* 723–8.

Rigby, K., Mak, A. S. and Slee, P. T. (1989) Impulsiveness, orientation to institutional authority, and gender as factors in self-reported delinquency among Australian adolescents. *Personality and Individual Differences, 10,* 689–92.

Rigby, K. and Rump, E. E. (1979) The generality of attitude to authority. *Human Relations, 32,* 469–87.

Rigby, K. and Rump, E. E. (1981) Attitudes towards parents and institutional authorities during adolescence. *Journal of Social Psychology, 109,* 109–18.

Rigby, K., Schofield, P. and Slee, P. T. (1987) The similarity of attitudes towards personal and impersonal types of authority among adolescent school children. *Journal of Adolescence, 19,* 241–53.

Rigby, K. and Slee, P. T. (1987) Eysenck's personality factors and orientation toward authority among school children. *Australian Journal of Psychology, 39,* 151–61.

Rump, E. E., Rigby, K. and Waters, L. (1985) The generality of attitudes towards authority: Cross-cultural comparisons. *Journal of Social Psychology, 125,* 307–12.

Rutter, M., Graham, P., Chadwick, O. and Yule, W. (1976) Adolescent turmoil: Fact or fiction. *Journal of Child Psychology and Psychiatry, 17,* 35–56.

Schibeci, R. A. (1984) Students, teachers and the assessment of attitudes to school. *Australian Journal of Education, 8,* 17–24.

Smetana, J. G. (1988) Adolescents and parents conceptions of parental authority. *Child Development, 59,* 321–35.

Steinbergh, L. (1981) Transformations in family relations at puberty. *Developmental Psychology, 17,* 833–40.

Straus, M. A. (1991a) Discipline and deviance: Physical punishment of children and violence and other crime in adulthood. *Social Problems, 38,* 133–54.

Straus, M. A. (1991b) New theory and old canards about family violence research. *Social Problems, 38,* 180–97.

Tuma, E. and Livson, N. (1960) Family socio-economic status and adolescent attitudes to authority. *Child Development, 31,* 387–99.

Weber, M. (1947) *The Theory of Social and Economic Organizations.* New York: Free Press.

Weir, S. (1978) Youngsters in the front line. *New Society, 44,* 183–93.

Widom, C. S. (1989) Does violence beget violence? A critical examination of the literature. *Psychological Bulletin, 106,* 3–28.

Willis, P. (1978) *Learning to Labour.* Sanson House, Farnborough.

Wilson, G. (ed.) (1973) *The Psychology of Conservation.* New York: Academic Press.

Wright, D. S. (1962) A comparative study of the adolescent's concepts of his parents and teachers. *Education Review, 14,* 226–32.

Youniss, J. and Smollar, J. (1985) *Adolescent Relations with Mothers, Fathers, and Friends.* Chicago: University of Chicago Press.

CHAPTER 10

Class and Hatred

David Jones and Helen Barrett

> There is, therefore, no cause for surprise if the workers, treated as
> brutes, actually become such; or if they can maintain their conscious-
> ness of their manhood only by cherishing the most glowing hatred, the
> most unbroken inward rebellion against the bourgeoisie in power.

> Engels 1972

Whilst some have seen hatred, prejudice and violence between social and cultural groups as essential for the healthy progress of the state (for example, Machiavelli 1965, Marx 1963), others have construed them as representing serious threats to social stability and well-being (for example, Lundberg 1939, Parsons 1951). It seems that where stratification exists (social class being but one of many forms of social stratification), tension can at times be expected between strata. According to Tumin (1985), 'arrangements and rearrangements by which certain selected portions of a population come to enjoy disproportionate amounts of property, power and prestige have always characterised human history' (p.2).

The ways in which tensions within social structures express themselves depend as much upon the kind of social structure as upon the nature and organisation of the social groups within them. From the beginning of history to the present day, countless examples are to be found of inter- and intra-group strife, sometimes involving open hostilities. Divisions have rarely been restricted to differences in social class; more commonly, differences in religion, ethnicity, language, political affiliation and geographical location are cited as bases for distrust and dislike. Nevertheless, the perhaps less overt role of social class in fostering hatred and distrust between social groups cannot be overlooked.

Operationalising the concept of social class has been problematic. The OPCS (Office of Population and Census Surveys) originally (1921–1971) identified five basic social class categories according to 'reputed standing within the community'. In 1980, this system was revised so that class was equated with occupational skill, though how 'skill' is determined has not always been clear. In acknowledgement of the less than satisfactory nature of the OPCS system, alternatives have been suggested which take into account factors such as ownership of the means of production, distribution of commodities, market location of particular occupations, (for example, Wright *et al.* 1982, Goldthorpe 1980).

Early attempts at categorisation using occupation of male head of household as the distinguishing variable may have been relatively satisfactory in terms of identifying so-called working class groups in communities dominated by large local industries. Such groups existed in dockland communities, mill towns, mining districts, and around iron and steel works. In these settings, families had many shared experiences: housing standards were similar, children made up the overwhelming majorities in local schools, and places of worship, shopping and medical facilities were communal. It was not unusual for children in such environments to grow up with a strong sense of in-group belonging and little experience of interaction with children from different backgrounds. But how relevant is this conception of social class to more cosmopolitan settings?

It seems significant that psychological research in Britain, perhaps more so in the last few decades, appears consistently to have omitted, or avoided, the issue of social class. This discussion is therefore undertaken rather on the understanding that we may be venturing 'where angels fear to tread'. Our approach is necessarily in the nature of a preliminary investigation; a search for evidence that social class is salient at all, let alone divisive, in childhood. Next, we explore the possibility that hatred in childhood might be fuelled by conscious or unconscious awareness of social class differences.

There are two immediate obstacles to this exploration. First, whilst some research has looked at associations between social class and children's performance (for example, educational achievement, linguistic behaviour, conduct), none seems directly to have assessed whether or how children perceive themselves in terms of social class membership. Second, although considerable work has been done on group processes amongst adults, very little attention has been given to the ways in which these processes might operate amongst groups of children (though there have been a few notable exceptions to this pattern).

We begin by considering the null hypothesis that social class is not salient in childhood. Recently, economic change or the lack of it has resulted in the break up or diversification of relatively closed communities such as those mentioned earlier. It has been argued that, as Britain's economic structure has become more diverse, class has become less relevant as a basis of social schism. Some have argued (for example, Jacques and Mulhern 1981) that increasing differences between workers in different economic sectors, labour markets and geographical locations have given rise to new divisions which render the term 'class' obsolete. Sectoral consumption cleavages distinguish more readily between social groups than occupation and material possessions have become the yard-stick for social identity, for example, whether you are self-sufficient on wages or a benefit claimant, whether or not you have property interests; amongst children, perhaps the importance given to designer labels on clothes reflects this trend. Others have argued that working class solidarity has been undermined in Britain since the 1950s and that self-interest and consumer-society individualism have led people to abandon the notion of class struggle. As Gorz (1982) puts it, the majority of workers have been relegated to a post-industrial proletariat which, with no job security or definite class identity, seeks private anti-work meanings. It has also been claimed that rising living standards have contributed to the erosion of class differences (Moorhouse 1983).

Marshall *et al.* (1988), by means of a survey, sought to examine the salience of social class as a concept informing adults' social identity. They found no obvious evidence of a lack of class awareness amongst respondents: over 90% put themselves in a particular class category; 73% felt class to be an inevitable feature of society; 74% thought social mobility difficult and only 19% thought it easy. Just over half of the respondents endorsed a picture of gross class inequalities and a similar proportion felt that important issues currently caused conflict between social classes. Marshall *et al.* argued that social class is by far the most common and seemingly most salient form of reference employed in the construction of social identities, as opposed to gender, feelings of locale or community, or consumption differences. They also claimed that 'informed fatalism' did not characterise their sample: 80 per cent of respondents thought wealth should be re-distributed down the hierarchy, 64% thought this would be possible and only 16% were 'fatalists'. Further, for most respondents, work was important, work-mates were often social friends and there was no evidence of widespread cultural privatism. The working class, they argued, is no more divided than it ever was.

Supposing that, as Marshall *et al.* suggest, considerations of class inform social identity, what evidence is there that children are aware of this identity and, if so, how may they become aware of it? Further, in view of the task we have undertaken in this chapter, we must also ask whether there is evidence that social class differences are associated with either conscious or unconscious hatred. If hatred is to be found in and between children because of their social class, where and by what means might we look for it? To hate can be defined as to see the object of one's hatred as despicable, to engage in enmity towards that object and to attempt to reduce or completely destroy its power to cause unbearable negative feelings. Such powerful emotions can be understood in situations where one individual appears to have grievously wronged another or when love and trust have been betrayed or rejected. It almost defies logic to explain how individuals in one group can develop intense negative feelings for individuals they may never have seen just because they belong to a different social order.

Puzzlingly, the issue of class inequalities, unlike racism and sexism, very rarely features in children's literature. Nor is children's literature unique in this omission. To a large extent, the same gap exists in research on children's friendships and in other studies of socialisation. Several possible explanations may account for this lacuna; for example as already mentioned, it may arise from difficulties of definition or because social class is not a salient feature for children. A third possibility is that the issue of social class differences is taboo. This possibility will be elaborated after consideration of the following rare example of the treatment of social class in children's literature.

In *The Water Babies* (Kingsley 1863), the main protagonist is ten-year-old Tom, a chimney-sweep. Initially, Tom is portrayed as stoically accepting his harsh lot, spending half his time crying from hunger, beatings and cold, the remainder joining in pranks with his peers. One of these pranks includes throwing half a brick at the legs of horses of richer people. The explanation given for this behaviour is that Tom was 'offended and disgusted' because a groom was 'so very neat and clean' and gave himself airs 'because he wore smart clothes'. Tom considered this groom a 'stuck-up fellow' (p.11). Later, in the course of his work, Tom chanced to enter the pristine bedroom of a well-to-do little girl and was astonished to see reflected in a mirror 'a little ugly, black, ragged figure, with bleared eyes and grinning white teeth. He turned on it angrily. What did such a little black ape want in that sweet lady's room?' Realising he was looking at a reflection of himself, Tom 'for the first time in his life, found out that he was dirty; and burst into tears with shame and anger and turned to sneak up the chimney again and hide' (p.26). In this example, class differences are reduced to cleanliness and described in terms identical with racist terminology. Later in the story, it becomes clear that dirt and sin are also conflated, with the implication, well noted by Leeson (1976), that the lower social classes are to be thought of as immoral as well as poor and ungroomed.

Kingsley's tale, as children's literature of the nineteenth and twentieth century has been, is predominantly concerned with the establishment and inculcation of middle class values. Throughout this literature protagonists are almost exclusively middle class while working class characters are generally represented as outsiders and sometimes as vagabonds or villains. Less dismissive treatments (for example Garnett's *The Family at One End Street* (1937)) continued to portray working class characters as inadequate in some respect, irresponsible if not overtly immoral, often of rather low intelligence and limited in verbal performance. Although the last decade or so has seen the emergence of some literature in which working class characters are more sympathetically treated, the predicament of the working class child has rarely been realistically addressed and children's literature (including some comics (Dorfman and Mattelart 1988)) can be seen to reflect institutionalised class prejudices.

Kingsley's portrayal of Tom's repulsion by his own dirtiness, his initial anger and disgust swiftly followed by his shame and wish to hide, graphically illustrates children's proneness to extreme moral positions in self- and other-appraisals. Boyden and Holden (1991) note how considerations very similar to those elucidated by Kingsley can still prevent working class children from attending school out of a sense of shame and inferiority. They cite Salazar's observations on child brickmakers in Bogotà: these children often fail to attend school because they are bullied and ridiculed by other children on account of their dirty and menial occupation (Salazar 1988). Whilst children in the UK are not, as a rule, presently under such pressure to work, incomes vary enough to ensure that the same standards of dress and cleanliness are not attainable by all children. Further, although the correspondence between self-presentation and social class may not be a simple one, the tendency to define one's place in a social group by means of dress is evident in most cultures. Inability to display respected designer labels may not lead to the same consequences as inability to hide one's brickmaker status but the resulting process of rejection seems not dissimilar. Perhaps more similarities will be found in situations where lower social class children are in a minority.

One final comment on *The Water Babies*: Kingsley's treatment of Tom is not only interesting in terms of the language he used to describe class differences and his conceptual confusion in conflating dirtiness (a sign of being at work) with immorality. It is also remarkable in that Tom is conceptualised as being able to (a) identify representatives of higher social classes, (b) see them as different from himself, (c) evaluate them as possessing inappropriate or unacceptable attitudes and, (d) take a 'class action' against them, albeit a low-level variant of this and not designed to strengthen the position of the lower class participants in any lasting sense, before having any clear idea of his own social identity. Kingsley also suggests that full awareness of one's social identity is not reached by everyday interactions: the necessary self-reflection can only be acquired by being presented with an image of oneself in the alternative social context.

Numerous theorists have agreed that class awareness, class consciousness and class action are distinct entities each arising from independent and unique conditions. It is argued (for example, Coser 1956, Waites 1987) that being aware of having an identity within a social system in which resources are distributed hierarchically regardless of need or merit represents a substantially different level of self-awareness from that involved in being conscious of differences between your own and other people's identities. Evaluating the nature of those differences involves operating at a yet more sophisticated cognitive level. In Piagetian terms, class *awareness* may involve no more than one-to-one mapping or identification whereas class *consciousness* involves perspective-taking, comparison, value-judgement and higher-order processes associated with later stages of cognitive development.

It has also been argued that an essential element in class conflict is that the parties involved are aware that they are in contention (for example, Weber 1947, Park and Burgess 1924). Class conflict and action which depend upon conscious, organised antagonism are thought not to arise until class consciousness has been achieved (for example, Morris and Jeffries 1970). According to Kriesberg (1972, 1983), however, where there are unequal power relations, conflict may arise not only without consciousness of the nature of differences but also without full awareness of one's own class identity. Indeed, participants may be in conflict without knowing it themselves. This situation, described by Marx (1963) as 'false consciousness', may arise under a number of conditions for example when participants are led to believe that existing unequal power relations and their consequences are legitimate, when participants recognise that there is an imbalance but deny it for fear of the consequences of overt acknowledgement and when some common benefits within a situation outweigh the cost to its participants. In these situations, participants' own interests fail to be recognised so that, when injustices are perpetrated, victims fail to take action to confront the underlying imbalance; rather they enact scenarios which may involve displacing their anger, denying it, introjecting it and displaying other defensive strategies amply enumerated by psychoanalytic theorists.

At this point, the third ('taboo') hypothesis concerning the relative absence of social class from children's literature can be elaborated. Children from a very young age are known to be capable of making fine distinctions between familiar and non-familiar people, for example infants within their first week can distinguish mother's from stranger's breast-pad (McFarlane 1975) and, often well before eight months, they evince 'stranger anxiety' (Bronson 1971). According to Kohlberg (1976), until they reach the level of 'conventional morality' (i.e. generally not before mid to late adolescence), children are thought not to internalise social rules, thinking of them as externally imposed injunctions. Might it be the case that, whilst before this stage children are capable of recognising differences attributable to social class, this awareness may not be present in a socially-acceptable form? Might it also be the case that making discriminations involves such strong affective responses that the ensuing defensive reactions obscure the initial more consciously-available perception? For example, if awareness of differences simply leads to a sense of helpless frustration, children from a very early age may develop strategies designed to prevent the necessity for feeling the full strength of their anguish or hatred. This process has been documented by Rivière: 'hate and aggression, envy, jealousy and greed felt and expressed by grown-up people are all derivatives, and usually extremely complicated derivatives, both of this primary experience (*dependence in the feeding situation and its incumbent frustrations*) and of the necessity to master it if we are to survive and secure any pleasure at all in life' (Klein and Rivière 1937, p.10). Whilst we may wish to dispute this location of the source of strong negative feelings, we may accede to the possibility that very powerful emotions in some way become transmuted so that they can be tolerated.

Displacement and introjection were interpreted as the principle mechanisms governing children's behaviour in the school setting described by Sennett and Cobb (1972). The majority of the predominantly working-class children in Watson school received fewer rewards for their work efforts than two boys whose values were more congenial to those of the lower middle-class teacher. Rather than conceptualising this imbalance as unfair, the children tended to accept the shaming they experienced as legitimate, directing their anger towards the two boys who were not shamed and calling them effeminate, weak 'suck-ups' (reminiscent of Tom's response?). Sennett and Cobb argued that children picked up a sense of their positioning within the reward schedule through their school experience fairly quickly and adapted to it passively. By the end of schooling, most boys were not in conflict with the school but had developed a subculture and begun to act 'as though they were serving time, as though schoolwork and classes had become something to wait out, a blank space in their lives they hope to survive and then leave' (p.83). Accepting the power of the teacher as legitimate, the children did not express direct resentment of the system which had alienated and belittled them. This situation reflected values more generally upheld within the community in which children were living: it was not uncommon for adults to feel both a sense of outrage at a system in which individuals were not equally respected and yet to accept that society had 'put (*cultured people*) in a position to develop their insides' and had therefore granted them the right to act as judges.

Kohn (1977) makes a similar point, arguing that upper class individuals have more sense of self-direction stemming from greater involvement at a policy-making level. In his study, lower class individuals, perceiving themselves as having no legitimate opportunity to challenge social rules, were more likely to conform passively. Class differences have also emerged in some studies of child-rearing practices (for example, Newson and Newson 1963, Farran and Ramey 1980). Given the existence of social class inequalities, accompanied by divergent expectations of adult social behaviour and differing experiences of social environments, it seems highly likely that children must often be sharply aware and perhaps discomforted by the social predicaments in which they find themselves. If we accept this premise, we must then consider the potential for resentment, expressed or otherwise. It is possible that, because the differences are so immutable and pervasive, children soon recognise them as not-to-be-mentioned (perhaps as their parents before them also shrank from publicly acknowledging their own parents' helplessness). And perhaps, just as the infant might have become fearful of its own destructive rage in the primary care-giving situation, the child, confronted by an intractable and unjust social system, experiences anew the need to protect itself against its own sense of outrage or alarm. The upper class child, too, cannot remain immune to a sense of the tension within so inherently imbalanced a system. Frustrations at the primary dyadic level are re-enacted at the societal level.

It is well documented that children from lower social classes achieve less academically than higher social class children. The arguments run that relationships between children, parents and teachers are more favourable to children from middle class backgrounds (Lareau 1989) and that, as middle class values are promulgated in schools, working class values are not permissible (Lee 1989). Children consequently tend to be disenfranchised according to class, gender and race.

This trend was noted by the socio-linguist Peter Trudgill, who, in a survey of teachers in Glasgow (Trudgill 1975), showed that only about half had attitudes which were favourable to the encouragement of children's natural use of dialect. Certain dialects were considered to be incorrect or wrong and children were therefore deterred from offering their linguistic contributions. On the other hand, teachers were thought to be 'snobbish' or 'toffee-nosed' by children who had become alienated and insecure within a system which openly rejected their social identity.

Trudgill's work was carried out in a climate perhaps still under the influence of Bernstein (Bernstein 1971), who attempted to chart class differences in language use and, through these, tried to demonstrate the relative inadequacy of working class dialects as conveyors and explicators of meaning. Bernstein is perhaps best known for his theory that working class speech employs 'restricted' linguistic codes whilst higher social classes utilize 'elaborated' codes. These class differences were thought to contribute to the educational disadvantages of working class children. One argument against Bernstein's position was that, although the socio-economic structure confers prestige on more formal middle-class speech patterns, this may also imply that informal, working-class styles have equal and opposing prestige (Labov 1966). Trudgill agreed with and enlarged upon Labov's observation: although, in his Norwich study, half of the dialect-speaking adult respondents belittled their linguistic ability saying things like 'I know I speak horrible' and 'I can't speak English properly', Trudgill argued that for male speakers working-class non-standard speech was shown to be highly prestigious. Nevertheless, he recognised that children using other than Received Pronunciation or Standard English (the dialect of the upper social classes) had fewer opportunities for social advancement as well as being subject to humiliations from both peers and teachers. To combat this, he argued, often against much opposition, in favour of 'a society free from dialect prejudice, where everybody can use their own dialect without fear of ridicule or correction' (Trudgill 1975, p.163).

It may seem that the notion that children hate each other or that adults hate children on the grounds that their dialect is 'incorrect' or their grammar 'not proper' must be an exaggeration of the facts. Yet, for a proportion of children, it does appear that dialect singles them out for ridicule. It is also the case that working class accents are often equated with low IQ or lack of education. It is arguable, then, that the negation and dismissal consequent upon prejudicial attitudes towards dialect both disempower and, in some social arenas, entirely remove all but a social elite. If we accept that annihilation is the end-point of hatred then this process could be seen to be synonymous with hatred, even if the full force of that emotion is not overtly displayed by participants.

Delinquency can be construed as a rejection of or rebellion against social rules. There has been considerable controversy about whether it can be said to arise from stresses which are particularly prevalent amongst lower classes.

Some, particularly psychoanalytic theorists, have emphasised the association between delinquency and emotional deprivation (for example Bowlby 1944). Others have argued that delinquent behaviour is a response to alienation which is clearly located within working class cultures where children are aware of the same desire for commodities but have less legitimate access to them (for example, Cohen 1955, Downes 1966). However, this account of the origins of delinquency would seem to overlook the fact that delinquency (actual rather than apprehended) is not restricted to the lower classes (Nye *et al.* 1967) any more than abuse or bullying appears to be (though Smith (1991) suggests that social class differentiation may be implicated in the higher rates of bullying to be found in Britain as compared to Scandinavia). Official statistics have appeared to suggest that violent crime, especially crime against property, is more common amongst the lower classes. This appears to have applied to juvenile as well as adult offences. However, the meaning of these statistics is unclear and, in terms of our remit in this chapter, we can only comment on the need for more research to look at the degree to which property inequalities (Weber's definition of social class differences) may, or may not, be associated with aggressive behaviour and the use of violence by and against children.

Research on delinquent groups has thrown light on some inter- and intra-group processes amongst youths. Gangs appeared, like adult groups, to be characterised by specific access codes and processes aimed at preserving the integrity of the group at the same time as polarising in- and out-group members (O'Hagen 1976).

In respect of access codes, the nature of which may be variable in gangs, Corsaro (1981) described how important these may be, even at nursery age: he observed that nursery children appeared to find access to groups quite difficult so that, once accepted, much of their behaviour could be interpreted as geared towards protecting their interactive space from intruders. McGrew (1972) and Goodenough (1931) also describe how newcomers to nursery groups display distinctly muted behaviours aimed, it seems, at observing the social context in an attempt to determine its frame of reference before trying to gain entry. Sociometric (or popularity) status may interact with socio-economic status in complicated ways; for example, Gottman *et al.* (1975) suggested that, once accepted, middle-class children appeared to be more popular if they engaged in positive verbal interactions whilst working-class children were more popular if they engaged in positive non-verbal interactions.

There also appears to be some inconsistent evidence that socio-economic class is significant in children's friendship choices, that is, children are more likely to choose friends from the social class of which they are a member (Neugarten 1946, Langworthy 1959). However, Langworthy (1959) also reported a tendency to choose peers with higher status and Dahlke (1953) claimed that social class was only important in senior school children's friendship choices (a finding contradicted by other workers). Other studies have reported finding that children from higher SES backgrounds have more positive others-concepts as a group than children from lower SES backgrounds; Zucker and Barnett (1977) have suggested that this difference is stronger at elementary school age, gradually decreasing as children approach adulthood.

The need for individual members to preserve the integrity of their own social group has been extensively described (for example, Merton 1949, Simmel 1955, Sherif 1967, Tajfel 1982). It is not within the scope of this chapter to do more than outline some of the findings perhaps likely to be relevant to groups of children, such as out-group stereotyping, effects of social contact and scape-goating.

Allport's seminal work on the nature of prejudice (Allport 1954) was not specifically focused on social class differences nor upon children, yet his findings remain pertinent to this discussion. He and his contemporaries shared a concern to understand how phenomena such as anti-semitism could arise and culminate in the inhuman torture and slaughter of fellow human beings. Work began to investigate how it was that members of one social group could perceive members of another social group in so negative a way as to appear to overlook the fact that out-group members were also human. Some felt that ignorance through lack of contact was implicated: in its original form, the contact hypothesis stated that association with persons from a disliked group could lead to greater liking and respect between group members (Cook 1978). Allport (1954), however, observed that increased contact could increase as well as decrease prejudice. Having outlined a taxonomy of variables which he considered important in determining the nature of inter- and intra-group relationships, he proposed that contact would increase inter-group harmony in situations where participants were of equal status, were pursuing common goals and had social/institutional support.

The process whereby out-group members come to be perceived with less sympathy than in-group members has recently become known as the 'out-group homogeneity effect': this effect refers to the perception of out-group members as less variable than in-group members. Linville et al. (1986) argue that increased contact with out-group members increases perceived variability and differentiation by making the number of exemplars both more numerous and more detailed. Others, however, have emphasised that out-group homogeneity effects are dependent not only upon familiarity or the number of exemplars available but on an attentional mechanism which causes in-group members to exaggerate out-group homogeneity at the same time as focusing more keenly upon in-group attributes (for example Park and Rothbart 1982). It has also been found that certain conditions modify out-group homogeneity effects; for example they increase when the out-group out numbers the in-group (Simon and Brown 1987) or when competition or the need for co-operation between groups is high (Judd and Park

1988), but decrease when the out-group is higher in status as well as less numerous than the in-group (Sedikides and Ostrom 1986).

Scapegoating has been seen as more likely to occur in small groups which are under threat from outside, require high membership commitment and have no room for internal conflict. It has also been suggested that, in societies where rigidity of structure inhibits realistic conflict, inner enemies may become targeted as scape-goats, or 'heretics' (Allport 1954, Simmel 1955, Coser 1956).

Clearly, further research is needed to investigate which, if any, of these processes might describe social class relationships between children. That they may be worthy of study seems well supported by this second excursion into the realm of children's fiction.

The Friends (Guy 1973), perhaps significantly, addresses a teenage readership. Very perceptively, Guy portrays the fear, disgust and contempt felt by Phyllisia, a newly-arrived West Indian child, towards the other members of her Harlem school-class. On the first page, we are told by Phyllisia, 'I did not like her. Edith always came to school with her clothes unpressed, her stockings bagging about her legs with big holes, which she tried to hide by pulling them into her shoes but which kept slipping up... Of course there were many children in this class that were untidy and whom I did not like... But at least they did not have to sit right across the aisle from me. Nor did they try to be friendly as Edith did – '. Phyllisia's antipathy towards Edith is based, it seems, almost exclusively on Edith's unkempt appearance, just as Phyllisia finds herself being rejected by another child who has prettier clothes than she does. Phyllisia's accent and cleverness also earn her the ill-feeling of the rest of the class. Gradually, in spite of her prejudice against what her father calls 'picky-headed ragamuffins', she and Edith become close friends, though hatred and contempt are never very far from the surface for Phyllisia and these emotions are directly linked with her prejudice against poverty – a prejudice which seems to have been bred largely from both her father's fear of his origins and his sense of shame about his current lowly occupation. The association between poverty and disadvantage within the education system is also well drawn in the teacher's cruel and unsympathetic treatment of Edith: Phyllisia's confusion, her readiness to blame Edith as the victim and yet her gradual recognition that fear underlies the teacher's injustice are powerfully conveyed as the reader is made aware of Phyllisia's conflicting loyalties. The friendship which grows between the two girls springs up in the face of opposition at least as strong as that between the houses of Montague and Capulet. Unlike Romeo and Juliet, though, who are portrayed as innocent great souls resonating with a love which transcends the feuds of the grown-ups, Phyllisia is far more amenable to the same fierce class prejudices as her father even while finding herself in need of and drawn towards Edith's street-wise protection and kindliness.

The Friends seems important not only in its demonstration of the intensity of childhood emotions arising from class differences and its recognition that these exist as a real issue for school children, but also because it draws attention to the way in which the attempt to overcome these prejudices can compel children to re-evaluate values transmitted through parents (though only the more dominant one in this case).

Until about the age of ten, children's friendship choices are thought to be highly influenced by parental constraints in both class conscious and other status conscious societies (Fine 1980). Perhaps somewhat more amongst upper than lower class parents, it is common for great sacrifices to be made (financial, practical and sometimes also emotional) to ensure that children learn to adopt desirable social values and are not exposed to situations which threaten or challenge those values. To the best of our knowledge, research has not shown whether class attitudes are consistent across generations. In the current climate of change in the social context of education, perhaps it is particularly apposite to examine the ways in which social class differences vary amongst and affect children in state-provided and other schools.

To conclude, though conclusions seem somewhat premature, social class is a highly complex variable, the nature and effects of which are probably largely covert, interactive and dependent upon specific social circumstances. We feel, however, that it is a potent factor which permeates the social world of all children and affects their life chances. And we tentatively suggest that it may be beneficial for the health and well-being of individuals in all social classes if more attention were paid to removing what almost appears to amount to a taboo on the issue of social class inequalities.

References

Allport, G.W. (1954) *The Nature of Prejudice.* Reprinted 1979, 1984, Wokingham: Addison-Wesley Publishing Co. Ltd.

Bernstein, B.B. (1971) *Class, Codes and Control. Vol. 1.* London: Routledge and Kegan Paul.

Bowlby, J. (1944) Forty-four juvenile thieves: their characters and home life. *International Journal of Psychoanalysis, 25,* 19–52, 107–27.

Boyden, J. and Holden, P. (1991) *Children of the Cities.* London and New Jersey: Zed Books.

Bronson, G.W. (1971) Fear of the unfamiliar in human infants. In Schaffer, H.R. (ed.) *The Origins of Human Social Relations.* London, New York: Academic Press.

Cohen, A.K. (1955) *Delinquent boys: the culture of the gang.* Glencoe, Ill:. The Free Press.

Cook, S.W. (1978) Interpersonal and attitudinal outcomes in cooperating interracial groups. *Journal of Research and Development in Education, 12,* 97–113.

Corsaro, W. (1981) Friendship in the nursery school. In Asher, S.R. and Gottman, J.M. (eds.), *The Development of Children's Friendships. Cambridge Studies in Social and Emotional Development,* Cambridge: Cambridge University Press.

Coser, L.A. (1956) *The Functions of Social Conflict.* London: Routledge and Kegan Paul.

Dahlke, H.O. (1953) Determinants of sociometric relations among children. *Sociometry, 16,* 327–38.

Dorfman, A. and Mattelart, A. (1988) How to read Donald Duck and other innocent literature for children. In Bacon, B. (ed.) *How much truth do we tell the children? The politics of children's literature.* Minneapolis: Marxist Education Press.

Downes, D.M. (1966) *The Delinquent Solution.* London: Routledge and Kegan Paul.

Engels, F. (1972) *The Condition of the Working Class in England in 1844: with a preface written in 1892.* Written in 1845, Translated by Wischnewetzky, F.K., edited by E.J. Hobsbawrn. London:Panther.

Farran, D.C. and Ramey, C.T. (1980) Social class differences in dyadic involvement during infancy. *Child Development, 51,* 254–7.

Fine, G.A. (1980) The natural history of preadolescent male friendship groups. In Foot, H.C., Chapman A.J. and Smith, J.R. (eds.), *Friendship and Social Relations in Children.* Chichester: John Wiley and Sons.

Garnett, E. (1937) *The Family from One End Street and Some of Their Adventures.* Reprinted by Harmondsworth: Puffin Books.

Goldthorpe, J.H. (1980) *Social Mobility and Class Structure in Modern Britain.* Oxford: Clarendon Press.

Goodenough, F.L. (1931) *Anger in Young Children.* Minneapolis: University of Minnesota Press.

Gorz, A. (1982) *Farewell to the Working Class.* London: Pluto Press.

Gottman, J., Gonso, J. and Rasmussen, B.(1975) Social interaction, social competence, and friendship in children. *Child Development, 46,* 708–18.

Guy, R. (1973) *The Friends.* Reprinted in 1987. Harmondsworth: Penguin Books.

Jacques, M. and Mulhern, F., (eds.) (1981) *The Forward March of Labour Halted?* London: New Left Books.

Judd, C.M. and Park, B. (1988) Outgroup homogeneity: judgements of variability at the individual and group levels. *Journal of Perspective in Social Psychology, 54,* 778–88.

Kingsley, C. (1863) *The Water Babies.* Reprinted in 1961. London: Victor Gollancz.

Klein, M. and Riviere, J. (1937) *Love, Hate and Reparation.* Reprinted in 1953. London: The Hogarth Press and the Institute of Psychoanalysis.

Kohlberg, L. (1976) Moral stages and moralization: The cognitive-developmental approach. In Lickona, T. (ed.), *Moral Development and Behaviour.* New York: Holt, Rinehart and Winston.

Kohn, M.L. (1977) *Class and Conformity. A Study in Values with a Reassessment.* London and Chicago: University of Chicago Press.

Kriesberg, L. (1983) *Social Conflicts.* 2nd edition, 1983. Englewood Cliffs, NJ: Prentice-Hall.

Labov, W. (1966) *The Social Stratification of English in New York City.* Washington, DC: Center for applied linguistics.

Langworthy, R. (1959) Community status and influence in a high school. *American Sociological Review, 24,* 537–9.

Lareau, A. (1989) *Home Advantage: Social class and parental intervention in elementary education.* London: The Falmer Press, Education and Policy Perspectives Series.

Lee, J. (1989) Social class and schooling. In Cole, M. (ed.) *The Social Context of Schooling.* London: The Falmer Press.

Leeson, R. (1976) *Children's Books and Class Society. Past and Present.* London: Writers and Readers Publishing Co-operative.

Linville, P.W., Salovey, P. and Fischer, G.W. (1986) Stereotyping and perceived distributions of social characteristics: an application to ingroup-outgroup perception. In Dovidio, J.F. and Gaertner, S.L. (eds.), *Prejudice, Discrimination, Racism: Theory and Research.* New York: Academic Press.

Lundberg, G.A. (1939) *The Foundations of Sociology.* New York: The Macmillan Co.

Machiavelli, N. (1965) Discourses on the 1st decade of Titus Livius (Book 1, Chap.1). In *Machiavelli. The Chief Works and Others, Vol. 1.* Translated by Gilbert, A. Durham, North Carolina: Duke University Press.

Marshall, G., Rose, D., Newby, H. and Vogler, C. (1988) *Social Class in Modern Britain.* London: Hutchinson Education.

Marx, K. (1963) *The Poverty of Philosophy.* Originally published 1847. New York: International Publishers.

McFarlane, J. (1975) Olfaction in the development of social preferences in the human neonate. In Hofer, M. (ed.) *Parent-infant Interaction.* Amsterdam: Elsevier.

McGrew, W.C. (1972) *An Ethogical Study of Children's Behaviour.* New York: Academic Press.

Merton, R.K. (1949) *Social Theory and Social Structure.* Reprinted in 1968. New York: Free Press.

Moorhouse, H.F. (1983) American automobiles and workers' dreams. *Sociological Review, 31,* 403–26.

Morris, R.T. and Jeffries, V. (1970) Class conflict: forget it! *Sociology and Social Research, 54,* 306–20.

Neugarten, B.L. (1946) Status in the classroom. In Warner, W.L., Havighurst, R.J. and Loeb, M.B. (eds.) *Who Shall be Educated? The challenge of unequal oppurtunities.* London: Kegan Paul, Trench, Trubner and Co.

Newson, J. and Newson, E. (1963) *Infant Care in an Urban Community.* London: Allen and Unwin.

Nye, F.I., Short, J.F. and Olson, V.J. (1967) Socioeconomic status and delinquent behavior. In Vaz, E.W. (ed.), *Middle-class Juvenile Delinquency*. London: Harper and Row.

O'Hagen, F.J. (1976) Gang characteristics: an empirical survey. *Journal of Child Psychology Psychiatric*, 17(4), 305–14.

Park, R.E. and Burgess, E.W. (1924) *Introduction to the Science of Sociology*. Chicago: University Chicago Press.

Park, B. and Rothbart, M. (1982) Perception of out-group homogeneity and levels of social categorization: memory for the subordinate attributes of in-group and out- group members. *Journal of Perspectives in Social Psychology*, *42*, 1051–68.

Parsons, T. (1951) *The Social System*. Glencoe, Ill:. The Free Press.

Salazar, M.C. (1988) Child labour in Bogotà's quarries and brickmaking. In Bequele, A. and Boyden, J. (eds) *Combating Child Labour*. Geneva: International Labour Organisation.

Sedikides, C. and Ostrom, T.M. (1986) *Status and ingroup/outgroup membership as determinants of person organization*. Presented at Annual Meeting of the Midwest Psychological Association, Chicago.

Sennett, R. and Cobb, J. (1972) *The Hidden Injuries of Class*. Cambridge: Cambridge University Press.

Sherif, M. (1967) *Group Conflict and Cooperation*. London: Routledge and Kegan Paul.

Simmel, G. (1955) *Conflict*. Translated by Wolff, K.H. Glencoe, Ill.: The Free Press.

Simon, B. and Brown, R. (1987) Perceived homogeneity in minority-majority contexts. *Journal of Perspectives in Social Psychology*, *53*, 703–11.

Smith, P.K. (1991) The silent nightmare: Bullying and victimisation in school peer groups. *The Psychologist*, *4*, 243–8.

Tajfel, H. (1982) Social psychology of intergroup relations. *Annual Review Psychology*, 33, 1–39.

Trudgill, P. (1975) *Accent, Dialect and the School*. London: Edward Arnold.

Tumin, M.M. (1985) *Social Stratification. The forms and functions of inequality*, 2nd ed. Englewood Cliffs, NJ: Prentice-Hall, Inc.

Waites, B. (1987) *The Class Society at War. England 1914–18*. Leamington Spa: Berg

Weber, M. (1947) *The Theory of Social and Economic Organisation*. Originally published 1921, translated by A.M. Henderson and T. Parsons. New York: Oxford University Press.

Wright, E.O., Hachem, D., Costello, C. and Sprague, J. (1982) The American class structure. *American Sociological Review*, 47, 709–26.

Zucker, K.B. and Barnett, D.W. (1977) *The Paired Hands Test*. Dallas, Texas: McCanon-Dial Systems.

CHAPTER 11

Gender and Hatred

Helen Barrett and David Jones

In time we hate that which we often fear.

Anthony and Cleopatra, I.iii.15

It is generally accepted that, across all cultures, gender acts as a central and major classifier, dividing people into two groups, male and female or, as some have suggested, male and non-male. Evidence from sociological and anthropological sources indicates that there is considerable cultural variation in both degree and type of differentiation, as shown in Mead's classic study of differences between the Arapesh, Tchambuli and Mundugamore cultures (Mead 1935). In most societies, however, males and females do not occupy equal status positions and it has been argued that females are the 'second sex' (De Beauvoir 1949), functioning, as their often decorative names might suggest, to serve the needs of dominant males or to nurture themselves through nurturing others (Eichenbaum and Orbach 1982).

In this chapter, we look briefly at gender role differences in society, focusing particularly on evidence of inequalities. We go on to outline stages through which children's concepts of gender are thought to develop and describe the nature of gender role differences in children. This provides the background to a discussion of the relationship between hatred and gender in childhood which centres upon the degree to which models of gender role development have made predictions concerning gender role relationships. Finally, we consider the role of child sexual abuse in producing patterns of hatred.

Gender role differences in society

Within many cultures a pattern of male dominance is observable, for example inheritance rules often favour the eldest son; in most institutions almost all top managerial posts are occupied by men; policy-making bodies often fail to include women sufficiently to represent their interests; on television, images of men (especially in portrayal of sports and recreational activities, but in many other areas also) vastly outnumber those of women, while male voices occupy considerably more airspace than female voices both on television and radio; in the arts, males again outnumber females in many spheres; a similar imbalance in reporting is evident throughout newspaper reports (for example, it is not rare for 80% of daily obituary and birthday listings to refer to males, implying that females of note are in a minority). In addition, according to statistics quoted in the *New Internationalist* (January, 1992), illiteracy amongst women is much higher than amongst men and, in many parts of the world, girls are less likely to be enrolled in secondary schools; when women do the same work as men, they are estimated to receive on average 30–40% less pay worldwide. In many parts of the world, women's freedom of movement is severely restricted: even in our own society, women may be considered to be 'asking for trouble' if they fail to obey conventions relating to where, when and how they should behave, and fashion dictates that basic items of clothing severely constrict parts of women's anatomy (for example, high-heeled, sharply-pointed, slippery-soled shoes).

These examples illustrate how women's work and females generally are viewed as secondary in status to men. Yet none of these details needs inevitably to entail resentment on the part of either party. A hierarchical distribution of power and prestige – indeed, inequality in itself – need not imply a competitive relationship.

However, there does seem to be evidence that inequalities between sexes can lead to unsatisfactory relationships in which distrust and hatred are manifest. Much of this evidence suggests that abuse of power may be irresistible, for example, domestic violence and other aggressive attacks by men on women (including rape) vastly outnumber attacks by women on men; epidemiological data on mental health appears to indicate that women are at least twice as likely as men to be treated for depression; the incidence of sexual harassment and the availability and nature of pornography also suggest the prevalence of less than respectful attitudes towards women. On a less aggressive but perhaps equally alienating level, clear distinctions are made within our culture between predominantly male-organised non-home and predominantly female-organised home work environments, for example, the former's incompatibility with child care arrangements.

These examples indicate that, despite the influence of feminism, female oppression is still a feature of the social environment for many children in most cultures. Whilst this situation appears to favour males, permitting them more freedom and control than women, it can be seen that the power structure places both males and females under tremendous pressure, forcing men to aspire to a position in which it may be difficult to feel validated, satisfied or successful.

Interestingly, though most women are not unaware of the ways in which their work is devalued, only a minority consciously takes steps to rectify this situation and to systematically challenge each instance of male pretentiousness. In the same way, men seem unwilling to make moves which might radically transform the power structure or their role within it. Indeed, the minority who do attempt to make changes are often perceived as inappropriately masculine or aggressive (if women), or 'wimpish' (if men).

Development of children's knowledge about gender

Intons-Peterson (1988) outlines children's development of gender concepts as follows: by about 24 months, correct identification of males and females is almost established; by three years, children can classify by gender activities, interests and occupations; gender constancy/stability (the knowledge that one's gender remains constant throughout the life-span) emerges at about four-five years; slightly after this, gender motive (the realisation that gender cannot change even if you want it to) and situational gender constancy (understanding that gender is stable over time and circumstance/place) emerge. She suggests that the initial distinctions are learned by reinforcement. Having accumulated experiences, children then learn to label these and develop a cognitive framework capable of organising stimuli relating to gender. Unlike adults, she argues, young children's gender concepts do not include information about secondary sexual characteristics: these are not incorporated until children are at least seven years old. It would appear that children's friendships do not show same-sex preferences until around the age of four or five (Foot *et al.* 1980). Within same-sex groups before the age of seven, it has been thought that males prefer smaller groups than females, though this situation appears to reverse in children over this age; in addition, girls' groups appear to be organised on a less hierarchical basis than boys' groups.

Evidence of gender differences relating to children

Within the discipline of psychology, an extensive literature documents the complex concept of gender, acknowledging its salience and recognizing its influence upon adults' behaviour towards children as well as children's regulation of their own and each other's behaviour. Whilst it is not within the scope of this chapter to describe all of these differences, nor to enter into any lengthy discussion with regard to them, it nevertheless seems important to give a brief account of some of the areas in which differences have been thought to exist. It is perhaps wise, though, to bear in mind the notion that, in many cases, the size and nature of differences has been disputed.

Parents' attitudes towards offspring

As Intons-Peterson and Reddel (1984) point out, the first question asked about a newborn usually concerns its sex. Further, a number of studies have revealed preferences, particularly amongst expectant fathers, for sons. Even in the early weeks of life, adults behave differently towards boy and girl infants and the tendency for mothers to be more highly praised on the birth of a son has not escaped the notice of many writers (for example Belotti 1975, Grabrucker 1988). It has been suggested that, before the age of three months, infant boys are touched and held more by parents (Lewis 1972) and may sleep less and be more irritable than girls (Moss 1967, Sander 1973). Girls at this age are looked at and talked to more than boys (Lewis 1972).

It has also been found that, in a group of infants rated as similar in length, weight and on Apgar score, fathers rate daughters as soft, awkward, weak, delicate and fine-featured but sons as firm, well-coordinated, strong, hard, alert and large-featured (Rubin et al. 1974). A number of differences have also been found between fathers' and mothers' behaviour towards same- and different-sex offspring, for example, in amount and type of holding, touching, playing, speech and punishment practices (White and Woollett 1981, Lamb 1981, Block 1978). These differences in parental practices towards boys and girls may increase as children get older and will be added to by teachers, other adults and other children; for example, it appears that court sentences for delinquent behaviour in adolescent girls are more severe than for boys (Elliott 1988).

Although this account of differences may give some idea of ways in which parental practices can vary with regard to male and female offspring, it must be remembered that these differences are by no means either universal or uniform throughout one society: social and economic factors as well as parity interact with gender differences in complicated ways, for example, whilst one study found that white middle-class North American mothers coo at and talk to girls more than boys (Thoman et al. 1972), another study within the same geographical area found that black lower-class mothers talked more to boys than to girls (Brown et al. 1975).

Gender differences in children's behaviour

With regard to gender differences in children's behaviour, findings have been perhaps even more controversial.

It has been suggested that the ability to distinguish between males and females can be shown in preverbal infants who are usually more responsive to the voice of a female than to a male adult (Clifton et al. 1981). Maurer and Maurer (1988) report a broad general tendency for newborn boys to be perceived as more active than girls on account of their greater body weight at birth: this, they suggest, makes movements of limbs in boys possible whilst movement in girls is more likely to be limited to smaller muscles (for example, those involved in smiling). Differences in activity levels were also reported in older children in the studies reviewed by Maccoby and Jacklin (1974), as well as small but significant differences in favour of male superiority in visuo- spatial and mathematical tasks and female superiority in verbal tasks (findings which have been much disputed). The other reported difference, and one of greater relevance to our discussion of the antecedents of hatred, is that males show more physical aggression than females. Both the higher levels of androgens in boys and the tendency for them to become more muscular as they mature have been posited as possible predisposing factors. However, in many cultures, boys are both exposed to aggressive behaviour by male role models and also, unlike girls, subtly but actively encouraged to be more physical in their play. Several reports also suggest that parents show greater tolerance of non-compliance in boys than in girls.

Studies of play behaviour and toy preferences have lent support to the notion that children's behaviour in this area is highly sensitive to social context and reflects both adult, own and peer expectations (Liss 1983, Fagot 1977). Liss (1983) considers that sex-role stereotyped differences in play behaviour and use of toys and behaviour afford different learning experiences for girls and boys; she argues that these practices can and should be altered so that girls and boys have equal opportunities to develop verbal and visuo-spatial skills. Vocalisation and speech patterns have been shown to differentiate between male and female children (Graddol and Swann 1989): for example, several studies have shown that, in the classroom situation, boys talk more than girls, are more effective at making themselves heard and in attracting attention to themselves, are more disruptive, and receive more attention from teachers. It has further been suggested that girls play a part in ensuring male dominance in this situation (Swann and Graddol 1988). Attention has also been drawn to the degree to which sexual harassment of girls infiltrates the school environment, particularly at senior school level (Jones 1985).

This necessarily brief sketch perhaps affords some clues as to the way in which early gender-based rivalries may develop between children. In the next section, we examine some of the theories put forward to explain the development of gender roles in children with the aim of trying to understand more about how different children adopting different gender roles might view each other.

Models of gender development

Due to the large number of theories about the development of gender concepts in children, this chapter only has scope to discuss those which are better known, i.e. the sociobiological, social learning theory, psychoanalytic and cognitive-developmental accounts. Our aim here is to consider the extent to which each account makes predictions concerning the likelihood of antagonism arising between children on the basis of gender differences, as well as to evaluate evidence supporting these explanations.

Sociobiological explanations of gender role differentiation

A number of workers have explored the possibility that biological factors may underpin behavioural (gender role) differences in males and females. One implication of this position is that biological differences between males and females exist in order to maximise chances of survival for the species. Although survival and reproduction of the species may be a common aim for both males and females, the means to this end need not involve cooperation – simply a competitive drive to select the most healthy, fertile and adaptable mate. Species-specific behaviours reflect pre-programmed roles developed by processes of evolution and may be geared less to the benefit of the individual, more in the interests of the species as a whole. Thus, whilst sociobiological arguments do not explicitly predict antagonism between males and females, they accept that rivalry and extra-individual considerations will inform behaviour and claim that behavioural differences such as male aggression or female submission can be reduced to differences in biological make-up.

Two main strands of evidence seem to have been put forward in favour of the biological basis of gender role differences: that chromosomal patterns are implicated in the development of sex-stereotyped behaviour and that testosterone levels are directly linked with aggression.

With regard to the issue of chromosomal patterns, unfortunately there is only scope here for the most rudimentary description and, since the precise pattern of anatomical and physiological differentiation is complex and not completely understood, readers are encouraged to consult other sources for fuller accounts (for example, Money and Ehrhardt 1972, Singleton 1986). Briefly, under conditions of normal development, sexual identity is determined by dimorphism in one of the twenty-three pairs of chromosomes in each cell of the human body. The chromosomes in this pair are usually referred to as the sex chromosomes. At conception, the pairing of two X chromosomes (XX) will result in a female and pairing of X and Y chromosomes (XY) will result in a male. All female parent ova contain only X chromosomes while the sperm of the male parent contain either X or Y chromosomes. It follows that the sexual identity of the newly formed embryo is determined by which of the father's sperm fertilises the mother's ovum. In order for the male reproductive system to develop, it seems that at least three conditions must obtain: Mullerian-inhibiting substances must be present to prevent the development of the female reproductive apparatus; sufficient gonadal androgens must be produced to permit the formation of male external genitalia and to facilitate specific organisational patterns in the brain; and the enzyme 5-alpha reductase must be present to convert testosterone into dihydrotesterone and to prevent androgen-insensitivity syndrome (a condition anatomically indicated by ambiguous external genitalia and sterile testicles). Excessively high intrauterine or foetal blood levels of androgens are thought to result in females having an enlarged clitoris or, occasionally, a penis with possibly an empty scrotum. These details may serve to illustrate that sexual development is a complex matter even without consideration of cultural influences, which may be more closely implicated in the production of gender divisions.

Whilst taking the overall position from a larger body of data on anatomical differences that gender assignment and cultural features are actually more influential than biological factors, Money and Ehrhardt (1972) reported that girls exposed to androgenic substances before birth were more likely to engage in tomboyish behaviour (i.e. the rough-and-tumble play thought to characterise the males of a number of species) and showed less evidence of maternal behaviours. They offered this as evidence of a possible link between biological differences and gender behaviours which may occur as a sequel to the masculinizing effect of androgens on the foetal brain. However, this suggestion was challenged, both on methodological grounds and in view of the fact that anatomically ambiguous females may not have been exposed to socialisation processes equivalent to those experienced by other females.

With regard to the hypothesised link between testosterone and aggression, several studies have found low positive correlations between testosterone levels and trait ratings of aggression and also higher correlations on ratings of aggressiveness by others in the person's environment. Such correlational evidence has to be treated with caution since the outcome of both aggressive and competitive encounters can influence testosterone levels (Archer 1991).

It would appear, then, that no conclusive evidence is available either to support or to refute the notion that gender differences are dependent upon biological sex differences.

A further point in relation to the argument against a purely biological explanation of gender differences is made by Graddol and Swann (1989), who note that distinct gender differences in speech intonation and voice pitch are distinguishable before the occurrence of biological changes in the voice apparatus at puberty. This suggests that non-biological influences play a part in the development of gender differentiation in children. It has also been demonstrated that children possess knowledge of and the capacity to perform the other gender's responses, but deliberately choose to suppress those not considered appropriate (Hargreaves 1977).

An alternative view point has been proposed by a now long tradition of feminist theorists who argue that gender is a purely social construct or, in De Beauvoir's well-known words, 'One is not born, but rather becomes, a woman'. This position appears to have much in common with environmentalist or social learning theory arguments.

Social learning theory accounts of gender role learning

Social learning theory (see, for example, Mischel 1970 for a fuller account) offers some explanation, in terms of reward, non-reward and punishment of particular behaviours, of how male and female children learn to reject other-gender behaviours. Essentially, it views children's behaviour as being shaped by adults and significant others so that rewarded behaviours are sought and imitated while non-rewarded and punished behaviours are avoided or feared. That other-gender items and characters become less important or interesting seems to be supported by evidence of attentional biases towards same-sex characters and same-gender behaviours (Mischel 1970). In itself, this finding need not imply that conscious hatred characterises relationships between male and female children, but it does predict that other-gender individuals will be perceived as less attractive than same-gender individuals.

Social learning theory has, however, been criticised on the grounds that, since much learning appears to be based on observation rather than upon imitation and reinforcement schedules alone, it fails to account fully for the active nature of children's adoption of engendered positions (for example, Hargreaves 1986). It would seem, then, that neither a strictly biological nor an environmental explanation can be said to account for gender role learning.

There is a more serious conceptual difficulty which must also be acknowledged, for many workers have suggested that gender is not a dichotomous variable but a complex psychological construction centring on the body, interactions with the bodies of others and the drives (Dahl 1988). Bem (1985) has proposed that people vary considerably not only in the degree to which they see themselves and others as belonging to a particular gender category but also in their ability to adopt behaviour characteristic of the other gender. According to gender schema theory, it is possible to classify individuals in terms of the degree to which they endorse beliefs and behaviours thought to be characteristic of gender role stereotypes. People classified as highly schematic on gender can fall into several categories: they can be high on masculinity and low on femininity, or vice versa; or high on both masculinity and femininity, i.e. androgynous. The set of beliefs and behaviours endorsed by androgynous individuals is thought to be the most likely to be adaptive, depending upon the cultural context: this argument is premised on the notion that the most situation-appropriate behaviour will often require females to engage in male activities (for example chairing the meeting) or males to take up the female position (for example nursing the baby). It is also possible to be gender-schematic or undifferentiated (low on both masculinity and femininity).

Clearly, if gender schema theory is correct, we must expect gender relationships to be far more complicated than a dichotomy would suggest and we must revise any simple assumption that male/female corresponds with masculine/feminine. Further, we must accept that conflict and differences in behaviour between males and females need not have any direct association with the issue of gender. Instead we can view gender conflicts as residing within individuals rather than, as we have hitherto implied, in a self/other interaction: if males or females are potentially equally capable of adopting masculine or feminine behaviours, then, within themselves, they may struggle with choices of gender positions.

It is beyond the scope of this chapter to explore the issue of whether such conflicts might be more intense for boys than girls or how decisions concerning choice of gender role might influence gender relationships or self-esteem. There does, however, appear to be some evidence that boys may receive more pressure from peers to conform to sex-role stereotypes than girls, who may engage more freely in some 'tomboyish' behaviours (Fagot 1977).

Kessler and McKenna (1978) have pointed out that, although within any possible list of items which differentiate males from females there are none that always and without exception apply to only one gender, yet, 'As we go about our daily lives, we assume that every human being is either a male or a female... even with biologically 'mixed' individuals... each one is placed in one of two mutually exclusive categories' (p.1).

The possibility that gender is not a simple dichotomy is one that seems to have been acknowledged within psychoanalytic theory, for Freud was aware of the bisexual nature of males and females as well as the non-correspondence between masculinity and femininity and biological sex (for example, Freud 1932).

Psychoanalytic theories of gender relationships

Unlike other theories discussed so far, which make very few predictions or statements about how male and female children interact, psychoanalytic theory has generated an enormous number of hypotheses in this area, few of which have been tested and many of which are not easily tested or falsifiable. Nevertheless, the effort to explore areas of experience which are difficult to examine using traditional experimental methods has yielded many interesting ideas and, in this section, an attempt will be made to give some, albeit rather limited, indication of the variety and range of these speculations.

Faced with the problem of trying to explain how boy and girl babies develop into men and women capable of heterosexual relationships, Freud developed a complex and not complete theory of psychosexual development of which only the points most relevant to gender relations can be mentioned here.

He postulated that, for the boy child, the prehistory of the Oedipus complex includes an identification with the father which gives way to Oedipal wishes, i.e. the desire to replace the father in mother's affections, a simultaneous hate for father and love for mother. Freud (1924) suggested that at around four years of age the actual sight of female genitalia leads to a realisation of sexual differences and the replacement of Oedipal by castration anxieties. Hereafter, the boy child despises females, feels disgust towards them and represses sexual interests (Freud 1923). At this point, the boy identifies with his father and tries to imitate the masculine sex role.

Even more controversially, Freud describes the little girl as identical with a little man until her realisation of genital difference (which occurs at the same point as in little boys): a female castration complex then arises in conjunction with penis envy. This leads the little girl to turn her sexual interests towards her father and away from her mother (Freud 1925, 1931).

Freud's later position (Freud 1932) was much complicated by his recognition of the potential of all individuals to adopt feminine and masculine positions. His ideas about the cause of shifts in gender positions or how the adoption of gender positions relates to biological sex or psychosexual stage, though numerous, were not formulated into a coherent, testable theory. Neither was he satisfied with his explanation of the processes of object change in girls – a shortcoming which has been seen by subsequent psychoanalytic theorists as a starting point for their own theories of sexual development.

One of the main challenges to Freud's psychosexual theories has been evidence that young children's gender awareness is observable before the age of four or five while their concepts of gender identity have been shown to be independent of knowledge about secondary sexual characteristics such as genitalia (Intons-Peterson 1988).

Of the many alternative psychoanalytic views on sexual development and gender relations, there is space here only to give one or two examples.

Deutsch (1925) claimed that female masochism is essential for the preservation of the species, females needing to be passive recipients in order to function effectively as agents of reproduction. By latency, she suggested, girls fantasise being castrated and raped by the father and need to view males as both aggressive and dominant. According to this theory, hatred or dread of males by females is therefore inevitable.

Horney (1932) proposed that the relationship between males and females is characterised by men's fear of the mother who dominates, frustrates and infantilises. Strategies adopted by males to free themselves from their need for a powerful mother include depreciation, avoidance, idealisation, abuse and hatred of women. Females' fear of males, she suggested, is underpinned by awareness of the vagina from the start of life and fear for destruction in Oedipal congress. Olivier (1989) develops these notions, suggesting that the relationship between boys and mothers is characterised by the seductive role of mothers who, as in the Oedipus myth, fall in love with their sons.

Klein's views add further to the complex picture provided by Freud with her introduction of the notion that objects (i.e., significant others, or parts of others) may be split into good and bad images. She suggests that relationships between children and their parents are characterised by extreme ambivalence, love and hate for the same object being the usual pattern. To this extent her theories do not specifically predict that hatred will arise in children on account of gender relationships, although both male and female children are described as being intensely fearful of attacks from others (Klein 1932).

Currently, theorists in the psychoanalytic tradition have continued to recognise the enormous complexity of gender relationships, emphasising particularly the way in which gender is constructed within social discourse. Unfortunately, there is not space to discuss these theories further here. To summarise, psychoanalytic theory has offered many hypotheses about the nature of gender relations in childhood but empirical evidence is needed before these ideas can be seen to be substantiated.

Cognitive-developmental theories of gender

Cognitive-developmental theory, like social learning theory, makes predictions about how children relate to others, specifically hypothesising that children will be unable to take non-egocentric view points until cognitive development has reached a fairly advanced level (that of concrete operational thinking, which is thought to emerge at around the age of seven years).

Workers such as Kohlberg (1966) proposed that young children first become aware of distinctions between the self and others and, subsequently, having learned that self and some others share certain attributes belonging to a gender category, begin to self-label and self-reinforce on the basis of group membership.

This explanation may fit with the notion that antagonism will exist between children of different gender categories since it is well documented that strong preferences are shown towards members of own's own social group whilst out-group members are de-individualised and distanced (see Brewer and Kramer 1985, Messick and Mackie 1989 for reviews of inter-group relations). However, besides the difficulty already mentioned in connection with social learning theory (that gender may not be a dichotomy), Intons-Peterson (1988) also points out that the timetable proposed by cognitive-developmental theory for the establishment of gender identity lags considerably behind that observed by other workers. Gender identity has been demonstrated at least as early as the second year (Lewis and Brooks 1974) or, in 75% of cases, by 24 months according to Thompson (1975): Kohlberg's theory would place it several years later.

Child sexual abuse

Child sexual abuse must rank as one of the greatest potential causes of hatred and distrust in both the child victims and their families. Sexual abuse is generally taken to mean involvement of dependent children and adolescents by a sexually mature individual in sexual activities which they may not fully understand and to which they are unable to give informed consent (Kempe and Kempe 1978).

Reported cases of sexual abuse do not adequately reflect the magnitude of the problem and more accurate estimates of prevalence have been obtained from survey studies of adult populations. Baker and Duncan (1985) questioned a British sample of 2019 individuals aged 15 years and over and reported that 12% of females and 8% of males described themselves as having been sexually abused before the age of 16. Finkelhor (1979) in a survey of 769 college students in New England obtained reports of child sexual abuse in 19% of girls and 9% of boys. Baker and Duncan (1985) estimated from their survey that a possible 4.5 million adults in Great Britain may have been sexually abused as children. Given the reluctance to make disclosures of personal experiences, this may still be a conservative estimate.

The nature of the abusive experience, frequency of the abuse, age of the child and relationship with the perpetrator are all thought to be important factors. In the Baker and Duncan survey, 49% of the abusers were known to the victims and 14% of the reported sexual abuse took place within the family. Bentovim and Boston (1988) analysed some of the characteristics of 274 families in which there had been child sexual abuse. The victims were 317 girls and 94 boys. Almost 40% of the abuse had been initiated when the child victim was under the age of 10 and over half of the children were abused for a year or more. The perpetrators were mainly men (96%); almost half were parents of the children (46%) and the largest other group were step-parents (27%).

In a clinic sample of 113 sexually abused children reported by Fitzpatrick and Fitzgerald (1991), 55 cases involved intra-familial abuse and in this group the largest single category of abuser was a sibling of the victim. All 16 of these sibling victims were girls and 15 of the abusing siblings were boys. The families in which sibling abuse took place were more likely to be two-parent families than a comparison extra-familial abuse group. The sibling abuse families also tended to have larger numbers of children.

This brief survey illustrates that unknown numbers of children are subjected to sexual abuse. Even when there is no physical contact involved, the experiences may be disturbing for the victims and give rise to intrusive thoughts and fears many years later. Clinical histories indicate that the ability to form trusting and loving relationships later in life may be impaired. Abuse within the family brings with it the additional problems of enforced secrecy and the association of sex with power. Disclosure of the abuse and the subsequent effects on family life can result in the victim being disbelieved and ostracised.

We can only speculate as to whether atypical family structures or early deprivation experiences impair the ability of children to form stable loving relationships in adolescence and adulthood. It has been suggested that adolescent boys whose self-image is modified by having an absent father (whose only apparent role had been to impregnate the mother) sometimes use promiscuous sexual activity in attempts to demonstrate their own masculinity (Miller 1986). Their lack of concern for the welfare of their partners approaches hatred. Similar promiscuous sexual behaviour has been reported for some boys who had been sexually abused by women.

Power and hatred in children

Given that children in our culture grow up to link sex differences with inequality, it is perhaps surprising that they express so little hatred towards members of the opposite sex and that they appear so readily to acquiesce in the adoption of sex role stereotyped behaviours. Although there have been some moves towards equality, differences still persist and appear amazingly resistant to change.

What might we need to do in order to effect changes? There seem to be no simple answers to this question. All children, girls and boys, need to feel wanted and to feel that they have equal opportunities. Although the evidence that we have reviewed indicates that biological differences may be relatively unimportant in the establishment and attainment of goals relating to gender identity, it is clear that parents and other carers of children have subtle influences on the sex-role development of children from the very start of life, and probably long before this too. They are often unaware and not in control of the role models which they provide in the exercise of power and the establishment of gender role relationships. Yet it does appear that there are ways in which this situation can change, on at least superficial if not deep levels; for example, fathers have been shown to be influential in encouraging the achievement orientation of their children, particularly their daughters, and steps could be taken to ensure that girls are enabled to be more active, boys less aggressive. Perhaps there is even a chance that fear and resentment of the other could be replaced by healthy rivalry or recognition of the value of differences between individuals so that hatred would not then need to develop.

References

Archer, J. (1991) The influence of testosterone on human aggression. *British Journal of Psychology, 82,* 1–28.

Baker, A.W. and Duncan, S.P. (1985) Child sexual abuse: A study of prevalence in Great Britain. *Child Abuse and Neglect, 9,* 457–67.

Belotti, E.G. (1975) *Little Girls. Social conditioning and its effects on the stereotyped role of women during infancy.* London: Writers and Readers Publishing Cooperative.

Bem, S.L. (1985) Androgyny and gender schema theory: A conceptual and empirical integration. In Sonderegger, T.B. (ed.) *Psychology and Gender. Nebraska Symposium on Motivation, 1984, Vol. 32.* University of Nebraska Press.

Bentovim, A. and Boston, P. (1988) Sexual abuse – Basic issues – Characteristics of children and families. In Bentovim, A., Elton, A., Hildebrand, J., Tranter M.and Vizard, E. (eds.), *Child sexual abuse within the family. Assessment and treatment.* London: Wright.

Block, J.H. (1978) Another look at sex differentiation in the socialization behaviours of mothers and fathers. In Denmark F. and Sherman J. (eds.), *Psychology of Women: Future directions of research.* New York: Psychological Dimensions.

Brewer, M.B. and Kramer, R.M. (1985) The psychology of intergroup attitudes and behavior. *Annual Review of Psychology, 36,* 219–43.

Brown, J.V., Bakeman, R., Snyder, P.A., Frederickson, W.T., Morgan, S.T. and Hepler, R. (1975) Interactions of black inner-city mothers with their new infants. *Child Development, 46,* 677–86.

Clifton, R., Morrongiello, B., Kulig, J. and Dowd, J. (1981) Newborns' orientation toward sound: Possible implications for cortical development. *Child Development, 52,* 833–8.

Dahl, E.K. (1988) Fantasies of gender. *Psychoanalytic Study of the Child, 43,* 351–65.

De Beauvoir, S. (1949) *The Second Sex.* Translated and edited by H.M. Parsley, 1972. Harmondsworth: Penguin Books.

Deutsch, H. (1925) Psychology of women in relation to the function of reproduction. *International Journal of Psychoanalysis, 6,* 405–18.

Eichenbaum, L. and Orbach, S. (1982) *Outside in... Inside out. Women's Psychology: A feminist psychoanalytic approach.* Harmondsworth: Penguin Books.

Elliott, D. (1988) *Gender, Delinquency and Society: A comparative study of male and female offenders and juvenile justice in Britain.* Aldershot: Avebury.

Fagot, B.I. (1977) Consequences of moderate cross-gender behavior in preschool children. *Child Development, 48,* 902–7.

Finkelhor, D. (1979) *Sexually Victimized Children.* New York: Free Press.

Fitzpatrick, C. and Fitzgerald, E. (1991) Sibling sexual abuse: family characteristics. *Newsletter of the Association for Child Psychology and Psychiatry, Vol. 13,* 10–3.

Foot, H.C., Chapman, A.J. and Smith, J.R. (1980) *Friendship and Social Relations in Children.* Chichester: John Wiley and Sons.

Freud, S. (1923) Infantile genital organisation of the libido. *S.E., Vol. XIX.*

Freud, S. (1924) The dissolution of the Oedipal complex. *S.E., Vol. XIX.*

Freud, S. (1925) Some physical consequences of the anatomical distinction between the sexes. *S.E., Vol. XIX.*

Freud, S. (1931) Female sexuality. *S.E., Vol. XXI.*

Freud, S. (1932) Femininity. *New introductory lectures on psychoanalysis. S.E., Vol. XXII.*

Grabrucker, M. (1988) *There's a Good Girl.* London: The Women's Press.

Graddol, D. and Swann, J. (1989) *Gender Voices.* Oxford: Basil Blackwell.

Hargreaves, D. (1977) Sex roles in divergent thinking. *British Journal of Education in Psychology, 47,* 25–32.

Hargreaves, D.J. (1986) Psychological theories of sex-role stereotyping. In Hargreaves, D.J. and Colley, A.M. (eds), *The Psychology of Sex Roles.* London: Harper and Row.

Horney, K. (1932) The dread of women. *International Journal of Psychoanalysis,* 13, 348–60.

Intons-Peterson, M.J. (1988) *Children's Concepts of Gender.* Norwood, New Jersey: Ablex Publishing Company.

Intons-Peterson, M.J. and Reddel, M. (1984) What do people ask about a neonate? *Developmental Psychology, 20,* 358–9.

Jones, C. (1985) Sexual tyranny: male violence in a mixed secondary school. Chapter 3 in Weiner, G. (ed.), *Just a Bunch of Girls.* Milton Keynes: Open University Press, Gender and Education Series.

Kempe, R. and Kempe, C.H. (1978) *Child Abuse.* London: Fontana Open Books.

Kessler, S.J. and McKenna, W. (1978) *Gender: An ethnomethodological approach.* New York: John Wiley & Sons.

Klein, M. (1932) *The Psychoanalysis of Children.* New York: Norton.

Kohlberg, L. (1966) A cognitive-developmental analysis of children's sex-role concepts and attitudes. In Maccoby, E.E. (ed.), *The Development of Sex Differences.* Stanford, CA: Stanford University Press.

Lamb, M.E. (1981) *The Role of the Father in Child Development.* 2nd ed., New York: John Wiley and Sons.

Lewis, M. (1972) State as an infant-environment interaction: An analysis of mother-infant interaction as a function of sex. *Merrill-Palmer Quarterly, 18,* 95–121.

Lewis, M. and Brooks, J. (1974) Self, other, and fear: Infants' reactions to people. In Lewis, M. and Rosenblum L. (eds), *Fear: The Origins of Behavior, Vol. II.* New York: John Wiley & Sons.

Liss, M.B. (1983) Learning gender-related skills through play. In Liss, M.B. (ed.), *Social and Cognitive Skills. Sex roles and children's play.* London: Academic Press.

Maccoby, E.E. and Jacklin, C.N. (1974) *The Psychology of Sex Differences.* Stanford: Stanford University Press.

Maurer, D. and Maurer, C. (1988) *The World of the Newborn.* Harmondsworth: Penguin books.

Mead, M. (1935) *Sex and Temperament in Three Primitive Societies.* New York: Morrow.

Messick, D.M. and Mackie, D.M. (1989) Intergroup relations. *Annual Review of Psychology, 40,* 45–81.

Miller, D. (1986) *Attack on the Self: Adolescent behavioural disturbances and their treatment.* NJ: Aronson.

Mischel, W. (1970) Sex-typing and socialisation. In Mussen, P.H. (ed.) *Carmichael's Manual of Child Psychology, Vol. 2* (3rd ed.). New York: John Wiley & Sons.

Money, J. and Ehrhardt, A.A. (1972) *Man and Women, Boy and Girl: Differentiation of gender identity.* Baltimore: Johns Hopkins Press.

Moss, H. (1967) Sex, age and state as determinants of mother-infant interaction. *Merrill-Palmer Quarterly, 13,* 19–36.

Olivier, C. (1989) *Jocasta's Children: The imprint of the mother.* Translated by Craig, G. London and New York: Routledge.

Rubin, J., Provenzano, F.J. and Luria, Z. (1974) The eye of the beholder: Parents' views on sex of newborns. *American Journal of Orthopsychiatry, 43,* 720–31.

Sander, L. (1973) *Twenty-four hour distributions of sleeping and waking over the first month of life in different infant caretaking systems.* Paper presented at the meeting for the Society for Research in Child Development, Philadelphia.

Singleton, C.H. (1986) Biological and social explanations of sex-role stereotyping. In Hargreaves, D.J. and Colley, A.M. (eds), *The Psychology of Sex Roles.* London: Harper and Row.

Swann, J. and Graddol, D. (1988) Gender inequalities in class room talk. *English in Education, 22(1),* 48–65.

Thoman, E.B., Leiderman, P.H. and Olson, J.P. (1972) Neonate-mother interaction during breast-feeding. *Developmental Psychology,* 6, 110–8.

Thompson, S.K. (1975) Gender labels and early sex role development. *Child Development, 46,* 339–47.

White, D.G. and Woollett, E.A. (1981) *The family at birth.* Paper presented to the British Psychological Society, London: December.

CHAPTER 12

Hate and Learning Disability
Issues in Psychoanalytical Psychotherapy with Children with a Learning Disability

Valerie Sinason

The beginnings of hate

In the fairy-tale 'Briar Rose' by the Grimm brothers, a baby princess is born. At the birth of the new baby princess the King has a great feast and invites many guests including all but one of the wise women in his kingdom. There are thirteen wise women but he only has twelve golden plates to serve them with so he fails to invite one. The wise women who come wish the princess many good things health, happiness, kindness, beauty. However, the unin-vited old woman, the thirteenth, says Briar Rose will prick herself with a spindle on her fifteenth birthday and die. Only the magic of the twelfth wise woman, who had not yet given her present, could mitigate the sentence. The Princess will not die but will sleep for a hundred years.

'Sleeping Beauty', like all good fairytales, offers us a deep understanding of many aspects of human life. However, instead of looking at the theme of an envious attack on adolescent sexuality or the female disowning of sexual feelings, I would like to start this chapter by looking at the death-wish, primary hatred, and its place at the birth of any baby. Then I will consider the specific ways hatred is experienced by children with a disability.

At the birth of a new baby parents hope for the best. We hope that our own good inner qualities and resources will outweigh the negative. We hope we have enough emotional food inside us to sustain the new relationship. However, something new, with all its unknown and untapped potential, arouses envy and hatred as well as love. The semi-humorous exhortation ascribed to the military – 'If it moves kill it' – is something that the hating part of us feels about everything new. The nausea experienced by many women in pregnancy is not necessarily only physiological. Sometimes it reflects ambivalence; the interplay between love and hate for the new being who will require so much and who may enter a far more comfortable world than its parents enjoyed.

Psychoanalytic theories of hate

Freud (1914) saw hate as older than love; something primordial, there right from the start at birth in the ego's repudiation of the outside world. As the polar opposite of love he also saw it as inextricably linked to love. He added (1923) that hate, as the polarity of love, points the way to the 'instinct of destruction' – the death instinct.

The wise woman who would have loved the baby turns easily to the instinct of destruction and tries to kill it. The act of exclusion maddened her and despite her wisdom and her capacity to care for others she turned to hatred and murderousness. Birth itself can be experienced as something painfully close to death. The historical effects of women dying in childbirth fleshes the co-existing primitive fear of the closeness of birth and death, love and hate.

Klein (1946) developed the understanding that feelings of love can only predominate when the death instinct is surmounted. If there are enough wise women, good feelings, then the older primitive hatred can be de-activated. When we have concern for others it helps to repair our hate and our fear that we have injured those we loved. 'It is only by facing feelings of hate, and thereby gradually bringing them together with other parts of the self, that they become less overwhelming' (Vol.4).

In other words, it is not only parents and other adults who struggle with their own fluctuations between loving and destructive feelings; the baby and child are similarly engaged. Wilfred Bion (1959) considered that the baby's primary aggression and envy would be exacerbated if the mother was unreceptive to her baby's dread. The mother's ability to respond to her baby's cries, to make a home for them and to return something that the baby can tolerate has a dramatic effect in modifying most babies' deathly feelings.

Sometimes postnatal depression, family trauma or emotional disturbance in the parents are the most powerful factors in the baby's or young child's emotional life. Sometimes it is the unique constitution of the baby that makes destructive forces predominate. Whatever the cause, the consequences of imbalance are severe. The novelist Henry James provides us with a painful example of the former case.

In his novel *What Maisie Knew*, James (1897) brilliantly describes the way separated parents project all their hatred and unwanted feelings onto their daughter Maisie. 'The evil they had the gift of thinking or pretending to think of each other they poured into her little gravely-gazing soul as into a boundless receptacle' (p.24). Slowly she becomes numbed on the outside. Bruno Bettelheim (1956) showed how many such traumatised and hated children could be driven to schizophrenia in a form of the illness that he saw as a reaction to extreme situations. Bettelheim was particularly aware of the catastrophic impact on the child when outside and inside life are both under threat (1980). He pointed out that if normal life continues around a personal tragedy we can stay sane, but if there is internal and external abandonment then there is an 'extreme situation'.

Klein (1952, p.367) comments that if, whatever the cause, a baby needs to split the forces of love and hate excessively then 'normal progress towards integration of the ego is disturbed. This may result later in mental illness'. Of particular relevance to our subject is her warning of the psychic consequences of such splitting: 'Another possible consequence is inhibition of intellectual development which may contribute to mental backwardness and – in extreme cases – to mental deficiency'.

The birth of a baby with a disability

If we consider the ambivalent feelings that exist over a normal baby, what is the impact of a baby with a disability? Here newness and difference come together in a painful way. How we define disability has to include not being like the norm. Such difference stirs up powerful feelings and fantasies. However much many loving parents and babies with disabilities bond, for others the situation is indeed what Bettelheim calls an 'extreme situation'. Philippa Russell (1991) clearly comments 'The birth of any child can be a traumatic as well as a happy event for the parents concerned. Parenthood brings alarming new responsibilities as well as pleasures. When a new baby has a disability, the initial diagnosis may be devastating for the parents'.

Parents of almost all religions, races and social class hope for a baby who is at least as healthy and attractive as they are. The birth of a baby with a disability is an almost universal blow. This means that if there are not adequate support systems right from the start then parents and babies are facing a delay in attachment. Philippa Russell points to the practical needs and high level of practical support needed in the day-to-day care of severely disabled children. Where children cannot be left alone the burden on parents – usually the mother – can be traumatic by itself, regardless of the hurt caused by the disability of the child.

New parents: The struggle between love and hate

Mr and Mrs Smith were in their thirties when she became pregnant. They had tried unsuccessfully for several years but Mrs Smith always miscarried. This meant they were initially too nervous to enjoy the pregnancy. 'We didn't know if it would die on us'. However, after the first four months had passed their confidence grew and they created a beautiful nursery room, full of soft toys and mobiles.

Baby Smith was born with a severe mental and physical disability. She was slightly premature and she needed intensive care for the first few weeks of her life. Mrs Smith on her first night at home, with her baby still in the hospital incubator, tore down the beautiful curtains with their nursery motifs and threw away the soft luxurious toys. 'I had made a palace for my baby but it wasn't for the baby I had', she cried later. The beautiful waiting space for the beautiful expected baby was frozen as if by a spell.

However, no prince would restore Baby Smith to normality. It was as if the uninvited wise woman had transformed the healthy wanted baby into a monster. Mr Smith withdrew into his work, working longer hours. Against his wife's wishes he spent thousands on an expensive new car needing to prove his economic potency at a time when his biological potency seemed to have produced 'damaged goods' – his bitter terms. The couple's sexual relationship ended; coming together had produced a catastrophe for them and so they withdrew from the comfort they could have given each other. Under their frozen behaviour was intense hatred for each other and the baby. 'We all felt like partners in crime', Mrs Smith said.

There was a resurrection of the loss experienced for the past miscarriages. Both partners saw the new baby as a grotesque reminder of the death of their past putatively normal children. Mannie Lewis and Sandy Bourne (Bourne and Lewis 1991) in their perinatal mortality workshop have well documented the frozen mask with which a mother looks at her new baby when she has not mourned for the past death. To have a disabled baby survive in the place of fantasised perfect babies was a further trauma for the Smiths.

When Baby Smith came home she was an object of hatred to both of her parents. 'I just hated her for the first months. I just wished she would die. I looked at the normal babies in the incubators. OK – some were small and some looked raw and unborn – but I would have taken any of them. I'd have swapped mine so quick! I just looked at her and looked at her willing her to die. One time, when she was not well, I did that and she started crying fiercely. I never knew she had such force in her – she was out to get me'. Mr Smith owned to creeping into her nursery at night to hear if she was breathing – partially hoping she would die. 'She would not die. She was too mean to give us what we wanted'. The hate in the parents, only partially owned, was projected into the baby who was then seen as the active murderous agent.

Mr and Mrs Smith did not have supportive families or friends and nor did they have adequate help at the start from professionals. The help they did receive was bright and breezy and they did not feel able to express any of their emotional distress. Mrs Smith had adopted the manically cheerful voice of the caring professionals. The disowned hatred in the family was only attended to when her daughter's destructive behaviour led to a referral. By then Sarah Smith was five years old. She had already been excluded from a special nursery and infant class because of her violence to the other children. She was banging her head as well as attacking other children and adults.

A visit to the Smith's showed an immaculate lounge with low shelves filled with ornaments – not a room for a child. In the corner of the room was a play-pen. Inside the playpen Sarah was rhythmically rocking, seemingly not noticing her forehead grazing against the wooden bars. There was a swelling on her forehead. A few soft toys were neatly piled at one corner of the playpen, clearly untouched.

'Someone to see you, isn't that nice?' said mother in a loud 'friendly' voice. Sarah did not look round but continued rocking and quietly banging and mother did not walk round to get facial contact with her. I said in quite a forceful tone that perhaps Sarah did *not* think it was nice. Perhaps she was fed up with all the people who came to see her and perhaps Mum herself felt quite tired out letting yet another professional into her home. Perhaps the two of them would much rather nobody came disturbing them.

There was a moment's silence in the room which came from Sarah stopping rocking, and then a little giggle from mother. 'I am sorry. Where are my manners?' I said I was not a usual guest and maybe her good manners weren't always helpful to her. Sarah had remained frozen and I asked mother if she thought Sarah would be able to talk to me. I was asking mother rather than directly speaking to Sarah as I wanted to establish her maternal authority.

'Want to talk to the nice lady?' asked mother brightly and then she giggled girlishly again and undid the side of the playpen. 'Hello little monster' she whispered, in an affectionate tone despite the name-calling. 'Do you need a new nappy?' Sarah let herself be lifted with an immensely wary expression on her face. She did not raise her arms but both her fists were clenched. Her dungarees were swollen with nappy pads. The padding to stop her leaking or smelling was as noticeable as the bruises on her forehead.

Sarah looked at me from her mother's arm and suddenly tugged my hair viciously. Her eyes were filled with hatred. 'Ouch' I said spontaneously and quickly lifted a hand to free my hair from her grip. 'Little monster' said mother harshly and placed her back in the pen. Sarah sat still for a moment, uttered a short discordant wail and then returned to banging and rocking. 'Want a cup of coffee?' asked mother brightly, readjusting her broken moment of hope.

I felt immensely sad for the pair of them. When mother was given a moment of support in which she was allowed to be angry at yet another professional entering her life she was able to be softer to her child. There was room for her loving feelings to be mobilised. However it remained to see whether Sarah, who had experienced such hatred from birth, could or would let go of her wariness or hatred. She did not reward her mother and her mother could not reward her and yet somehow there was good feeling there.

After several weeks of visits Sarah stopped attacking me. Slowly it could be noticed that mother always sat Sarah on her lap facing away from her, not looking into her eyes. When I wondered aloud whether mother was scared that Sarah would not like to look at her face, both mother and child looked riveted at me. A tiny smile crossed Sarah's face. It had empowered her to see her mother as needy for her attention. The French psychoanalyst Maude Mannoni (1967) described a child not looking at his parents' eyes for fear of seeing his own death and I had also become very aware of the disabled child's need for visual contact in therapy.

When I commented on Sarah's smile her mother looked at it in surprise. 'Does that mean she cares about me?' she asked and burst into tears. Sarah then punched wildly and screamed but the knowledge of her smile stayed with us.

On my next visit Mrs Smith pointed to something new in the playpen – a toy mirror. 'The little monster has quite a nice face really, when you get used to it. Especially if she smiles'. Again, to my surprise Sarah showed a real smile – not the false appeasement smile adopted by so many children and adults with a disability which is responded to equally falsely by their careers.

Hatred and murder: visible and invisible

Where there is not adequate support there can be either a devastating disowning of hatred or an infliction of it. In David Cook's brilliant and pioneering novel 'Walter', about a man with learning disabilities, here are mother and disabled son struggling with their knowledge and fear of each other's hatred.

> Her awareness of his dependence weighed heavy. If she were to smile, he would smile back, but he would watch her still. And smiling once wasn't enough; she could not smile all the time... Walter was like a puppy, licking her hands for approval, like a stray dog at the Dog's Home, who, if she did not take him home, would be put down... If only Walter had been born a dog and not a human child, how easy it would be to end her sense of responsibility. A vet with a pill or an injection, administered while she protested love and kindness, could free her. (1980, p.46)

A German psychiatrist, Johannes Meyer-Lindenberg (1991) has just documented the way German psychiatry concretely followed such a fantasy. An estimated 100,000 mentally ill or disabled patients were murdered under the Nazi regime under the guise of 'a merciful death'. The disowned hatred in that terminology was soon to be found in the Nazi 1942 circular which spoke contemptuously of 'creatures unworthy of life'. Many individuals connected with the field of learning disability have to struggle with the existence of an internal death-wish and a guilty awareness of the external one.

This is a very complicated and painful arena. Medical advances mean that a woman can find out if she carries a foetus with a disability and have an abortion. Unless religious beliefs automatically make an abortion wrong, it needs acknowledging that for many women it is possible to have an abortion without feeling or being murderous and it is possible to feel and be murderous to a baby because of *not* having had an abortion. It all depends on how the primitive feeling is processed. Being sentient and unwanted can for some be a terrible life-sentence.

Nevertheless, for many children and adults with a learning disability there can at times be a disturbingly fine line between the concept of wanting to abort a foetus so that it does not develop into a baby and be born and killing them once they are born. That line is far harder to keep in mind when the child knows he is not wanted and is actively hated. As Micheline Mason (1990) comments, 'There is plenty of room for debate here (genetic counselling) but remember that people with congenital disabilities who may be part of the debate are likely to experience the debate as a personal issue – "should I be allowed to live"' (p.205).

'I had my baby even though I knew she was going to be handicapped because I'd had measles. I somehow could not manage to have an abortion because that felt like murder. Now I wish I had', said one mother. Another mother who already had two children decided on an abortion after her amniocentesis revealed a disability. 'We decided we had enough difficulties without the extra burdens we felt a new baby with a handicap would involve us in. I did not want to have a baby that I ended up hating and wishing wasn't born. An abortion is not a casual event – it is painful. But I am relieved we did it. The worst sin is bringing an unwanted child into the world'.

Children with mild, severe and profound learning disabilities have taken in the meaning of amniocentesis. Only in the last few years have I really been able to take on board the terror some of my child patients have of being killed: their profound and sophisticated knowledge of their own unwantedness. In a letter to *Child: Care, Health and Development* Micheline Mason (1981) commented 'I was a few days old when the seriousness of my disability was discovered. I can remember the change in the attitude of the people around me from calm and loving to panicky and hostile. A message clearly and firmly slipped into my unconscious saying that people would prefer it if I died'.

Knowledge of the level of social, parental or staff hatred can make the handicapped child more vulnerable to physical and sexual abuse. It is even harder to say 'no' when you are physically dependent for survival on others and know they wish you were dead (Sinason 1992).

Tina, aged seven, had profound learning and physical disabilities. She could not walk, wash, toilet, feed or dress herself. She had little speech. She had been abandoned by her parents at the age of two. The staff who tended to her changed their jobs every few months so there was no secure attachment figure. When she was ill with pneumonia an assistant said to me in a loud voice 'Poor thing – she'd be better off dead, wouldn't she I mean she'd be doing all of us a favour and herself too'. Another assistant was even blunter. 'It would be just like to her to last out instead of giving all of us a break'. The staff guilt and hatred was projected onto the ill Tina, aged seven who was seen as the agent of all their misery.

I needed to acknowledge the real hatred that she had experienced. When I said 'perhaps you worry I will be like A and B and just hope you will die and not bother to know what you are thinking and feeling', she lit up. 'Poo on them!' she whispered and then giggled. When it was time for me to go she looked angry. I said, 'perhaps me going makes you feel like pooing on me'. This time she laughed really loudly. 'Piss off' she ordered. From another child that might have been extremely offensive! However, for Tina it was a major step. It took many months of work, however, to realise that Tina had been abused chronically by a staff member. How could she protest when she knew how hated she was?

Primitive fear as a source of intra-personal hatred

The fear of a baby with physical or learning disabilities was experienced concretely in different times and cultures. The 'changeling', for example, the ugly goblin child who was substituted for a stolen healthy baby, embodied an image of disability. Someone had stolen or killed the normal wanted baby and put a monster in its place. Where parents have not worked through their feelings of anger about the birth of their baby, the baby is made even more monstrous; it includes the damaging projections of its parents. The same applies to workers later on in the child's life.

Sometimes, the hatred that is projected into the baby or child is so powerful that it cannot be surmounted. The Hungarian psychoanalyst, Sandor Ferenczi (1929, p.105) saw unwanted children as 'unwelcome guests of the family' who could easily get colds, psychosomatic disorders, epilepsy... and who want to die. He saw the deaths of such children from a variety of illnesses as unconscious choice. Although he was working at a time when medical advances in child-care were nowhere as advanced, he nevertheless understood that a child needed love to want to stay alive in the world. Indeed, he felt that a child, being near to birth, was also near to non-being and could easily seek an exit from life.

It is hard enough being an adult who is hated in a primitive way. The impact of racism and prejudice for all minorities can be impossible to process. The hatred that some children and adults with a learning disability face comes from a similar source.

Here is Frank Thomas (1987) writing a moving diary about his work with adults with learning disabilities while a nursing assistant. Despite changing attitudes, this conversation could be heard in hundreds of places all over the country. Although it is spoken by an orderly, that title could also be replaced by many others. 'David comes up for dinner. The orderly hands it to him. "Looks like shit", she tells him as he is about to eat his main meal of the day' (p.35). Or here is the Charge Nurse: 'How the fuck can you be hungry? You've eaten two bowls of this muck already. Oh, sod you, here's another one, hope it makes you sick... You are a filthy lot, don't know why I bother' (p.33). Staff need support, just as parents do, and faced with lack of training and lack of support there is room for hatred to grow larger than positive feelings. In a similar way in the wider community racism is fed by economic and emotional disadvantage.

Here, for contrast, are some extracts written by a mixed ability group of school children I worked with on this subject.

Some were siblings of children with learning and multiple disabilities and some had minor physical disabilities. They were considering the impact of prejudice that children with disabilities feel just from walking down the street. Once they realised they could express negative as well as positive feelings they quickly showed an ability to discriminate between the hurt of the disability – what it evokes in the wider society – and the impact of emotional disturbance that can co-exist with the disability. As this was work done over two decades ago, the language is slightly different.

> My brother is a cripple
> look at his feet
> His hands, his head
> it's a bit out of shape
> so feel sorry and do not hate.

John, aged 11

> The clouds gather in the sky
> and he sits down to cry
> Life for him, life is no fun
> He feels like a criminal on the run.

Steven, aged 12

> When he goes out
> all they do is mock him
> They call him names and copy what he does
> I tell him to ignore them
> but he sits down and cries.

Mark, aged 12

> The neighbours look at me
> they pretend not to see my mongol sister
> They look at her as if she is an alien
> I only want to take her for a walk
> but everywhere I go everyone looks.

Jenny, aged 13

Tony is very clumsy and his face is large. When he sees a tree he breaks branches and starts eating the leaves. People run away from him or they say horrible things and make sure he hears.

Susie, aged 9

Once when he walked out alone – just to try
a little boy spat in his eye
and then he fell over onto the road
he screamed for help with a voice like a toad.

Martin, aged 11

As I walk slowly down the street people stare at me and sometimes they laugh. They laugh at the way I walk. Ever since I was born I had a limp in my right leg. It looks quite funny and I feel terrible. I can't really blame people for staring. But I do feel awkward. One girl about my age in the street started calling me 'lefty' and all sorts of horrible names. Then another girl asked me the time. I'm sure she knew the time – she just wanted to mock me by getting closer.

Sarah aged 13

After the children had been given the freedom to explore their negative feelings they were able to feel empowered. Humour and affection showed through as well as ordinary sibling rivalry.

When they called him spastic we just shouted back 'just be glad you aren't'. When I wanted Mum to look at my schoolwork John signed he needed the toilet. Every time she came to help me he signed again. I punched him. Mum shouted I shouldn't punch him because he can't walk. But his arms are perfectly strong enough and he punched me back and then we both fell about laughing and Mum told us both off.

Invisible hatred

The referral letter was a familiar one. George, aged 10, was a happy, loving boy with Down's syndrome. It was just that he knocked staff unconscious with his head-butts or made them need medical attention because of deep bites. He came from a 'happy' school where there was a choice of a 'lovely' walk or 'lovely' painting and the signs for children who did not have verbal speech included 'happy' and even 'not happy' – but not 'hate' or 'anger' or any colloquialism. 'Of course we don't provide signs for words like "hate"', protested the head-teacher. 'This is a happy school. You won't see anything about hate here'.

Faced with the unspoken despair felt by many of the children at this school; faced with the unworked-through grief of the parents and the fear of the teachers that they had little to offer, it is not surprising that some schools develop an 'happy' atmosphere. Without staff support groups it is rarely possible for institutions that work for children or adults with disabilities to avoid taking the 'happy' road or some other equally defensive side-turning.

However, censoring the spoken language of hate, anger, despair and envy does not make those issues go away. Rather, it creates disowned, split-off acts of violence. These two situations represent two sides of the same coin. When we cannot bear to deal with the feelings that painful predicaments evoke there is a tendency either to idealise or denigrate. The person with disabilities can be idealised as an inspiring saint who is loving and happy or else written off as worthless, devoid of any worthwhile meaning.

Bettelheim showed how one traumatised Maori child took four months to learn the words 'come', 'look', 'and' and only four minutes to learn linked angry aggressive words like 'butcher-knife', 'gaol', 'police', 'sing,' 'cry', 'fight'. In linguistic research I have been carrying out in the Tavistock Clinic Mental Handicap, Psychotherapy and Psychology Research Workshop I have similar findings. With the treatment of psychoanalytical psychotherapy, children and adults quickly show their vast knowledge of 'hate' words. Their knowledge is not surprising – they have heard them in all sorts of settings over many years. What did surprise me was the enormous discrepancy in vocabulary between 'hate' words and supposedly positive words.

Mary, aged 10, for example, had severe learning disabilities. Her favourite words at school were 'nice', 'alright', 'happy', 'smart'. In one year of therapy her language within the therapy room included over forty negative adjectives, including 'tea-bag', 'scum-bag', 'spastic', 'toilet-face', 'shit-head', 'disgust-ing', 'sickening'. This discrepancy was equally true for adults. Eighty six per cent of all adjectives used in therapy by all patients, child and adult, represented the illegitimate but corrosive understanding of hatred and pain. In other words, the real emotional understanding of my patients was hidden in illegitimate words that they did not initially feel they had a right to use. Their knowledge of those words and the feeling and meaning behind it could not enrich their performance intelligence as they experienced it as secret knowledge – knowledge of hatred. The moment I made clear that those words were important and used them myself and helped them explore their anger with me, their vocabulary was able to increase.

My interest in the inhibition of language development due to fear of owning knowledge of received or internally felt hatred came from as a result of an early assessment that I described in 1986 (Sinason 1986).

This extract is from the assessment of an obese, severely retarded, hemiplegic, epileptic boy of 13.

Me:	Your teachers asked me to come because they felt you were feeling quite sad lately.
Patient:	No. Happy all time.
Me:	Happy all the time?
P:	Yes.
Me:	Happy when you have a fit?
P:	(long pause) No. But happy all time.
Me:	Not happy when you have a fit but otherwise happy?
P:	Yes.
Me:	Happy about being in a wheelchair?

P: (slowly) No. (Getting louder and sounding clearer) No. Not happy. Sad. Angry. I'm sad and I'm angry.

Speech ability, language knowledge, grammatical structure, feeling, all improved immediately once it was made clear the false happy self was not required.

At the Tavistock clinic we have been offering individual and group psychoanalytic psychotherapy to patients with mild, severe and profound learning disabilities for over twelve years, as well as offering ten week and one year courses to professionals. The importance of mobilising healthy anger has been central in the work with both clients and workers. However, healthy, differentiating anger can only be used when it is allowed to separate from its close cousin hate.

For example, when Sandra threw her stinking and filled incontinence pad face-down on my therapy room floor I could not speak for a while. The smearing effect of her action and the smell in the room filled me with such a sharp feeling of fury that I could only think of disinfectant, opening the window and wishing to end the session. Only when I had adequately processed my own feelings could I then say: 'You really want to stink my room out and show me how angry you feel but I can't really think with that smell in the room so I am going to have to open that window and disinfect the floor before we continue'.

Often, it is necessary to explore feelings of guilt before hatred and anger can be usefully separated. Guilt at not having a disability can have a corrosive influence on parents and workers in making all anger be experienced as illegitimate. Then hatred, disowned, becomes even more frightening. The patients sense the unworked – through hatred and guilt in their workers and perpetuate a smiling denial of negative feelings. A *folie à deux* is thus perpetuated to the disabling of all. When we ask students to offer an adjective that describes their feelings at work we often hear positive ones: inspiration, hope, affection, commitment, humour. Slowly negatives appear: useless, uncomprehending, worn-out, tired, bored, angry. Only after both are linked together is there freedom from idealisation or denigration.

References

Bettelheim, B. (1956) Childhood Schizophrenia. *American Journal of Orthopsychiatry* pp.507–18.

Bettelheim, B. (1980) *Surviving and Other Essays, 6th edition.* New York: Vintage Books.

Bion, W (1959) Attacks on linking. In W.R. Bion (ed) *Second Thoughts: Selected Papers on Psycho-Analysis.* New York: Jason Aronson.

Bourne, S. and Lewis, E. (1991) *A Review of Perinatal Morality Literature.* Tavistock Clinic Publication. Available from the Librarian.

Cook, D. (1980) *Walter.* Harmondsworth: Penguin.

Ferenczi, S. (1929) The Unwelcome Child and His Death Instinct. In M. Balint (ed) (1955) *Final Contributions to the Problems and Methods of Psychoanalysis.* London: The Hogarth Press.

Freud, S. (1915) Instincts and their Vicissitudes. In Vol. 14 *The Standard Edition of Sigmund Freud* (1973). London: The Hogarth Press and The Institute of Psychoanalysis.

Freud, S. (1923) The Two Classes of Instincts. In Vol. 19 *The Standard Edition of Sigmund Freud* (1975). London: The Hogarth Press and The Institute of Psychoanalysis.

Klein, M. (1952) Weaning. In *Love, Guilt and Reparation and Other Works* (1975). London: The Hogarth Press and the International Psychoanalytic Library.

Klein, M. (1961) *Narrative of a Child Analysis Vol. 4.* London: The Hogarth Press and the International Psychoanalysis Library, 1975.

James, H. (1897) *What Maisie Knew.* Harmondsworth: Penguin Modern Classics, 1966.

Mannoni, M. (1967) *The Child, 'His Illness' and the Others.* London: Penguin.

Mason, M. (1981) Letter. *Child: Care, Health and Development, 7,* 183–86.

Mason, M. (1990) Genetic Counselling: Abortion v Sterilisation. In *Disability Equality in the Classroom: A Human Rights Issue.* London: ILEA.

Meyer-Lindenberg, J. (1991) The Holocaust and German Psychiatry. *British Journal of Psychiatry, 159,* 7–12.

Russell, P. (1991). In S. Segal and V. Varma (eds.) *Prospects for People with Learning Difficulties* (ed.) London: David Fulton.

Sinason, V. (1986) Secondary Mental Handicap and its Relationship to Trauma. *Psychoanalytic Psychotherapy, Vol. 2.* No. 2, 131–54.

Sinason, V. (1992) *Mental Handicap and the Human Condition: New Approaches from the Tavistock.* London: Free Association Books.

Thomas, F. (1987) In J. Ryan and F. Thomas (eds) *The Politics of Mental Handicap.* London: Free Association Books.

List of Contributors

Dr Ved P. Varma
is a former teacher and educational psychologist. His many previous books include *How and Why Children Hate* and, as co-editor with Barbara Tizard *Vulnerability and Resilience in Human Development*

Dr Martin Herbert
is Professor of Clinical Child Psychology and Consultant Clinical Psychologist, Child Health Directorate, Plymouth Health Authority

Robert Bocock PhD
is Senior Lecturer in Sociology, The Open University

Helen Barrett PhD
is Research Fellow, Department of Psychology, Birbeck College, University of London and Lecturer in Psychology, Thames Valley University

Francis M.J. Dale
is Principal Child Psychotherapist, Child and Family Guidance Service, Torquay

Dr Christopher Dare
is Senior Lecturer, Department of Psychiatry, Institute of Psychiatry, University of London and Honorary Consultant, the Psychotherapy Unit, Maudsley Hospital

Dr Kedar Nath Dwivedi
is Consultant Child, Adolescent and Family Psychiatrist, Northampton

Kevin Epps
is Senior Clinical Psychologist, Glenthorne Youth Treatment Centre, Birmingham

Neil Frude, PhD
is Senior Lecturer in the School of Psychology, University of Wales. College of Cardiff

Dr Robin Higgins MB, Bch (Cambridge), DPM, BMMS
is a former consultant child and family psychiatrist

Dr Clive Hollin
is Senior Lecturer in Psychology, The University of Birmingham and Research Psychologist, Glenthorne Youth Treatment Centre

David Jones PhD
is Senior Lecturer in Psychology, Birbeck College, University of London

Nandini Mane
is the Project Worker, Working Group Against Racism in Children's Resources

Jocelyn Emama Maxime' PhD
is Principal Clinical Psychologist, London Borough of Hackney

Valerie Sinason
is Consultant Child Psychotherapist, Tavistock Clinic Child and Family Department and Day Unit and Psychotherapist Convenor of the Psychotherapy and Psychology Mental Handicap Research Workshop at the Tavistock Clinic

Subject Index

Name Index